PENGUIN BOOKS

THE
SALAD GARDEN

JOY LARKCOM is a leading authority on growing
vegetables and possesses an unrivaled knowledge
of unusual salad plants. A well-known broadcaster
and writer, her influential works include *Oriental
Vegetables*, the complete revision of the Royal
Horticultural Society's *The Vegetable Garden
Displayed*, and *Grow Your Greens*. In 1992 she was
awarded the RHS's Veitch Memorial Medal, and
was Gardening Writer of the Year.

THE SALAD GARDEN

JOY LARKCOM

PHOTOGRAPHS BY

ROGER PHILLIPS

Published in cooperation with
the New York Botanical Garden Institute of Urban Horticulture

PENGUIN BOOKS

To my dear mother

PENGUIN BOOKS
Published by the Penguin Group
Penguin Books USA Inc., 375 Hudson Steet, New York, New York 10014, U.S.A.
Penguin Books Ltd, 27 Wrights Lane, London W8 5TZ, England
Penguin Books Australia Ltd, Ringwood, Victoria, Australia
Penguin Books Canada Ltd, 10 Alcorn Avenue, Toronto, Ontario, Canada M4V 3B2
Penguin Books (N.Z.) Ltd, 182–190 Wairau Road, Auckland 10, New Zealand

Penguin Books Ltd, Registered Offices: Harmondsworth, Middlesex, England

First published in the United States of America in hardcover
and paperback editions by The Viking Press 1984
Published in Penguin Books 1989
This edition published in Penguin Books 1996

10 9 8 7 6 5 4 3 2 1

The Salad Garden was conceived, edited, and designed by Frances Lincoln Limited,
4 Torriano Mews, Torriano Avenue, London NW5 2RZ

LIBRARY OF CONGRESS CATALOGING IN PUBLICATION DATA
Larkcom, Joy.
The salad garden
Includes index.
1. Vegetable gardening. 2. Salads. I. Title.
SB321.L33 1984 635 83–40382
ISBN 0 14 02.5144 8

Printed in Hong Kong

CONTENTS

SALAD GROWING

INTRODUCTION

If anyone had asked me ten years ago what to grow for a salad, I would probably have suggested only half a dozen vegetables – lettuce, radish, tomatoes and so on. Since then I've been on a voyage of discovery, finding all along the way more and more plants that can be used in salads. Today my list numbers between 100 and 150 plants, and the purpose of this book is to share what I have learnt about them with other gardeners and salad enthusiasts.

The highlight of my 'decade of discovery' was 1976 when my husband, Don, and I, with our two young children, spent a year touring Europe in a caravan. Our main purpose was simply to learn about traditional and modern methods of vegetable growing, and to collect the seed of local varieties of vegetables, which, like the wild animals of this planet, are vanishing fast.

Moving in a large southward arc, we travelled from Holland to Hungary, through Belgium, France, Spain, Portugal, Italy and Yugoslavia. We gleaned information from seedsmen, seed catalogues, and the backs of seed packets, from markets and market gardeners, peasants, cooks, botanists and housewives. We managed to collect quite a number of old local varieties of seed (over 100 samples are now safely housed in the seed bank since established in the UK), and we certainly learnt a great deal about horticultural methods. But we were totally un-prepared for the tremendous number of salad plants we found, particularly plants grown for the colder months of the year. In Holland, Belgium, France and Italy, we found beautiful varieties of lettuce, chicory and endive that were previously unknown to us; in Belgium we 'discovered' claytonia, that pretty escapee from the American continent, and sparkling iceplant; and in Italy, in early spring, we saw people parking their cars on motorways to scour the fields for young leaves of wild plants – our first inkling of that vast neglected heritage of wild plants that can be used raw. Coupled with these new

Right *The kitchen garden at Barnsley House, one of the best modern examples of the formal French potager, where, within the confines of formal beds, vegetables are grouped so that their ornamental qualities are displayed to the full. Fruit trees, garden flowers and herbs can all be fitted happily into the formal potager as, of course, can salad plants, many of which are grown primarily for the beautiful colors and the texture of their leaves and flowers.*

Left *Purple salsify and yellow scorzonera flowers, used both in salads and as cooked vegetables, make wonderful splashes of color in the garden. In the past it was commonplace to cultivate flowers grown for culinary and medicinal purposes among the vegetables.*

Below left *Ornamental cabbages are such decorative vegetables that they are often used in park bedding schemes. Their colors deepen in cold weather: in autumn and winter, and in mild areas in spring, their bright, crinkly leaves make a wonderful addition to a salad.*

Far left *One of the nine squares in the reconstructed Renaissance garden at Château Villandry in the Loire valley. Within each square the beds are arranged in symmetrical patterns. Chards, ornamental kales and cabbages, blue-leaved leeks and 'Salad Bowl' lettuce create solid patches of color.*

plants were new ideas on how to grow salad plants, particularly the cut-and-come-again concept. This extends from broadcasting patches of seedlings, which can be cut up to five times, to cutting mature heads of chicory, endive and lettuce and leaving the stumps to resprout.

At about the same time, suspecting another untapped treasure trove of useful salad plants, I began to try out some of the Chinese and Japanese vegetables which were becoming available in the West.

As a result, we turned our garden into a small experimental market garden, supplying unusual vegetables to wholefood and health shops. Perhaps here I should give my definition of a salad plant: it is either any plant that tastes good raw or it is any plant that is good eaten cooked and cold.

The time now seems ripe for introducing these salad plants to a wider audience. More and more people are concerned about the quality of fresh food, and what finer guarantee of 'purity' is there than to grow your own salad plants? They are ideal for the small modern garden.

This book covers both well-known and 'new' salad plants. Unfortunately, it was impossible to cover all the well-known plants in great depth, but further information on these can be found in the standard texts recommended in the appendix. Precedence was given to new plants, but here two problems have to be squarely faced. Firstly, since much less is known and has been written about them, they must be approached in a somewhat experimental frame of mind. Whenever possible, try different sowing times and methods, and different varieties, and see what works in your area and what you personally like best. Several mail-order seedsmen are now stocking these unusual seeds (see p.167 for suppliers).

My experiments with the more unusual plants in this book, and the advice given, have been based on the conditions discussed below, and it is not always easy to predict how some plants will perform in more extreme conditions.

In my part of the world, in most winters temperatures fall to about −10°C/14°F, there is relatively little snow, and the snow rarely lies for long. The first frosts normally occur towards the end of October or early November, the last around the middle of May: but there is enormous variation from one year to the next. Similarly, maximum summer temperatures fluctuate a good deal, ranging from around 20°C/68°F in poor summers to around 32°C/90°F in hot summers. Average annual rainfall is about 9cm/22in, spread fairly evenly throughout the year.

As many salad plants mature rapidly, especially when grown as seedlings or using the cut-and-come-again methods, it is safe to say that they would be suitable for growing at *some* time of year in all parts of the continent. For example, many of the leafy salad plants do best in a temperate climate. They could be grown in New England during the summer months, but in the autumn or spring in the southeast, and in winter in the southwest.

In areas with severe winters, more reliance must be placed on the use of protective cropping to extend the season, on root crops which can be lifted and stored for winter, on plants which can be lifted and forced indoors, on seed sprouting and the growing of seedlings in flats indoors. Where summer temperatures are high there are compensations in the ease with which tomatoes, sweet peppers, cucumbers and leafy salad plants like amaranthus can be grown.

As for the more common salad plants, there is today an enormous, continually changing choice of varieties. On the whole, I have recommended only those varieties that I have grown or otherwise know myself, but there are many other excellent varieties. Follow the popular gardening press to keep abreast of good new ones.

Most salad lovers would prefer to grow their plants organically. Our own garden is run on organic lines, without artificial fertilizers or chemical sprays. We have encountered no special problems in growing organically, and believe our plants are more robust, and better flavored, and remain fresh longer as a result.

Finally, a word on the photographs, taken especially for this book by Roger Phillips. Most of the plants illustrated were grown in my garden in one season, and an unusually odd season it was. We had more than twice the average rainfall in April, followed by an exceptionally cold May, and a very long drought in summer. So, as can happen in any garden, we had our failures, and a few specimens were not as good as we would have liked. Even so, I hope the photographs convey something of the fun, variety and color that can result from growing, and making, your own salads.

JOY LARKCOM   DECEMBER 1983

SALAD GROWING

PLANNING THE GARDEN

Salad plants cannot be grown successfully unless the garden is well organized. This chapter looks at several key aspects of planning, starting with the soil and site and the steps that can be taken to improve them, and the layout of the beds and paths. The garden also has to be planned so that, within the limitations imposed by its size and the climate, there is a continuous supply of salad plants: here the emphasis is on intensive space-saving systems which give quick returns. Lastly, the garden can be planned so that it is a place of real beauty, utilizing to the full the color, texture and form of the main vegetables and flowers grown for salads.

SOIL AND SITE

As salad plants are usually eaten raw, they *must* be succulent and tender. If they have to struggle for existence in poor soil, contend with alternating periods of drought and waterlogging, or be buffeted by cold and searing winds, they will inevitably become coarse and toughened. They deserve the best soil and best position – fertile, well-drained soil; warm, sunny, sheltered sites.

Soil

Most of us, of course, have very little choice as regards soil: it's simply a question of making the best of what we have. We are most probably gardening on loam, but may have anything from very light, rapidly draining sand to heavy, apparently intractable clay.

Very light soil, being well drained, has the advantage that it warms up rapidly in spring and is therefore marvellous for early salad crops; on the other hand, its nutrients, or plant foods, are washed out rapidly and in hot weather it is, of course, liable to suffer from drought. Conversely, clay is a cold, ill-drained soil in winter and may become baked hard in summer, but it is a rich storehouse of plant foods and can be very fertile once it has been brought under control.

Whatever the soil, everything must be done to improve and maintain its fertility. The many interlocking factors involved in creating a fertile soil are discussed more fully on pp.33-7. From the planning point of view, what matters is the continual need to work other materials into the soil. With light soils you need to increase their ability to hold water and their supply of nutrients; this can be done by working in peat and well-made compost. With loams and heavier soils you need to improve the aeration and drainage. The drainage can sometimes be improved by working sand and coarse grit into the top spit of soil, but the best method is to dig in plenty of bulky organic matter, such as strawy manure. This will provide food for the burrowing and casting earthworms, whose 'cemented' burrows create marvellous drainage and aeration channels in the soil. They also liberate the nutrients in the soil, making them available to the plants.

All this heavy material has to be transported in wheelbarrows or by some other means, so it goes without saying that your salad plot should be as accessible and as level as possible.

Water supply

A nearby supply of good water is also important. Leafy salad vegetables consist largely of water, and may need frequent watering, especially during their 'critical'

As heavy loads of manure are constantly being wheeled into the vegetable garden, beds should be as accessible as possible – narrow beds flanked by paths are convenient and functional.

periods (see p.39). If deprived of water they suffer stress and their quality deteriorates. Underwatered radishes, to take one example, will be cracked, woody and unbearably hot rather than crisp and succulent – and who wants a woody radish? So in areas where water shortage is likely, bear this in mind when siting your salad plants; the shorter the distance that watering pots have to be carried or hoses trailed, the better.

Drainage

Poor drainage can be a serious problem. For most salad plants, other than a few of marshy origin such as celery, fennel and Chinese cabbage, waterlogging is fatal.

A drainage problem is usually obvious. If water lies on the surface for several days after heavy rain, or is found when digging down, say, 30cm/12in, or if there are no worms, or if the soil is grayish, blueish, blackish or mottled rather than brown, something must be done. As mentioned above, poor drainage can often be improved over a period of a few years simply by digging in large quantities of bulky organic matter. If the problem is more persistent, it may be necessary to make a few trench drains to remove the excess water (see diagram). A drain can also be incorporated into a garden path, meandering through the garden if necessary.

In more serious cases it may be necessary to lay a network of drains with clay or plastic pipes in them, emptying into an outlet such as a ditch, or a French drain or sump. Expert help should be sought on the type of drains to use, and on their layout, depth and spacing, as well as the gradient at which they should be laid. Drainage can also be improved by the use of raised beds.

Occasionally, poor drainage is caused by an underlying hardpan, possibly due to a mineral deposit or to compaction caused by heavy machinery or by continual rotovation at the same depth. Where this occurs the only remedy is to break up the hardpan with a spade, mattock, or small backhoe.

Shelter

If vegetables are sheltered from even light winds their yields can be increased by up to 50 per cent. Salad plants, of course, are particularly vulnerable to the damaging effects of wind, so in any exposed garden it is worth erecting some kind of windbreak.

The ideal windbreak should act as a filter to the wind, and should be about 50 per cent *permeable*. Wind tends to leap over a *solid* barrier, creating an area of turbulence on the leeward side. A hedge, fence or windbreak netting are all suitable. In small gardens 1.2-1.5m-/4-5ft-high fencing is generally more appropriate than trees or hedging which compete with the crops for nutrients, moisture and light, and may cast shadows.

Although the initial expense is high, it is often feasible to surround an exposed garden with some kind of paling, wooden or lath fencing (the small gaps are necessary to

Vegetables benefit enormously if sheltered from wind. Here, nylon netting secured to posts makes an effective windbreak.

Trench drain
Most drainage problems can be corrected by digging out a trench about 30cm/12in wide and 60-90cm/24-36in deep across the lower end of a slope or on either side of a level site. Fill the lower third of the trench with rubble before replacing the soil.

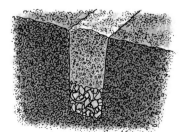

provide a 'filter') or nylon windbreak netting secured to posts. Netting lasts for several years, but erect the posts securely, reinforcing the corner posts if necessary. In strong winds they will, of course, have to take tremendous strain.

On a smaller scale, strips of netting or burlap sacking about 30-60cm/12-24in high can be strung between beds or rows of vegetables. These can cut down the wind most effectively. Plants can also be used as temporary windbreaks. Sweetcorn or maize is grown as a windbreak in Holland; Jerusalem artichokes, sunflowers, even chicory or a 'hedge' of cardoons can be used.

A windbreak is effective for a distance of between six and ten times its own height. Where possible, it should be sited across the path of the prevailing wind. In city gardens, wind often funnels through the gaps between buildings, which should be closed by erecting a windbreak that extends several feet beyond the gap on each side. However, take care never to close a gap at the lower end of a slope, or a frost pocket can be created.

Ever since salads have been grown, a premium has been put on the very early crops, raised in sheltered sites on south-facing slopes. Enterprising market gardeners in the past have even created slopes for growing early salads, while in the large walled kitchen gardens of the European gentry the earliest salads were grown in south-facing beds at the foot of the walls. This position would become very hot and dry in midsummer, but early in the year it is a prime site.

The most exciting sites I have ever come across for growing early salad plants are the *maceiras* on the north Portuguese coast – remarkable beds excavated out of sand dunes. Vines are trained against the sloping sides to keep the sand in place, and tall grasses planted around the top as shelter from the strong, salt-laden sea winds. The sun reflects off the gleaming white sloping sandy sides into the beds, creating an exceptionally warm and sheltered microclimate. Kept fertile with seaweed and irrigated with networks of little canals, up to four crops are produced every year from these sites – the first being very early salad plants. This, of course, is a unique situation. But with ingenuity a warm fertile spot can be found or created in most gardens, and used for growing early salad plants.

Cloches, polyethylene tunnels and greenhouses are all forms of shelter. These are discussed fully on pp.41-4.

GARDEN LAYOUT

Every garden is unique, and its layout will inevitably be influenced by the amount of space available and the way the vegetables are grown. Let's make the assumption that space is scarce and that the salad garden will be cultivated, as far as possible, on organic lines.

Where there is little space, it follows that everything must be grown as intensively as possible. This generally means that traditional rows, which have a lot of wasted space between them, will be abandoned in favor of a 'block' system, with plants grown closely together, generally at equidistant spacing. Where possible, trailing and climbing plants such as cucumbers and tomatoes will be grown up trellises and supports to save ground space, and, where a harmonious arrangement can be achieved, vegetables will be mixed in with flowers in the more formal beds.

The necessity to preserve the structure of your soil also has a bearing on garden design. (For an account of the role of soil structure, see p.34.) The important point to bear in mind is that soil structure is a particularly fragile quality, and is very easily destroyed, for example, by digging heavy soils, such as clays, when they are wet, and by simply treading on any type of soil, again, especially when wet. It is, therefore, very important to lay out the garden so that the need to walk on the soil is minimized, or better still, eliminated.

Bed size and shape
This leads naturally to the use of small beds, particularly narrow beds, which can be worked from the path. In the old days, fields and gardens were often laid out in beds 1.5m/5ft wide, so that the center of the bed could be reached from either side: even today, market gardeners all over the world still cultivate their land in strips, ranging from 1 to 2m/3 to 6ft wide. They have found, through years of experience, that narrow beds are both practical and efficient.

My personal preference is for beds about 1m/3ft wide, with 30cm/12in paths between them. This might be considered an extravagant path-to-bed ratio, but it is a width which seems 'comfortable' to me. It allows all the digging, cultivation and harvesting to be done from the paths without ever having to tread on the soil, and in winter low polyethylene tunnels fit over the beds. My beds are

A salad garden can be both practical and pleasing to the eye. Here, in the author's own garden, an attractive effect has been created by growing vegetables in patches of contrasting textures and colors, by intercropping, and by growing flowers in the vegetable beds. In the left-hand bed, starting from the front, are pot marigolds, alfalfa, red 'Salad Bowl' lettuce seedlings, rocket, Abyssinian cabbage 'Karate' and shungiku. In the right-hand bed, onions are intercropped with 'Tom Thumb' lettuce.

permanent, so that all resources are concentrated on them, and their fertility is continually being improved.

Incidentally, in the Northern Hemisphere, to make maximum use of sunshine, beds should ideally be orientated from north to south for summer crops, and from east to west for early and late crops. In practice this is rarely possible.

The potager

A very attractive concept for growing vegetables is the formal layout of the French kitchen garden, or *potager*. This evolved in the sixteenth and seventeenth centuries, when many new exotic vegetables were being introduced into Europe, mainly from the Americas. They were considered so curious and interesting that people wanted to watch their progress from the terraces of their country houses or *châteaux*. But if they were to be visible – vegetables were normally hidden discreetly out of sight – then they had to be arranged in patterns in formal beds like the flowers. So the classic *potager* was born.

The best known example of a reconstructed *potager* is at Château Villandry in the Loire Valley in France.

Another inspiring example is Rosemary Verey's recently created *potager* at Barnsley House in Gloucestershire. Here an essentially rectangular garden is divided into four squares: a metal urn, surrounded by lavender, decorative vegetables and standard roses, is the central focal point. Within each of the principal squares the beds, which range in width from about 60cm to 1.5m/2 to 5ft, are arranged in different geometric patterns to delightful effect. This garden demonstrates well that a vegetable garden can be a beautiful place. The many salad plants with decorative qualities which lend themselves to this type of treatment are discussed more fully on pp.20-22.

Paths

Thought must also be given to the paths between the beds. They should be hard, clean and well-drained, so that any salad plants that flop onto them will stay clean, rather than be soiled with mud. The choice of material depends on what is available. In my own garden I use sawdust, which quickly settles into a firm, dry surface. Mud from boots and wheelbarrows will form a layer on top, which can easily be 'sliced' off. The sawdust base can be 'topped up' from time to time. Similarly, wood and bark chippings can be used to make a pleasant-looking and serviceable path.

Very attractive paths have been made at the Barnsley *potager*, with old bricks and small cement blocks carefully laid in patterns (see below).

Although narrow, 30-45cm/12-18in paths are quite serviceable for most purposes, in a garden of any size it is useful to have the occasional wider path, say up to 60cm/24in wide, for pushing wheelbarrows with large loads.

Rotation

Crops from the same botanical family or closely related groups should not be grown every year in the same piece of ground. The theoretical reason for this is that most soil pests and diseases attack only a limited range of plants but if the plants they attack are always present, there will be a serious buildup of pests and diseases. In practice, many soil pests are fairly mobile so there is little point in simply moving a crop a few yards away. Moreover, some pests and diseases, such as clubroot and some species of eelworm, can remain in the soil for up to six or seven years,

so rotation would have to be practiced over a long cycle to be really effective. This is obviously impractical in the typical small garden.

However, especially when growing organically, there is no doubt that rotation over a two-, three- or preferably four-year cycle is sound preventive medicine. (It is, incidentally, far easier to work out a flexible rotation plan where a garden is divided into numerous small beds rather than a few large ones.) So, whenever possible, follow each crop with a crop from an unrelated group (see below).

The main groups for rotation purposes are: the **potato** family *(Solanaceae)* (potatoes, tomatoes, eggplants, peppers); **legumes** (all peas and beans); **brassicas** (such as cabbages and cauliflowers, and all other members of the cabbage family, including radishes, Chinese cabbage and mustards, turnips, swedes and kohlrabi); the **onion** family (including leeks and garlic) and **umbelliferous** vegetables (carrots, parsnips, parsley and celery).

As far as possible, plan your garden so that plants from each of these main groups are grown in a different bed each year, returning to their original beds, ideally, one year in every four or five.

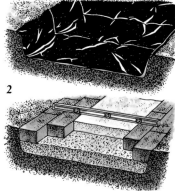

In the formal potager *at Barnsley House the paths are made from old weathered bricks and small concrete blocks. They are laid, as shown below, in 10cm/4in deep channels lined with polyethylene to prevent weeds (1). A 5cm/2in layer of sand is laid over the polyethylene to make a level base for the path (2).*

1

2

SPACE-SAVING SYSTEMS

In the past, gardeners have been overgenerous with space, tending to give each plant far more room than it really needed. We now know the optimum spacing for most vegetables that will enable us to get the highest yield from a given area. Scientists have also shown the inefficiency, in most cases, of the traditional method of growing plants close together in rows, with the rows spaced far apart. Within the rows, plants will compete fiercely for the limited resources of nutrients and moisture, and deprive each other of sunlight, yet in the space between the rows, where there is no competition, weeds will flourish. With equidistant spacing this is avoided.

Each individual plant should be seen as the center of a circle, from which it draws its nutrients and moisture, the radius varying with the size of the plant and its demands. A cauliflower, for example, naturally draws from a far greater area than, say, a lettuce. The most economic way of utilizing the soil – the storehouse of both nutrients and moisture – is to space plants so that their 'circles' just overlap (see diagram). This effect is achieved by planting in staggered rows with equidistant spacing in both directions, that is, with the same space between the plants *in* each row as there is *between* the rows themselves.

When the plants are mature, each will more or less just touch its neighbors, forming a leafy canopy over the soil. This, incidentally, is a very effective means of weed control, as far fewer weed seeds will germinate when deprived of light.

Spacing can be a useful tool: it can be used to control the size and quality of many vegetables, and also the speed with which they mature. With onions, for example, close spacing will produce pickling onions, moderate spacing small cooking onions, and wide spacing very large

Seedling crops look attractive when growing and make very intensive use of the ground. The purslane above was sown in spring in an unheated polyethylene tunnel for an early crop.

onions. The same principle holds true for carrots, cabbages, leeks and many other vegetables. The quality of calabrese heads and self-blanching celery stalks will, to some extent, be improved by closer spacing than is normally advised, and tomatoes will mature earlier when grown relatively close.

The most extreme example of close spacing is the use of seedling crops, the best known being garden cress, grown by generations of children on blotting paper on a windowsill. When cress is sown in ordinary soil rather than on blotting paper it will grow much taller and after it has been cut, it will grow again. In fact, several cuts can normally be made from one sowing.

Quite a number of plants can be used at the seedling stage in salads, and many of them, like cress, will produce several cuttings. This makes them highly productive, and ideal for small gardens. Growing seedling crops is discussed more fully on pp.48-50.

Intercropping

A whole range of space-saving techniques comes under the general heading of 'intercropping'. Some plants, such as most brassicas, grow much more slowly than others, and will not occupy their allotted 'circle' until they have been in the ground for several months. In their early stages, when they are still small, it is therefore often possible to grow a fast-growing crop alongside or around

Equidistant spacing
The best possible use of ground is made when plants are grown with equidistant spacing rather than in traditional widely spaced rows. Imagine each plant as the center of a circle, as in the diagram right, and space the plants so that their circles overlap. The dotted circles indicate the area the full-grown plants will occupy.

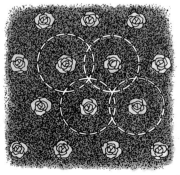

them, which will be ready for use and cut before the entire space is required by the slower-growing plant.

In much the same way, it is not always necessary to wait for a crop to be cleared before planting its successor. There may be space to plant the successor alongside so that it can get established rather than languish in a crowded seedbed. By the time it needs more space, the first crop will be ready for harvesting. There is more scope for this last type of intercropping when plants are grown in rows rather than when grown with equal spacing between them.

Undercropping is another form of intercropping, where upright plants are combined with ground-hugging or trailing crops. A very useful plant for this system is sweetcorn, since its stems are sturdy, and the plants stand well, particularly if earthed up. The leaves create only a little shade, so that the ground beneath can be put to good use: trailing squashes and cucumbers, pickling cucumbers, dwarf green beans, lettuces, iceplant and Japanese mustard 'Mizuna' are just some of the vegetables I've grown successfully beneath sweetcorn.

Similarly, when tomatoes are grown pruned and staked, twisted up strings or tied to canes, it is practical to grow summer herbs such as parsley, marjoram, savory or basil on the ground between them. Herbs can also be grown between cucumbers, climbing green or runner beans, or among asparagus – for some reason parsley does very well in an asparagus bed.

One year I grew the climbing, round, South African squash 'Little Gem' up a 'tepee' of four canes, each set at

Above *An example of undercropping, in which the Japanese mustard 'Mizuna' is planted beneath sweetcorn. The 'Mizuna' will continue to be productive long after the sweetcorn has been harvested. Sweetcorn is an ideal subject for undercropping as the leaves only shade the ground lightly. A wide range of low-growing and trailing plants can be grown successfully beneath it.*

Left *A useful example of intercropping: garden cress is sown around young cabbage plants when they are planted out. The fast-growing cress can be cut a couple of times before it needs to be uprooted to allow the cabbages space to develop to maturity. This is an intensive use of ground.*

the corner of a 1m/3ft square, the canes being tied together near the top (see below). The four squashes were sown under glass jars to help them to germinate, one at the foot of each cane. At the same time, a dozen lettuces were planted in the square. While the squashes germinated and started to climb the canes, the lettuces grew steadily so that they were ready for cutting before the squashes had clothed the canes and blocked out all the light. Climbing cucumbers can also be grown this way, undercropped initially with lettuces or any other fast-growing crop, but the foliage of squashes, with its pretty gray markings, makes a particularly striking feature grown up a tepee of canes.

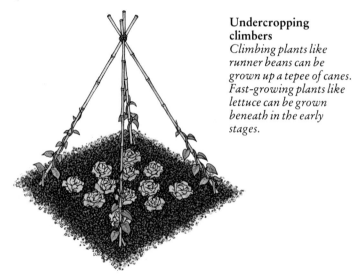

Undercropping climbers
Climbing plants like runner beans can be grown up a tepee of canes. Fast-growing plants like lettuce can be grown beneath in the early stages.

Chervil and dill are examples of two plants which work well in tandem. Both, once established, will more or less perpetuate themselves from self-sown seed. If grown in the same spot, the chervil will germinate in autumn and grow in winter, running to seed in spring. And then, just when it is dying down, the dill will germinate and carry on throughout the summer.

There are countless intercropping and undercropping permutations, and everyone can develop their own favorite combinations, geared to their own conditions. In areas with high rainfall or low light conditions, excessive intercropping may result in rampant, jungly growth or an increase in disease. Study the growth and performance of plants in your garden to work out what is feasible. The main principle is to combine plants which grow particularly quickly or slowly, or those with complementary growth habits. Be careful, though, not to overdo it. Both sets of crops must have enough space, light, moisture and nutrients to develop fully. Such very intensive use of the ground will make heavy demands on your soil, which must be kept fertile and well watered.

Once the crops are established, it pays to water them really well and then mulch them, both to help retain moisture in the soil, and to stifle any weeds which would be another source of competition if they were to germinate. There must, of course, also be room to cultivate, if necessary, and to reach the crops for harvesting – all factors which are sometimes overlooked in the excitement of 'getting in as much as possible'. Plants suitable for intercropping are given in the table below.

SUGGESTIONS FOR INTERCROPPING AND UNDERCROPPING

INTERCROPPING COMBINATIONS		UNDERCROPPING COMBINATIONS	
Fast-growing plants that mature rapidly and/or can be used young	**Slow-growing plants that can be intercropped in early stages**	**Tall-growing plants**	**Low-growing plants**
Summer radishes	Cauliflowers, cabbages, sprouting broccoli, Brussels sprouts	Sweetcorn	Trailing squashes and cucumbers
Small lettuces such as 'Tom Thumb' and 'Little Gem'	Parsnips, turnip-rooted parsley, salsify, black salsify	Climbing squashes and cucumbers on supports	Corn salad, iceplant, land cress, Mediterranean rocket, 'Mizuna', shungiku*
Early turnips	Bulbing onions, shallots, celeriac	Climbing green beans and runner beans on supports	Dwarf green beans*
Seedling crops such as garden cress, coriander, Mediterranean rocket, salad rape, white mustard, endive	Globe artichokes, cardoons	Tall varieties of Brussels sprouts	Seedling crops*
		NB: Sweetcorn can be combined with any of the low-growing plants, but the other tall-growing plants listed can be combined only with those from groups marked with an asterisk.	

Further examples of four different types of inter-cropping, with suggestions on how they might be dealt with, are as follows:

IN-ROW INTERSOWING Slow-growing root vegetables such as parsnips can be 'station sown' (see p. 27), and a few seeds of, say, radish, scallion or Mediterranean rocket, or small lettuce, sown between each 'station'. Alternatively, you could mix the seeds of the radishes with carrots (or any of the other slow-germinating root crops listed above) and sow them in a row together. In this case, the radishes will act as 'markers' for the carrots, which are fairly slow to germinate.

Another possibility is to intersow Abyssinian cabbage 'Karate' with radish, alternating three or four 'Karate' seeds with three or four of the radish. ('Karate' and radish could also be sown in alternate rows, with the rows no more than 5cm/2in apart). This is a very useful combination when used in an unheated greenhouse in early spring with a forcing variety of radish which produces little leaf, since by the time the radishes are large enough to be pulled, the 'Karate' will normally be ready for its first cut.

MIXED PATCH SOWING Radish and carrot seed can be mixed together and sown in a patch; or lettuces, purslane, claytonia, carrots, radishes and parsnips could all be mixed and allowed to come up in their turn – the parsnips lasting until winter. This combination was suggested by the seventeenth-century diarist, John Evelyn.

Mixed packets of salad seeds, containing up to a dozen different species of salad vegetables, can sometimes be bought. If not, mix your own salad 'cocktail' with, say, cress, Mediterranean rocket, chervil, 'Salad Bowl' lettuce, 'Sugar Loaf' and red Italian chicory. These will give a continuous supply of salad throughout the year, different plants maturing in succession.

INTER-ROW AND INTER-PLANT SOWING Try intersowing rows of radishes and seedling garden cress, coriander, Mediterranean rocket or endive between newly planted rows of shallots, leeks, bulbing onions, brassicas or newly sown carrots. These same plants might also be

Left *An example of intercropping, with 'Tom Thumb' lettuce and round spring carrots interplanted between onions. All were sown in soil blocks (the onions were multi-seeded) and were planted at the same time. The lettuces and carrots will be harvested before the space is required by the maturing onions.*

Above *A patch of mixed salad seedlings. Packets of mixed salad seed may contain as many as a dozen different species of salad plants which mature in succession over a 12-month cycle. The patch above includes several varieties of lettuce, endive and chicory, as well as dandelion, chervil, rocket and buck's horn plantain.*

sown, in circular or square patterns, around brassicas, celeriac or globe artichokes when they are planted out. Take a couple of cuts from the seedling crops before the brassicas start to overcrowd them or the seedlings run to seed (as they will in hot weather).

INTER-ROW AND INTER-PLANT PLANTING Lettuces, some of the smaller oriental mustards, claytonia, purslane or shungiku can be planted between slow-growing plants and will normally provide a picking or two before they are encroached upon. Corn salad and land cress can be planted under Brussels sprouts in the autumn in mild areas, and will grow there happily until spring.

CONTINUITY

One of the greatest challenges for the owner of a small salad garden lies in ensuring that there are always some salad plants ready for use. Nothing is more wasteful of space than gluts which are followed, almost invariably, by shortages. A row of bolting lettuce is a depressing sight, however fond you are of lettuce soup.

Given the vagaries of weather and climate, gardening is bound to be an inexact science. The modern gardener, however, has an array of techniques and knowledge at his disposal which make 'continuity', to use the commercial grower's jargon, far more attainable than in the past. The use of varieties and crops which mature at different seasons, protected cropping, staggered sowing, planting and transplanting are all tools which help to solve the glut/gap problem.

Choice of plant

In the post-war years plant breeders have developed many new varieties of edible plants – all notable for certain characteristics and qualities. These might be resistance to disease, uniformity, heaviness or quality of crop, or ease of harvesting. Many plants have been developed specifically to enable the commercial grower to supply the market over a longer season – perhaps by filling a previously existing gap. (Such is the case with the Japanese overwintering onions which, in temperate climates, fill a gap in the supply of fresh onions in early summer.) By selecting carefully from the many available salad plants, therefore, the private gardener can extend his season considerably.

Protected cropping

Protected cropping is a term which embraces all forms of growing under cover (see p.41). It has definite advantages in that it not only enables the actual cropping period to be extended, but also makes it easier to maintain a steady supply of salad vegetables. It is worth remembering that a 0.5°C/1°F rise in temperature is equivalent to moving 100 miles south.

In spring, for example, seed can be sown under cover (perhaps in a heated propagator) to get earlier plants for planting out; the first salad crops can also be grown to maturity under cover. Similarly, in autumn and winter a surprisingly wide range of salad crops can be grown under cover, benefiting as much from the shelter as from the slight gain in temperature.

In summer protected cropping is useful in cold and northern regions, where heat-loving summer crops such as tomatoes, peppers and cucumbers cannot normally be grown successfully outdoors. Grown under cover there is a much higher chance of success.

Staggered sowing and planting

Staggered sowing and planting are an obvious means of preventing the whole crop from maturing at the same time. With quick-maturing crops which 'go over' after reaching maturity, such as hearting lettuce and summer radish, it pays to make small but frequent sowings. Similarly, the lifting and transplanting of seedlings can be staggered, or staggered cropping can be obtained by selecting different-sized seedlings for planting.

Using individual soil blocks

Raising plants in individual soil blocks (see p.28) has much to offer from the point of view of maintaining continuity, making maximum use of garden space and contributing to the appearance of the garden. It is always useful to have a few seedlings 'at the ready' to pop into any vacancy which may arise.

Seedlings grown crowded together in a seed flat or seedbed deteriorate fairly fast if they are not planted out. The robust seedlings obtained by raising plants in small pots or blocks without any competition from neighboring plants are much more suitable as gap fillers. 'Salad Bowl' lettuce, 'Mizuna' and corn salad are the sort of plants which are useful for this purpose. A few spares of each are all that is needed to handle emergencies.

DECORATIVE PLANTING

It has always been one of my dreams to create a garden of outstanding beauty in which every tree, shrub and plant is not only lovely in itself, but is also edible or practical in some other way. The Americans have coined the term 'edible landscape' to describe this concept. I'm not sure I like the term, but I love the idea.

Salad vegetables must be the easiest group of plants to weave into an edible landscape, as so many of them are beautiful in color, texture and habit. They can be used as eye-catching features, to create a tapestry of patches and patterns, worked into formal and informal flower beds, or used as decorative edges.

Feature plants

Probably the most handsome of all vegetables is the cardoon, with its lovely gray foliage and thistle-like leaves and heads, growing over 2m/6ft high. It is normally cultivated for its young stems, which are blanched and then cut in its first season. But it can be left in the ground and grown as a perennial. A single plant makes a magnificent focal point in a central position, or a row of cardoons can be grown as a hedge. The herbs angelica and lovage can be used in the same way; they grow into enormous, shiny-leaved handsome plants with dramatic seedheads.

Globe artichokes grow less tall than cardoons but have the same decorative qualities. They can also be planted in rows as hedges or used for demarcation purposes. So can the humble rhubarb. Though not, of course, a salad plant, it can make a handsome weed-smothering boundary to the salad garden.

'Feature' plants with misty fern-like foliage will make attractive soft-textured clumps. Examples are sweet cicely and the green and bronze forms of the perennial fennel, both of which will grow 1.2-1.5m/4-5ft high. The fennels will combine beautifully with borage, though the latter may become cumbersome in mid-age and require supporting or trimming.

For color in early summer, allow several chicory plants to run to seed. The clear blue flowers open in the morning and close in early afternoon – a dramatic sight, as the spikes of some root and asparagus chicories can be over 3m/10ft tall. Red-leaved orach is used in salads when it is young, but any plants left to seed create a brilliant splash of coral coloring in the autumn.

Some of the climbing vegetables are very colorful. A good example is the runner bean – first introduced into gardens as an ornamental plant. They and climbing green beans always look effective trained up trellises or grown up tepees of canes or strings. Exceptionally pretty is the old-fashioned variety, 'Painted Lady': the flowers are like apple blossoms. The purple-podded green climbing beans also have lovely dark foliage and mauve flowers in keeping with the pods. For additional drama, climbing beans can be trained up trees or even up sunflowers – but firm staking will be necessary with the latter.

Salad patches

One of the prettiest ways of working a salad garden is to grow plants in small patches of triangles, squares or

Left *A handsome cardoon with an edging of chives.*

Above *The pretty flowers of a root chicory, towering over 2m/6ft tall.*

Right *An 'edible landscape' of vegetables in the potager at Barnsley House. Bushes of lavender and ornamental cabbages and kales cluster around the central urn.*

irregular shapes. The most suitable salad plants for this purpose are those with pretty or colored foliage and a fairly even growth habit – coriander and red lettuce, for example – so that the patches look uniform rather than ragged.

Patches can be created by direct sowing of seedling crops (see p.48), which are normally short-lived, or by transplanting young plants. For a continually full, tapestry effect, always have something ready to replace a seedling patch when it is finished. Some subjects, such as 'Karate', Mediterranean rocket, purslane, red and 'Sugar Loaf' chicory, can be treated as seedling crops to start with, then thinned to allow a smaller number of plants to mature.

Seedling crops with pretty foliage include garden cress, coriander, dill, mustard, alfalfa, fenugreek, curly endive and curly cutting lettuce. It's a nice idea to mix the seed of carrots and a variety of annual flowers and broadcast them together. The result is a colorful patch with flowers blooming among the carrot foliage. The carrots are pulled when they are ready.

For colored patches, use red lettuces, beets and golden purslane and red Italian chicories – though these will only turn red or variegated in autumn. Very attractive dense effects can be created with salad rape, 'Sugar Loaf' chicory, green purslane and coriander – all of which can be direct-sown.

Vegetables which will make effective patches when *planted* are 'Karate', 'Mizuna', shungiku, asparagus peas, iceplant, 'Ragged Jack' kale, other dwarf and ornamental cabbages and kales, and tomatoes.

It's great fun planning patches so that there are contrasts of color, texture and form. And don't overlook the fact that intercropping can also result in very attractive effects, especially when there are contrasts. For example, small, round-headed lettuces are set off particularly well by the slender blue-green upright leaves of onions or leeks.

Edges

Edges in vegetable gardens should keep a neat, low profile. In summer, lively edges can be created with 'Salad Bowl' lettuce, especially the richly colored red and green varieties, and the curly-leaved Italian 'Lollo' varieties, which have red and green forms. When red and green varieties are planted alternately, the effect is striking. Golden purslane and shungiku also make pretty edgings if picked frequently to keep them compact. In winter, corn salad, land cress and claytonia can all be grown as attractive edgings.

Many herbs can be used in this way. Parsley, which runs to seed after a year, and chives, which are best divided and renewed every two or three years, are traditional edging herbs. Let the chives flower in early summer – the purple heads look marvellous and can be used in salads – and then cut them back for a second crop. Sorrel and alpine strawberries make satisfactory edges, but need renewing every few years.

Evergreen edges can be achieved with a variety of salad herbs. Salad burnet, for example, though a perennial, sows itself annually. (The leaves of the young seedlings are more palatable than those of the older plants.) Other suitable herbs are hyssop (which is pretty in flower and has the merit of attracting bees and butterflies), winter savory, upright thymes, variegated marjoram and the neat winter marjoram, rue (renew it periodically with cuttings taken in spring) and southernwood (which will need hard clipping to keep it trim).

Edgings of flowers transform the appearance of a vegetable garden. Pansies will flower throughout the year; *Bellis perennis* (the double form of English daisy) in spring, summer and autumn; nasturtiums in summer and pot marigolds for much of the year. All of these can also be used in salads. *Limnanthes douglasii* (the poached egg flower) also makes a cheerful edging, and attracts bees and hoverflies while Chinese chives make a delightful permanent edging.

Salad plants in flower beds

There's a lot of scope for incorporating salad vegetables into flower beds and borders. Fairly large plants usually look best in groups of three or four; smaller plants in larger groupings, depending on the size of the beds. As a general rule, flowers grow well on less fertile soil than vegetables, so where the two are being mixed, work plenty of compost into the areas where the salad vegetables will be grown, and keep them well watered.

Borders, ideally, should be composed of plants of differing heights, with, say, taller plants such as sunflowers, climbing beans or cardoons at the back, and single plants of globe artichokes and asparagus (and, in summer, ornamental cabbages and kales) in the middle. Asparagus peas, bush tomatoes and dwarf green beans can all be worked into beds, and smaller colorful plants such as the red lettuces, 'Mizuna', red chicories and claytonia can be fitted in quite naturally at the front.

Dry sunny places will suit purple and variegated sage, clary sage, lemon balm and thymes. The lovely variegated mints can be productive occupants of moister ground or shadier corners. Remember, too, that a number of garden flowers are both edible and decorative.

Right *Clumps of garlic chives with their graceful white flowers make a dainty edging in the vegetable garden. The plants are perennial; both the leaves and flowers can be used in salads.*

Below *Red forms of the Italian 'Lollo' lettuce make a neat border in a vegetable garden. They stand for many weeks without running to seed and, pretty and colorful as they are, would not be out of place in a flower garden.*

PLANT RAISING

Is it worth going to the trouble of raising your own plants, rather than buying them ready for planting out? The answer must certainly be 'yes, if you can'. It's fun and it is satisfying but, above all, you have a far greater choice of varieties if you raise your own, since nurserymen inevitably concentrate on the most popular, but by no means most interesting, varieties. You also avoid the risk of introducing soil-borne diseases such as clubroot and eelworm into your garden.

Where it proves necessary to buy, choose sturdy, strong-looking plants, if possible grown in individual containers, rather than those poor plants wrenched out of crowded seed flats. Where appropriate, harden them off before planting outside (see p.32).

SEED

The majority of salad vegetables are raised from seed: the better the seed quality, the greater the chances of a good crop. In most Western countries, minimum standards of purity and germination are laid down for the more important vegetable seeds, so you can be fairly sure of buying seed which was of reasonable quality when it was packeted. However, seed does deteriorate with time and in adverse conditions, losing its viability (ability to germinate).

Where possible, buy seed in hermetically sealed foil packets; these enable it to remain viable much longer than in the traditional paper packets. Always beware of seed packets that have obviously been subjected to damp or very dry conditions: the chances of good germination are slender.

Storing seed
Seed should be kept dry and cold. A lot of germination failures stem from using old seed or seed which has been kept in damp garden sheds or hot rooms indoors. Ideally, seed should be stored at temperatures below freezing: in fact for every 5°C/9°F rise above zero, the storage life of seed is halved. So keep it in an airtight tin or jar in a cool room with a bag or dish of silica gel in the container to absorb any moisture. If possible, use cobalt-treated silica gel, which turns from blue to pink when moist. When it becomes pink, warm it in an oven until it has dried out, then return it to the seed tin. Ordinary silica gel will, of course, need to be dried out periodically. If you cannot get hold of silica gel, a handful of cooked rice grains in the tin or jar (a device used in the tropics to absorb moisture) will perform much the same function.

The natural viability of vegetable seed varies according to the species. Brassica, tomato and legume seed can, under good conditions, keep for up to ten years; lettuce, endive, and chicory will normally last for four or five; but with the onion and leek family germination drops off after the second year; and for roots like parsnip, salsify and black salsify, which lose their viability very rapidly, fresh seed only should be used.

Saving your own seed
Amateur gardeners are usually advised against saving their own seed, as it is unlikely to match the quality of bought seed. However, it is worth saving some seed of those salad vegetables used as seedlings, not least because if you broadcast seedling patches on any scale, you will need far more seed than the average seed packet contains. It is also handy sometimes to save the seed of an unusual salad plant which has been difficult to obtain, or of a particularly beautifully colored lettuce or chicory. However, seed saving is best undertaken in areas with a dry climate in the period when the seed is ripening.

Seed should be saved only from the very best plants, never from those that are diseased or have gone to seed prematurely. If possible, keep the plants isolated from

Storing seed
Vegetable seed should always be stored in cool, dry conditions. Packets can be kept in airtight cookie tins with a bag of silica gel to absorb moisture. The illustration, right, shows the blue silica gel in its dry, natural state; the illustration, far right, shows how the gel turns pink when damp.

other varieties so there is no chance of cross-pollination. Keep them well watered when the flowers and seedheads are forming. They may need staking so that they don't fall over, soiling the seed pods, and running the risk of becoming diseased by trailing on the ground. Once growth has ceased no further watering is required. It is best to allow the seed pods to dry naturally on the plant, but in persistently damp weather uproot the plants and hang them under cover until completely dry.

When the pods are brittle, the dry seed can be shaken out on a newspaper and stored in envelopes or jars, but I sometimes leave garden cress seedheads, for example, hanging in the greenhouse, taking them down and crumbling the seed pods directly onto the ground when I want to sow.

Seed saving is feasible with a number of plants, such as chicory, endive, lettuce, landcress, corn salad, chervil, 'Mizuna' and borage. To ensure that quality is maintained, it is advisable to start again with commercial seed every few years.

Sowing methods

Vegetable seeds are sown either **outdoors**, directly in the ground *in situ* or in a nursery bed from which they are eventually transplanted into their permanent positions, or **indoors**, a loose term to describe sowing seed in a seed

Seed can be saved from crops like garden cress, above, and Mediterranean rocket, but the seed pods must dry off thoroughly.

TYPES OF SEED

Seed is now sold in various forms, apart from ordinary 'naked' seed.

PELLETED SEED Individual seeds are coated with a protective substance, making each seed into a small, round ball. This makes them much easier to handle and sow with precision. The coating breaks down in the soil, but it is important to ensure that the pellets remain moist until this point, or they may not germinate.

CHITTED (PREGERMINATED) SEED Seed can be germinated indoors. Put it on moist blotting paper, until the tiny radicle is no more than 6mm/¼in long. It can then be sown in potting mix or outdoors. Chitting speeds germination when soil temperatures are low. Chitted seed of tender plants (such as cucumbers) is sometimes available from mail-order seed firms, to save the necessity of sowing in a heated propagator.

SEED TAPES AND SHEETS Seed is embedded in tapes or tissue-paperlike sheets, which are laid on the ground or in a seed flat and covered lightly with soil to germinate. They must be kept moist. Since the seeds are already spaced out evenly, very little, if any, thinning is required.

F_1 *SEED* A number of modern vegetable varieties are designated 'F₁ hybrids'. These are obtained by crossing two parent lines, which are of exceptional purity because they have been 'inbred' for several generations. The resulting F_1 seed is of outstanding quality, evenness and reliability. Since F_1 hybrids will not breed true the seed should not be saved.

DISEASE-FREE SEED Many varieties of vegetable have now been bred with resistance to particular diseases. Sometimes seed is guaranteed free of certain seed-borne disease: In some cases it can be treated against seed-borne diseases which would become evident after germination. Lastly, seed is sometimes dressed when packeted with fungicides that combat diseases likely to attack the seed or seedling during the germination phases.

flat or pot in any protected position such as a green-house, windowsill, frame or cloche. The choice of method depends on local climate, on the type of salad vegetable and the purpose for which it is being grown.

Outdoor sowings are made for robust vegetables which germinate easily, for vegetables that dislike being trans-planted, for seedling crops that are sown thickly and harvested young and for hardy crops, such as peas and beans. A nursery or seedbed is used primarily to save space for vegetables that either have a long growing season or occupy a lot of space when mature. In their early stages, they can be grown relatively close together in the seedbed, during which time the ground they will eventually occupy is used for another crop. A seedbed can be used to gain time if ground space is not available when seeds should be sown.

Indoor sowings are often used to give plants an earlier, protected start when conditions outdoors are still un-favourable, so that bigger and better plants or earlier-maturing ones can be grown. In cold areas, half-hardy vegetables, such as tomatoes, peppers and green beans, can be raised indoors to increase their chances of matur-ing during the summer. Out-of-season crops of ordinary vegetables are often obtained by making exceptionally early sowings under cover.

SOWING OUTDOORS

A lot of good seed sown outdoors never germinates, often because it was sown when the soil was too cold, too wet, too dry or too lumpy. Choosing the right conditions for sowing, and preparing the seedbed well, are crucial to success.

Here, perhaps, the term 'seedbed' should be explained. It is used, rather ambiguously, both for *any* piece of ground in which seed is sown, and also for an area put aside for raising seedlings that will later be transplanted.

Preparing the seedbed
Seedbeds are often put in an out-of-the-way corner of the garden – perhaps near a hedge – where the seedlings are deprived of light and moisture and develop into sad, drawn specimens. Always make the seedbed in an open position; the soil does not need to be rich but it should, if possible, be weed-free. In soil that is suspected of being full of weed seeds, it is worth preparing the seedbed first, then allowing the weed seeds to germinate, and hoeing them off before sowing the salad crop.

The surface of the seedbed needs to be free of clods, lumps and stones, and raked to a fairly fine tilth – about the size of breadcrumbs. A fine tilth is particularly important when sowing small seeds, but larger seeds, like peas and beans, can cope with a rougher surface. The soil should be reasonably firm – where possible leave it to settle for a few weeks after digging.

The mechanics of making a seedbed vary with the soil. Sandy and light soils are easily raked down into a good surface in spring, but clay and loam soils are naturally much lumpier (some clay soils are unsuitable for seedbeds but can be improved by working in compost and sand). The bed should be dug over in autumn and exposed to winter frosts which help to break down the lumps. Once they have started to dry out in spring, rake them down,

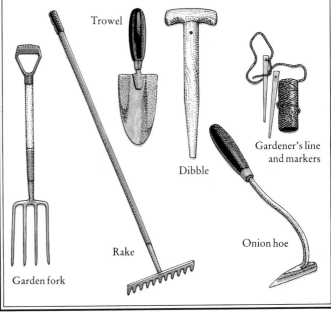

TOOLS FOR SOWING
These are the basic tools used in preparing the soil and in sowing. Always buy the best quality you can afford. The illustration below shows a standard garden fork, rake, trowel, dibble, gardener's line and markers and an onion hoe, which comes in handy for making a wide drill.

Trowel

Gardener's line and markers

Dibble

Rake

Onion hoe

Garden fork

breaking up the larger clods with a fork or the back of the rake; if this proves difficult, fork the soil over lightly. Then rake backward and forward several times, removing small clods and stones, until a smooth surface is obtained. It is important to choose the right moment to tackle the soil. If it sticks to your shoes, it would be best to wait a few more days until it has dried out a little. (You can cover the ground with cloches to make it dry faster.) If the soil is too dry, water it before raking it down.

Preparing a seedbed
1 *Breaking up the clods of earth with a garden fork.*

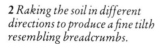

2 *Raking the soil in different directions to produce a fine tilth resembling breadcrumbs.*

3 *Testing the soil temperature with a soil thermometer prior to sowing the seed.*

Different seeds germinate at different soil temperatures. As a general rule, the higher the temperature, the faster the germination, although for most vegetables there is an optimum temperature for germination, and some seeds (such as butterhead lettuce and onion) germinate poorly at temperatures above 24°C/75°F. Soil temperature can be taken with a soil thermometer, which should be inserted 5-8cm/2-3in deep in the soil to obtain a correct reading. There is little to gain by sowing prematurely in cold soil: as likely as not, the seed will rot or become diseased. If you are unable to sow straightaway for any

reason, cover the prepared seedbed with a light mulch of straw or dried leaves to protect it from strong drying spring winds or heavy rainfall.

Methods of sowing

Seed can be sown in drills, broadcast or sown individually, the choice of method depending on both the type of crop and the size of seed.

SOWING IN DRILLS In this method a narrow slit, or drill, is made in the soil with, say, a trowel. The depth of the drill will depend on the size of the seed being sown: as a rough guide, seeds need to be buried at least twice their depth. It is important to sow the seed thinly as, in most cases, seedlings have to be thinned out when they have germinated. The more they are spaced out when sown, the less thinning will need to be done later.

Drill sowing
1 *Having marked out the row with a gardener's line, make a shallow drill with a trowel.*

2 *Taking a pinch of seed from the palm of the hand, sow it thinly and evenly along the drill.*

3 *Press the seeds into the bottom of the drill.*

4 *Use an onion hoe to cover the seed with a fine layer of soil.*

STATION SOWING In this variant of drill sowing two or three seeds are sown fairly close together at a 'station', then a gap is left, then another group of seeds sown, and so on along the drill. It makes thinning easier, and enables a fast-growing crop to be sown between stations of slower-growing ones (see p.17). For a crop that will eventually be thinned to 20cm/8in apart, station sow the seeds at half the distance of the final spacing – 10cm/4in apart. Pelleted seed is very useful for station sowing.

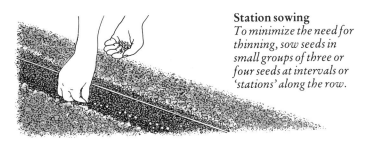

Station sowing
To minimize the need for thinning, sow seeds in small groups of three or four seeds at intervals or 'stations' along the row.

If you have to sow in drills in very dry conditions, make the drill, then water only the base of it (not the ground surrounding it) until it is almost muddy. Sow the seed in the moist drill and cover with *dry* soil. The latter acts as a mulch, preventing evaporation, and ensures that the ground stays moist until the seed has germinated. In dry weather cover the seedbed after sowing with a light mulch, or with clear polyethylene film, to keep the surface moist. It must be removed as soon as the seedlings are through, or they become drawn.

In very wet conditions, the drill can be lined (and the seeds covered) with potting mix, or well-rotted leaf mold, to make a dry 'bed' for the seed.

BROADCASTING This is the old-fashioned method of sowing seed by scattering it over the surface. It is still very useful for seedling crops that require little or no thinning, and sometimes for fast-growing salad plants such as radishes or early carrots. It is also a useful space-saving method.

Prepare the seedbed as already described, taking special care to ensure that it is free of weeds. Then scatter the seed over the surface as evenly as possible. Crops used at a very young stage, like garden cress, can be sown thicker than, say, radishes or 'Sugar Loaf' chicory, where individual seedlings will eventually need more space to develop.

After sowing, cover the seed by raking gently first in one direction, then at right angles to it. Because the seed is so near the surface, there is a greater risk than normal of it drying out in hot weather, in which case cover the bed with a thin mulch or polyethylene film until the seed has

germinated. Alternatively, fine soil or compost should be sifted over it.

A similar effect to broadcasting is obtained by sowing in very close drills about 5-8cm/2-3in apart, or in broad drills about 15cm/6in apart, with 15cm/6in between the drills. These will be easier to weed than a broadcast patch.

SOWING INDIVIDUAL LARGE SEEDS Very large seeds, such as peas, beans and cucumbers, can be sown simply by making a hole in the soil with the point of a small dibble and dropping the seed into it, but make sure the seed touches the bottom of the hole and is not suspended in midair. Seeds can be sown outside in this way under a jam jar, to give them an early start, the jar acting as a minicloche. Sow two or three seeds per jar, thinning to one seedling after germination.

Sowing large seeds
To encourage germination large seeds can be sown under a jam jar, which acts as a minicloche. Sow several seeds together, thinning to the strongest seedling after germination. Remove the jar as soon as the seedlings are through.

Thinning

Seedlings grow very rapidly and if they are overcrowded, will fail to develop properly and become diseased, so they must be thinned as soon as they are large enough to handle. It is easiest if the ground is moist, so water beforehand if necessary. Try to minimize disturbance to the remaining seedlings by simply nipping off the unwanted ones just above soil level. It is best to thin in stages, each time thinning so that each seedling stands clear of its neighbor. Clear away the unwanted seedlings, as their smell may attract the plant's natural enemies.

Thinning

1 Pinch off surplus seedlings just above ground level.

2 Firm the soil back around the remaining seedlings.

SOWING INDOORS

Raising plants indoors is best seen as a multi-stage operation in which certain phases are sometimes omitted or merged with others. The key phases are: **sowing**, in which seed is sown, generally in a small container, in fine-textured potting mix or a special growing medium, and is usually put in the warmth to germinate; **pricking out**, in which seedlings are transplanted into a larger container with richer, coarser mix so that they have space and nutrients to develop; **potting on**, in which seedlings are moved into individual pots of richer potting mix; and **hardening off**, in which plants are acclimatized gradually to lower outside temperatures before being **planted out** in their permanent positions.

With modern mixes and propagators it is deceptively easy to germinate seedlings, and, at this stage, they take up very little space. Once they are pricked out and/or potted on, they need more room, good light and some warmth, and you may well find it difficult to meet these conditions. Since it can take some time from sowing to the moment when soil conditions and temperatures are suitable for planting out, beware of sowing more plants than you have room to cater for; plants deteriorate and are likely to become diseased if subjected to overcrowding or extremes of temperature and poor light levels.

Sowing containers

Almost any container can be used for sowing seed (see below). For most seedlings, it need hold no more than 2.5cm/1in of potting mix, but should have drainage holes in the base. Where a propagator (see opposite) is being used, choose containers that will fit into it economically, as heated space is always at a premium. Although seed is traditionally sown in seed flats, small or shallow pots, it can also be sown in individual soil blocks. These can either be handmade (see below) or can take the form of reusable molded 'cellular' seed flats, compressed peat

Types of container

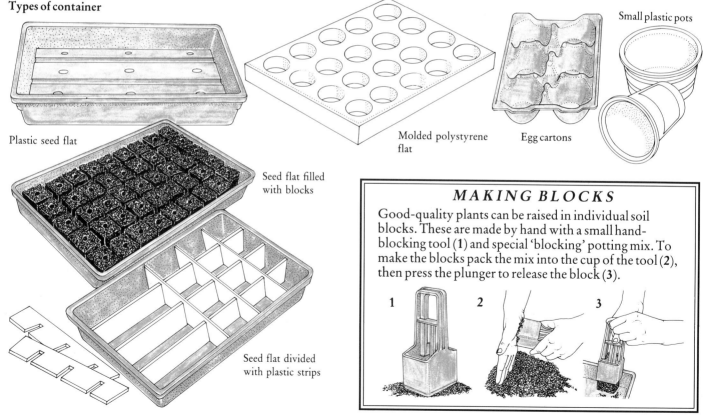

Plastic seed flat

Molded polystyrene flat

Egg cartons

Small plastic pots

Seed flat filled with blocks

Seed flat divided with plastic strips

MAKING BLOCKS

Good-quality plants can be raised in individual soil blocks. These are made by hand with a small hand-blocking tool (**1**) and special 'blocking' potting mix. To make the blocks pack the mix into the cup of the tool (**2**), then press the plunger to release the block (**3**).

pots, or seed flats divided into single compartments. Improvised containers, made from small plastic pots or egg cases, can be used just as successfully. (Don't forget to create drainage holes: make them with a knitting needle or sewing bodkin.)

Although patented sowing flats are sometimes fitted with removable plastic domes to keep the surface of the potting mix moist, other containers can equally be kept moist by covering them with a piece of glass or by slipping them into a plastic bag until the seed germinates.

Potting mix

A potting mix must be a good medium for germination, the seed's main requirements at this stage being air, warmth and moisture. The ideal mix is even in texture, retains water well and is sterile, or at least as free as possible from weed seed and disease spores. Both peat-based and soil-based potting mixes (such as the ProMix formula mixes) are sold for garden use.

Seed can also be germinated successfully in inert mediums such as sand, perlite or vermiculite, but, as these have no nutritive value, seedlings must be transferred rapidly to a stronger potting mix.

Peat-based mixes have the advantage of being very light to handle, but they dry out rapidly and are awkward to rewet once dry. Soil-based mixes, which should be made from finely sifted sterilized loam mixed with peat and sand, are heavier to handle but retain moisture better. Adequate potting mixes can be made up by sifting topsoil from a hardwood forest through a 12mm/½in mesh sieve, or by mixing two parts of good-quality peat with one part of builder's coarse silver sand. Potting mixes can be watered with a very weak solution of liquid seaweed fertilizer to promote healthy growth, and to provide nutrients for the seedlings once they are past the germination stage. Garden compost is *not* suitable for germinating seedlings – it is far too rich and would simply encourage sappy, disease-prone seedlings. Specially formulated blocking mixes with adhesive properties are normally used for soil blocks.

Methods of sowing

Although seed is generally sown in seed flats or pots, soil blocks are very useful, as they eliminate the need to prick out. With soil blocks, one or at the most a few seeds are sown in a small block of compressed potting mix. The

PROPAGATORS

Seed germination is faster and more successful in warm soil. Propagators are used to supply a source of 'bottom heat' below the seed flat to raise the soil temperature to 13°-16°C/55°-60°F. Propagators range from very simple units heated with an electric light bulb, to electrically warmed plates or coils placed beneath or within a seed flat to elaborate automated, self-watering units. A propagator can also be built on a greenhouse bench using insulated electric cables buried in sand. Propagators can also be designed to run in conjunction with gas, oil and kerosene greenhouse heaters. The seed flat must always be covered to prevent the potting mix drying out.

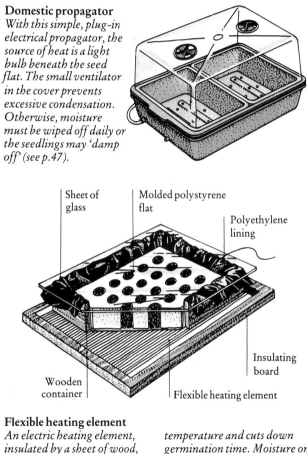

Domestic propagator
With this simple, plug-in electrical propagator, the source of heat is a light bulb beneath the seed flat. The small ventilator in the cover prevents excessive condensation. Otherwise, moisture must be wiped off daily or the seedlings may 'damp off' (see p.47).

Sheet of glass
Molded polystyrene flat
Polyethylene lining
Insulating board
Wooden container
Flexible heating element

Flexible heating element
An electric heating element, insulated by a sheet of wood, will help to ensure success when germinating seeds. It keeps the container at an even temperature and cuts down germination time. Moisture on the glass above the polystyrene container should be wiped off daily.

seedling grows without competition and develops into a strong plant with a vigorous root system. The block is planted out as one unit, so there is no root disturbance and the plant 'gets away' beautifully.

With soil blocks there is no risk of seedlings becoming overcrowded and, if they hang about before planting, there is less likelihood of deterioration. Because of the protective nature of the block, they can often be planted under conditions where planting of normal 'bareroot' transplants would be impossible. Also, plants which normally dislike being transplanted, such as Chinese cabbage, can be successfully transplanted if raised in soil blocks.

Blocks are also useful for raising plants in small gardens and for maintaining continuity. It is easy to sow a dozen or so lettuce blocks every week or ten days. If you want, say, no more than ten winter savoy cabbages, sowing a dozen blocks would be enough, rather than sowing a whole seed flat. A seed flat holding, say, 40 blocks could, in theory, house 40 different vegetables.

SOWING IN SEED FLATS If using soil-based mixes, first fill your container to within 12mm/½in of the top with the potting mix, gently pressing your fingers along the container edges and into the corners to make sure they are filled. If using a peat-based mix, fill the container to the rim, then tap it once or twice on the worktop, and water it with a fine nozzled pot. Allow it to drain for 5-10 minutes to avoid compaction. Press the surface of the mix smooth using a small board or, for a round container, the bottom of a flower pot. Then stand the container in a dish of water until it has soaked up moisture. If a peat-based mix has become very dry, moisten it in stages, with repeated damping and turning, rather than leaving it to soak for several hours.

Sow the seed thinly on the surface, if possible spacing individual seeds no closer than 12-25mm/½-1in apart. Push the seeds carefully off a piece of paper, or pick them up individually on a wetted knife blade or on the moistened tip of a piece of broken glass. Dangerous though this sounds, it works beautifully – the seed drops off as it touches the potting mix.

Then sift a little dry potting mix over the seeds to cover them, pressing the surface down smoothly as before. If moisture doesn't seep up from below to the surface of the compost, water it gently using a fine nozzle on the pot, or a fine mister for small seeds.

Finally, put the container in a propagator and cover with a glass sheet or polyethylene film or put in a plastic bag to keep it moist. Remove the covering for about half an hour a day to let the air circulate and wipe off any moisture; this helps to prevent seedling 'damping off' disease (see p.47).

SOWING IN BLOCKS When using soil blocks, one seed is normally sown in each block. If the viability of the seed is in doubt, test it by sowing some first on moist blotting paper, or sow several seeds in each block, thinning to one per block after germination by pinching out the surplus seedlings at soil level. Small seeds can be sown using the 'glass' method already described.

In some cases, with onions, leeks and beets for example, commercial growers have found it possible to raise several seedlings in one block and to plant them out as one unit *without* thinning. They should be planted somewhat further apart than single seedlings would have

Sowing in flats

1 *Fill the seed flat to within 12mm/½in of the top, levelling the surface with a piece of board.*

2 *Sow seeds very thinly on the surface. Here a piece of glass is used to space individual seeds 12-25mm/½-1in apart.*

3 *Sift a thin layer of potting mix over the seeds to cover them. Press it smooth after sowing.*

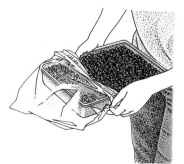

4 *Slip the seed flat into a plastic bag to keep the potting mix moist until the seed germinates.*

been, but each plant develops into the normal size. This saves handling time and space in the early stages. The rows, because they are slightly further apart than usual, can then easily be intercropped in the early stages. Small lettuces, for example, can be grown very successfully between rows of multi-seeded onions or beets.

Germination

After sowing, put the seed containers somewhere warm to germinate, in a propagator, or in a heated cabinet or above, but not directly on, a radiator. Avoid a position in direct sunlight where the seedlings would shrivel as soon as they germinated. Any seed flats that have been kept in a warm, dark place must be brought into the light as soon as there are signs of germination, or the seedlings will become weak and etiolated and will never make strong plants. It is a good idea to examine seeds daily as they may germinate very fast. Most vegetable seeds germinate within four to ten days.

Once the seedlings have germinated they tend to grow rapidly. They need good light (but not direct sunlight) and warmth, although in most cases temperatures 3-6°C/5-10°F lower than those needed for germination will suffice during the day; at night, aim to keep them at least frost-free. Any covers on the containers should be wholly or partially removed to give the plants adequate ventilation. Keep the mix moist but do not overwater. With peat-based blocks line the base of the container with plastic film to prevent the mix drying out.

If you are using individual blocks and find that the plants are outgrowing them when it is still too early to plant outside, transfer some of the blocks to another seed flat and pack the space between them with loose potting mix. The roots will grow into it, so plant growth will not be checked: at this stage they can be fed with liquid fertilizer diluted to quarter- to half-normal strength. They must, of course, be hardened off before being planted out (see overleaf).

Pricking out

Seedlings should never be allowed to become overcrowded, and should be pricked out as soon as they are large enough to handle, generally when they have two or three small leaves.

Use commercial soil- or peat-based potting mixes. If making your own potting mix, combine three parts of peat with one part of sand or 3mm/⅛in grit. For every 9 liter/2 gallon bucket, add 28g/1oz of general fertilizer (double this quantity for tomatoes) or, if you are growing plants organically, several handfuls of well-rotted garden compost. Alternatively, you can use seaweed-based fertilizer, provided it is diluted according to the manufacturer's instructions.

Pricking out
1 *First water the seedlings thoroughly, and fill the container into which they are being moved with moist potting mix; then level it as for sowing. Using a small dibble, ease out the individual seedlings, holding them by their leaves to avoid damaging the root hairs.*

2 *Make a small hole in the potting mix just large enough for the seedling's roots, and insert the seedling with its lower leaves just above the surface*

3 *Press the soil gently around the base of the stem. Space seedlings about 4cm/1½in apart and keep them out of direct sunlight until they are well established.*

Potting on

Most salad plants – lettuce and endive, for example – can be planted out direct from the seed flat once they have developed a good root system and provided outdoor conditions are suitable. Larger, less hardy plants, such as tomatoes, need to be grown under cover longer, and moved into individual pots of about 8cm/3in in diameter. Similarly, plants that will be grown to maturity in large pots should first be moved into pots of an intermediary size, to stimulate root growth.

Standard potting mix is normally used for potting on. Where a soil-based potting mix is used, fill the bottom third of the pot with drainage material, such as a few pieces of broken pot, then cover it with a layer of dried leaves or coarse fibrous material. This is unnecessary with a peat-based mix, which is very well drained unless firmed too hard. Water after planting.

Potting on
Water the plant which is being moved, then ease it out of its container. Holding it so that the bottom of the stem is 2.5cm/1in below the rim of the new pot, pack potting mix gently around the roots. Tap the pot on the bench to settle the potting mix and firm around the stem with the finger tips and water.

Hardening off
Before they are put outside, plants need to be gradually acclimatized to colder, more exposed situations, preferably over a two- to three-week period. Start by increasing the ventilation indoors; then move the plants into a sheltered position outside during the day, bringing them in at night. If you have a cold frame, simply remove the lights during the day and replace them at night. Finally leave the plants out day and night before planting.

Hardening off is especially important when using peat-based rather than soil-based potting mixes, which lead to lusher, softer growth, more susceptible to checks after planting.

PLANTING OUT

Planting out is inevitably a shock and setback to the plant, so whatever is being planted, whether seedlings from a seedbed, seed flat or soil blocks, or a pot-grown plant, try to minimize the disturbance.

Plants vary in their optimum size for planting (some dislike being transplanted altogether) but, as a general rule, the younger they can be transplanted, the better. Although normally sown *in situ*, roots such as carrots and parsnips *can* be transplanted when very small. Always try to plant in overcast weather or in the evening.

How to plant
Assuming the ground has already been dug over and prepared, rake it reasonably smooth; the soil should be pleasantly moist, so water several hours in advance if necessary. Then water the seedbed or seed containers, again preferably in advance, to let the water soak through thoroughly. Dig up the plants with a trowel, holding them by the leaves or stem, and make a hole in the ground large enough to accommodate the roots without cramping them. Then, holding the plant in the hole, replace the soil around its roots. Firm the soil around the stem with your fingers. Check that the plant is firmly anchored by giving a leaf a tug. If the plant is wobbly, replant it more firmly. If necessary, water the ground around the plants and mulch them, provided they are not so small that they would be swamped by the mulch.

In hot weather you can shade the plant for a few days. Cover it with a cone, made either from newspaper or from a large envelope (see below), cut down one side and opened into a triangular shape. Floppy-leaved plants like chicories and spinach can be trimmed back to a couple of inches after planting to minimize water loss.

Planting out
1 *Water the plant well beforehand, then turn the pot upside down and tap the rim on a hard surface to loosen the root ball.*

2 *With a trowel, make a hole just large enough to take the roots without cramping them. Holding the root ball at soil level, fill in the soil around the roots, firming it around the stem with the finger tips. Give a leaf a tug to ensure the plant is firm.*

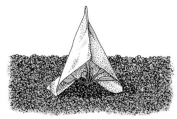

3 *A plant tends to wilt after planting and in sunny weather may need to be shaded for a few days to reduce evaporation. Make a shade from newspaper or from a large envelope, slit down one side and opened out into a triangular shape.*

GARDEN PRACTICES

Good-quality vegetables can be produced only if they are grown well, that is manured, watered, mulched, kept free of weeds, pest and diseases, and protected from the elements. This chapter looks at some of these aspects of plant care as well as the question of growing vegetables in containers, stressing those features that are most relevant to salad plants. For more detailed information, consult one of the standard texts recommended on p.167.

MANURING

The soil should be looked upon as a larder. In fertile soils plants find all the nourishment they need, and when they die and eventually rot, the nutrients they extracted from the soil during their lifetime are returned to it. This is what happens in nature. But in a cultivated garden plants are removed and the nutrients lost: so the larder must be replenished by the use of fertilizers and manures.

Fertilizer

This term is generally used to describe a concentrated, manufactured and, therefore, 'artificial' substance containing nitrogen (N), phosphorus (P), or potassium (K), or a mixture of the three. Artificial fertilizers supply nutrients in a form which plants can use almost immediately. Some concentrated liquid feeds derived from natural sources, such as seaweed extracts, are also called fertilizers.

Manure

This term implies a bulky 'organic' substance, derived originally from plants or animals. Farmyard manure, garden compost and seaweed are examples of useful manures. Bulky manures provide food for worms, bacteria and other beneficial organisms and, after they have been broken down by the micro-organisms in the soil, are converted into humus, from which plant nutrients are released. They supply a wider spectrum of nutrients than artificial fertilizers, over a long period, but in smaller, less concentrated, less predictable quantities. Humus also plays a major role in improving soil structure.

The use of fertilizers

Fertilizers are used to 'top up' the supplies of nutrients in the soil. Plants need N, P, and K in large quantities, and various minor and trace elements obtained from the soil in lesser quantities. Broadly speaking, N is important for leaf growth (so leafy crops like brassicas require large amounts), P for early growth and K for general plant health and ripening. Nitrogen is always the nutrient most likely to be in short supply as it is very soluble and is therefore washed out of the soil in winter; most soils have reasonable reserves of P and K.

In practice, nutrients have to be applied in a balanced form, N balanced by smaller quantities of P and K, or plant growth is unbalanced. The simplest way of doing this is to buy a brand name compound fertilizer, in which N, P, and K are mixed in suitable proportions. Fertilizers are applied either as a 'base dressing' a few weeks before sowing, or as a 'top dressing' during growth. Granular and powdered forms are spread on the ground and watered in; liquid forms are diluted and watered onto the ground; some can be sprayed directly onto the foliage.

On average soil, where reasonable quantities of manure or compost are being used, an annual base dressing of compound general fertilizer (N:P:K = 10:10:10), applied at the rate of 60-90g per sq m (2-3oz per sq yd) would be sufficient.

Artificial fertilizers are widely used to give quick results and high yields, but they make almost no contribution to the long term fertility of the soil. They are a form of 'force feeding'. The lush growth which results is 'soft', prone to pest and disease attacks, susceptible to setbacks in poor weather and, many people feel, poorly flavored. It is also very easy to give an 'overdose' of artificial fertilizers. In my view, it is better to build up the fertility of the soil with manure and compost, and, where necessary, boost plant growth with a seaweed extract or homemade liquid manure such as 'black jack' which is gentler in action and cheaper.

BLACK JACK Suspend a sack of well-rotted animal manure mixed with grass clippings and soot, if available, in a large tub of rainwater. After several weeks it will be ready. Dilute the liquid to the color of weak tea. It can

then be used as a good general purpose liquid fertilizer.
COMFREY FERTILIZER Use a 90 liter/20 gallon lidded container such as a barrel, with either a tap or a pipe at the base, which can drain off into some kind of pitcher. Stuff the barrel with fresh, young comfrey leaves, fill it with water, and replace the lid. After about four weeks clear liquid can be drawn off. Dilute 570ml/1 pint with 2.2 liters/½ gallon water. The solution is rich in potassium, making an excellent feed for tomatoes.

The use of manures

Manures are not only a source of nutrients, but help to improve the soil's fertility. They do this partly by providing food for earthworms, which work in a remarkable variety of ways to improve the soil. The more organic matter in the soil, the faster the earthworm population increases, and the richer the soil becomes. But once their food supply diminishes, they die or move away and fertility drops.

Manures also improve the soil 'structure'. Put simply, this is the arrangement of particles in the soil, and governs its workability, aeration, drainage and ability to hold moisture. To get good soil structure, clay particles must be broken down into crumbs, and sand particles built up into aggregates. Humus, because of its unique physical and chemical properties, is the main agent for bringing this about.

All this explains the organic gardener's maxim: 'Feed the soil, not the plants'. Feed the soil regularly with manure, and you'll grow fine salad crops. Wherever possible, work in manure annually: I try to dig in *some* manure or compost every time a piece of ground is cleared. As a rough guide, farmyard manure should be used at the rate of at least 6kg per sq m/10lb per sq yd and poultry manure, which is more concentrated, at about half that rate.

What can be used for manure? Possibilities include any animal manure (the more it is mixed with litter and straw the better), spent mushroom compost (use sparingly on limey soils), rotted straw, sewage sludge and municipal waste (these last two only if free of toxic metals), and seaweed (piled in a heap first so that the rain can wash off the salt). Sawdust and peat have little nutritive value and are best combined with animal manures. All these materials can either be used fresh or alternatively can be composted.

Garden compost

In modern industrialized society it is often difficult to find a supply of manure, and many gardeners have to rely on making compost from household and garden waste. It is not easy to make enough. Compost shrinks enormously in decomposing, and the final pile can seem a pitiful amount to spread over the garden. But the enthusiast will always find ways of collecting more raw material. In cities, market stalls and supermarkets throw out enormous quantities of vegetable waste: in the countryside, weeds, young nettles and bracken, and leaves can be gathered; and horse manure is often available.

COMPOST BINS

The object of a purpose-built bin is to generate high temperatures, so that waste decomposes rapidly killing weeds and weed seeds, pests and disease spores, and producing a homogenous end product looking like soil. This requires relatively large quantities of waste materials, kept in well insulated bins approximately 1m/3ft wide and 1m/3ft high, though they can be any length. If two bins are made

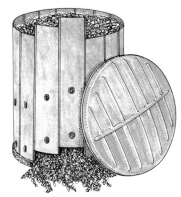

Compost bins
Left *A patented compost bin is useful for a small household, though its capacity is generally too small to create enough heat to break down very coarse material. Waste is put in the top and several months later removed from the base.*

Right *A purpose-built compost bin constructed as described.*

side by side one can be maturing while the other is being built up. The bin is normally a permanent construction sited in an out of the way place on well-drained soil.

It must be strong as the raw material is heavy and bulky. The side and back walls can be constructed of insulating material such as cinder blocks, bricks, lumber or straw bales (these, of course, would need to be replaced annually). The front can be made of loose boards slipped behind upright posts. This enables the pile to be built up and dismantled in stages.

COMPOST PILES Compost can be made in simple piles or in purpose-built bins (see below). The simplest method is to stack suitable garden and household waste in a pile, keeping it covered with black polyethylene sheeting. Once it is about 1.5m/5ft high, leave it covered. After about a year it will be ready for use. The disadvantage of this method, apart from being slow, is that high temperatures are not generated so weed seeds, pests and disease spores may not be killed nor will the coarser, woodier material be completely rotted. Nevertheless, organic material is eventually returned to the soil, and that is what really matters.

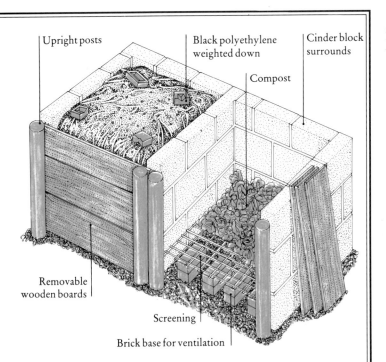

Upright posts

Black polyethylene weighted down

Cinder block surrounds

Compost

Removable wooden boards

Screening

Brick base for ventilation

The base of the pile should be raised at least 10cm/4in off the ground for ventilation and drainage. Make the base from brushwood, rubble, clay drainage pipes, or double rows of bricks with 5cm/2in gaps between them. Heavy duty screening can be laid over the drainage base to hold the compost in place.

Nutrients are very easily washed out of a compost pile by rain, so wherever possible keep the pile covered, both when it is being made and once it has been completed and is maturing.

BIN COMPOST Construct the bin as shown below left. The best way to build up the bin, although it requires discipline, is to premix the materials in a plastic sack, either adding a sack at a time, or waiting until there are enough sackfuls to make a layer about 20cm/8in deep.

Any material that will rot can be used, though coarse or woody material, such as cabbage stalks, should be shredded or chopped. Just avoid having a solid mass of any one substance, such as lawn mowings or leaves (see below). Do *not* use diseased plant material, weeds that have gone to seed, or roots of perennial weeds such as ground elder or couch grass. These should all be burnt without delay.

The bacteria which bring about decomposition need air, moisture and a source of nitrogen, found naturally in leafy green material or animal manure. There is plenty of nitrogen in a summer pile, but in autumn and winter a source should be added, sprinkled on each 20cm/8in thick layer or, preferably, with the premixed wastes. This can be poultry or other manure (roughly one bucket per sq m/sq yd), ammonum sulfate (115g per sq m/4oz per sq yd), seaweed extract or brand name compost activator (at the rates recommended by the manufacturer).

When the pile reaches the top of the bin, cover it permanently with black polyethylene, punctured with 2.5cm/1in diameter holes about 30cm/12in apart, to ensure ventilation. Then cover the pile with permeable but insulating material, such as several inches of soil, matting, or a thick layer of straw.

A pile made in summer will normally be ready for use in two or three months; a winter pile in eight or nine.

Leaf mold

Autumn leaves are best made into leaf mold. Pile up fallen leaves and transfer them to a wire-netting frame, preferably sited in a dry shady place. The leaves decompose slowly, taking about two years to make a pleasant, fibrous mold useful for potting mixes and, when sifted, for sowing mixes. After only one season, however, the partially rotted leaves can be used as drainage material in flower pots, or for mulching.

Incorporating manure into the soil

Bulky manures and compost are either dug into the soil, or spread on the surface, depending on the soil and the state of the manure. Fresh manure and compost is spread on the surface, allowing the worms to work it in gradually. If it is dug in, there will be a loss of nitrogen from the soil in the early stages of decomposition. *Well-rotted* manures and compost can be dug in, or used to mulch growing crops. Traditionally, heavy soils are dug over roughly in the autumn, so that frost action can help break up the clods. Manure is worked in during digging. The soil may be forked over again lightly in spring.

Alternatively, heavy soils are sometimes ridged up in winter, the ridges being covered with manure. I use a single central ridge on a 90cm/36in wide bed; but two 45cm/18in ridges could also be used. The ridges ensure good drainage while still permitting frost to penetrate. By spring, the soil has generally broken down beautifully and the manure can be easily forked in.

Light, well-drained, and sandy soils are best covered with manure in winter, but dug over in spring. The manure protects the surface from winter weathering which would destroy the structure and wash out nutrients.

In most years it is quite adequate simply to fork over the soil to the depth of the spade (one spit deep). Every third year or so it is beneficial to dig more deeply (see below). This breaks up any hardpan which may be forming in the soil, impeding drainage, and enables manure to be worked into the ground at a deeper level. This, in turn, encourages plants to root more deeply – the best insurance against drought.

Soil acidity

As mentioned earlier, most vegetables grow best on a slightly acid to neutral soil. Soil acidity is related to the

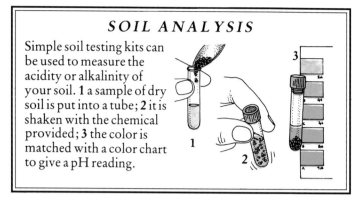

SOIL ANALYSIS

Simple soil testing kits can be used to measure the acidity or alkalinity of your soil. **1** a sample of dry soil is put into a tube; **2** it is shaken with the chemical provided; **3** the color is matched with a color chart to give a pH reading.

amount of calcium (lime or chalk) in the soil, and is measured on the pH scale, which ranges from 0 to 14. The neutral point is 7, the pH of distilled water. Soils with a pH below 7 become progressively more acid, those with a pH above 7 more alkaline, though the normal range is between pH 4 and pH 8. The change from one pH level to the next represents a tenfold increase in acidity or alkalinity.

In humid climates there is a tendency for soils to become progressively more acid, as rainfall washes calcium out of the soil. This is particularly marked on light, well-drained soils and in industrial areas with atmospheric pollution.

Don't worry about acidity unless plants are not growing well, or if there are few worms, or if the soil looks sour with moss growing on the surface. In this case test the soil with a simple soil analysis kit or pH meter. Raise the pH level to around 6.5 by the addition of lime over several successive seasons. Ground limestone is normally used,

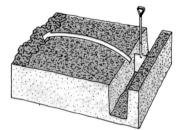

Double digging
1 *Make a trench one spade deep and about 38cm/15in wide across the bed, and remove the soil to the far end of the strip. Keep the manure handy in a wheelbarrow.*

2 *Fork over the soil at the bottom of the trench, then put in a good layer of manure or garden compost, or whatever is being used.*

3 *Fill the trench with soil from the next strip, then fork soil and manure together so the manure is spread evenly through the soil.*

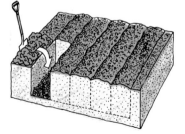

4 *Continue in this way to the end of the strip, then fill the last trench with soil from the original trench. Double digging is normally necessary only one year in three.*

and is sprinkled over the surface in autumn. (Never apply it at the same time as manure or fertilizer.) On sandy soils it can be applied at the rate of approximately 270g per sq m/½lb per sq yd. Use double the rate for loamy soils, and treble the rate on clay soils or those very rich in humus. However, never lime unless it is necessary; over-liming can cause many problems.

WEEDING

The salad grower looks upon weeds with a kindlier eye than most gardeners because quite a number of them, especially in the seedling stage, make tasty, nutritious additions to a salad. But they will compete with the salad crops for water, nutrients, light and space, and must, therefore, be kept under control.

Perennial weeds
Weeds are grouped into two categories, perennials and annuals. Perennials are those that live on in the soil from one year to the next. They often have invasive creeping root systems like couch grass (*Agropyron repens*) or ground elder (*Aegopodium podagraria*), or deep, stubborn tap roots, such as the broad-leaved dock (*Rumex obtusifolius*) and dandelion (*Taraxacum officinale*). Learn to recognize the perennial weeds in your garden with the help of a good wild-plant book, and dig them out without mercy. Remove even small pieces of root and burn them. Most perennials disappear relatively fast when ground is cultivated regularly.

Annual weeds
Short-lived annual weeds cause the most problem in the salad garden, perpetuating themselves by seeding once or even several times a year. One plant can produce an enormous number of seeds, but even starved little annuals will drop a few unnoticed seeds.

Undoubtedly the most important factor in the battle against annual weeds is to prevent them going to seed in the first place. Weed seed can remain viable in the soil for a good many years. In weed-ridden gardens there is a huge reservoir of weed seed in the soil, waiting for favorable conditions to germinate.

Shallow cultivation disturbs the weed seeds near the surface, with the result that about half are destroyed, either by germinating and dying or through exposure to birds and so on. After about seven years of cultivation they would be reduced to a fraction of the original number, demonstrating the truth of the old proverb, 'one year's seeding, seven years' weeding'. Deeper cultivation will bring up seed from the lower levels, perpetuating the problem, so in weedy soils confine cultivation to shallow hoeing in the growing season.

When previously undisturbed soil is cultivated, there is a great flush of weeds in the first year. Hoe them off and, if you have time, let a second crop of weeds germinate before sowing or planting. If possible, avoid cultivating during the growing season or only cultivate shallowly to prevent further weed seed being brought to the surface. Keep the crops mulched: this is a very effective means of preventing weeds from germinating.

Contrary to previously held belief, it is now thought that weeds *between* rows are much more serious competitors to growing crops than those *within* rows, and should be removed first. Where possible, grow plants at equidistant spacing in a 'block' rather than in rows. A great many leafy plants eventually make a canopy over the ground when grown at equidistant spacing, effectively preventing weeds from germinating. As soon as the seedlings are through the ground can be mulched.

With crops sown in the open, weed competition, in most cases, starts to become really serious about three weeks after the crop has germinated. So, if necessary, postpone weeding until that point: but remember, by then it is urgent!

The best tool for weeding in an intensively cultivated salad garden is the small hand or onion hoe, as it enables you to get really close to the plants. If hoeing is done in wet weather, weeds should be put straight on the compost pile, otherwise they may reroot. Weeds that have gone to seed, however, should be burnt.

Weeding
A small onion hoe is an extremely useful tool for weeding in the salad garden as it enables one to get very close to plants.

WATERING

Growing plants need a constant throughput of water, which is taken in through the roots and evaporated through the leaves. They need enough water to keep them turgid: if they lose turgidity and wilt, growth is checked. But it's a fallacy to assume that the more watering, the better. Watering washes nitrogen and other soluble nutrients out of reach of the roots, it can reduce the flavor of vegetables like tomatoes, and it discourages the deep rooting that allows plants to draw on deeper reserves of nutrients and moisture in the soil.

Watering primarily stimulates the growth of the leafy parts of a plant. This, of course, is what is wanted with salad vegetables like lettuce and cabbage, grown for their leaves; but with crops like radish and onion, grown for their roots, overwatering can have a detrimental effect by encouraging leaf growth. As is explained later, plants have differing water requirements which vary according to their stage of development. These factors must all be taken into account if watering is to be as efficient and effective as possible.

Avoiding watering

Everything should be done in the salad garden to conserve water and minimize the need for watering. The following cultural practices work toward this end:
1 Work in as much bulky organic matter as possible to increase the water-holding capacity of the soil. (This has a particularly dramatic effect on light, well-drained soils.) Work it in deeply to encourage deep rooting. **2** Keep the soil surface mulched to prevent evaporation – far more water is lost through evaporation than drainage. **3** On sloping ground, cultivate *across* rather than down the slope, to minimize erosion and water loss through surface

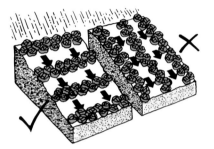

Conserving water
In a sloping garden, plan your beds and crops to run across, rather than down, the slope. This helps to cut down on moisture loss through surface run-off, and also helps to prevent soil erosion.

WATERING EQUIPMENT

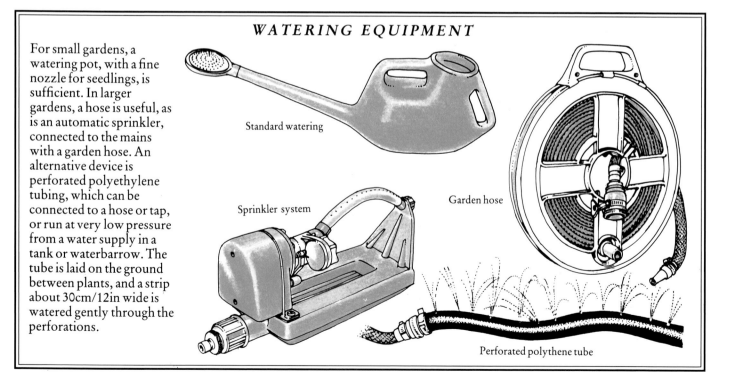

For small gardens, a watering pot, with a fine nozzle for seedlings, is sufficient. In larger gardens, a hose is useful, as is an automatic sprinkler, connected to the mains with a garden hose. An alternative device is perforated polyethylene tubing, which can be connected to a hose or tap, or run at very low pressure from a water supply in a tank or waterbarrow. The tube is laid on the ground between plants, and a strip about 30cm/12in wide is watered gently through the perforations.

Standard watering

Sprinkler system

Garden hose

Perforated polythene tube

run-off. **4** In dry weather, during the growing season, cultivate as little as possible and only very shallowly as deeper cultivation brings moisture to the surface, which will then evaporate. Once the top few inches of the soil have dried out, they act as a mulch and the rate of evaporation is slowed down. **5** Keep the ground weed-free: weeds both compete for water and evaporate water through their leaves. **6** Erect artificial windbreaks in windswept gardens, as wind increases evaporation.

How to water

Always water gently and thoroughly. Large water droplets damage both the soil surface and young seedlings, which should always be watered with a fine sprinkler or with a pot with a fine nozzle.

With established plants, direct water to the base of the plant. With those spaced far apart, confine watering to a circular area around each stem, leaving the soil between dry. This will discourage weed germination between the plants. With large plants, such as tomatoes or zucchini, sink a clay pot into the ground near the stem of the plant, and confine watering to the pot. The water seeps slowly through to the plant's roots without evaporating.

When plants are grown close together they make heavy demands on moisture in the soil and will need generous watering if they are to make lush growth. The same is true of seedlings grown as 'cut-and-come-again' crops.

The most common fault is to underwater. The soil, in fact, becomes wet layer by layer, and until the top layers are thoroughly wet, the root zone beneath will remain dry. After watering, test how far water has penetrated by pushing your finger into the soil; the result is often illuminating. With a few exceptions, heavy but infrequent waterings are far more beneficial than frequent, light waterings. Light soils will, however, need more frequent watering than heavy soils, although somewhat less water would be required at each watering.

Watering large plants
An efficient, labor-saving method of watering single plants is to sink a porous clay flower pot into the ground near the plant, watering into the pot. Water seeps slowly through to the roots with far less moisture loss from evaporation than normally.

KEY PERIODS FOR WATERING

GERMINATION Seeds will not germinate in dry conditions, so seedbeds or drills must be watered in advance of sowing.

TRANSPLANTING This is a delicate, critical stage for plants. They should be transplanted into moist but not waterlogged soil, and kept moist until they are established. Root hairs are generally damaged by transplanting so the plant can only absorb a little water at a time. In this case, frequent watering – daily in dry weather – is necessary, giving the plant no more than 140ml/¼ pint each time.

LEAFY VEGETABLES Leafy vegetables such as the brassicas, lettuce, endive, spinach, celery and zucchini require a lot of water throughout growth. In the absence of rainfall, they would benefit from waterings of about 9-14 liters per sq m/2-3 gallons per sq yd a week. Where regular watering is difficult, however, limit watering to a single, very heavy watering – about 18 liters per sq m/4 gallons per sq yd – 10-20 days before you estimate the plant is ready for harvesting.

FRUITING VEGETABLES For tomatoes, cucumbers, peas and beans – all vegetables grown for their fruits – the most critical time for watering is when the plants are flowering and the 'fruits' start to swell. Heavy watering at this stage increases their yields. Full details will be given where appropriate.

ROOT CROPS These need enough water for steady growth, but too much water encourages lush foliage rather than root development. In the early stages, water them only if the soil is in danger of drying out, at the rate of at least 4.5 liters per sq m/1 gallon per sq yd a week. More water is required in the later stages when the roots are swelling.

MULCHING

A mulch is a protective layer on the soil. It can be organic material, such as compost, leaf mold or even cardboard, that will eventually rot into the soil, or inorganic material such as polyethylene film. Stones, gravel and sand are traditional mulching materials in hot climates in various parts of the world.

The main purpose of a mulch is to conserve moisture, but mulching has a number of very useful secondary effects. It helps to control weeds by inhibiting both the germination of weed seeds and their subsequent growth – any weeds which do germinate are easily pulled out of a mulch. It improves soil structure by protecting the soil surface from the destructive influence of heavy rain, by minimizing the effects of treading on the soil and, in the case of most organic mulches, provides food for worms which, in turn, contribute in a number of ways to soil fertility.

Mulch also helps keep the soil moist, enabling plants to extract soluble nutrients from the soil. Provided the mulching material is clean, it helps ensure sprawling plants like cucumbers and tomatoes stay clean, and prevents disease spores splashing onto the foliage and fruit.

Mulching keeps the soil cooler in summer and warmer in winter. There is, therefore, less frost penetration and it is easier to dig roots out of the soil. When stone, gravel and sand mulches are used in a greenhouse, the heat they radiate at night raises the night air temperatures.

Types of organic mulch

A wide range of organic materials can be used for mulching. As a general rule, they should be as well rotted as possible, making them easier to spread on the ground around the plants, and increasing the chances that any diseases, weed seeds and toxic substances they may contain will be destroyed.

Ideally, a mulch should be slightly loose-textured so that rain can penetrate. Suitable materials include: animal manures, garden compost, seaweed, old straw, dried bracken, dried leaves, spent mushroom compost, and cotton waste. Wood derivatives such as sawdust, wood shavings, pulverized and shredded bark and also pine needles can all be used but are improved by being composted for several months beforehand or by being mixed with animal manures. Lawn mowings are a convenient mulching material, but are best left to dry for a day or so before use, or they form a 'gooey' mat. Newspapers, cardboard and old carpeting make good mulches.

A tip taken from Mel Bartholomew's book, *Square Foot Gardening*, is to drill holes in a pile of newspapers or carpet squares, so they can be slipped over growing plants. Unsightly though these are, they appear to be very effective.

Peat can be used for mulching, but has the disadvantage that it tends to absorb any rain before it permeates the soil.

The remains of an organic mulch can be dug in at the end of the season, although by then earthworms will often have done the job for you.

How to mulch

The thicker the mulch, the more effective it will be. The limiting factors are the amount of suitable material available, the time and energy one can devote to mulching and the size of the plants. You must not swamp small or medium-sized plants, though tall plants such as tomatoes will grow happily with a mulch 15-20cm/6-8in deep; normally you will have to be content with a mulch a couple of inches deep. You can plant through a mulch by scraping it to one side, and replacing it around the plant after planting, but do not sow in mulched ground, as birds are likely to scratch around and disturb the seeds. It is preferable to sow in open ground and to start mulching when the seedlings are just through.

When to mulch

The important thing about mulching is that it maintains the *status quo*. Don't mulch when the soil is very cold, very wet or very dry – all conditions which discourage plant growth – because the soil will stay that way. Mulch when the soil is warm and moist – the soil temperature should be at least 6°C/42°F and preferably higher.

In practice, the most convenient and often most suitable time to mulch is after planting. But if you are planting in spring, make sure the soil has warmed up before mulching; in summer, water well after planting and then mulch to cut down on subsequent watering.

Vegetables which are being overwintered in the soil, such as celeriac and root crops, can be mulched with a thick layer of straw or bracken in the autumn.

Polyethylene film

Many types of polyethylene mulches are available and new forms are constantly coming onto the market. Black films are best for weed suppression, but tend to keep soil cool. The perforated black films are useful because they allow some rain to penetrate. Transparent films do little toward weed suppression, but warm the soil in spring and cut down evaporation. Opaque white films are sometimes used for mulching, as they reflect light up onto the plants, helping tomatoes, for example, to ripen. They are not very effective as weed suppressors. However, this failing is overcome with dual-purpose black and white films, where the black surface is laid downward, preventing weeds from germinating while the white upper surface directs light toward the plants.

Polyethylene films are normally available in strips and are laid at planting. There are two methods. The first is shown below. In the second method, plant first, then unroll the film over the ground and cut the slits above the plants, easing them through. Anchor the edges of the film as shown below. Both methods, to be honest, are fiddly. Adopt whichever you find easiest.

Large seeds, such as sweetcorn, are sometimes sown through holes punched in film, the leaves being eased through when the plants are large enough. Water in the gap at the base of the plant. Potatoes are often grown under black polyethylene to avoid earthing up.

Polyethylene film tends to attract slugs. Look out for them and remove them.

Mulching takes time and effort, not least in finding suitable mulching materials. But the lovely moist, crumbly soil that develops under a good mulch is an excellent reward for your trouble.

Planting through polyethylene

1 *Lay the film on the bed to be planted with a little spare film on each side. Use a trowel to make slits in the soil about 10cm/4in deep on each side of the bed.*

2 *Slip the edge of the film into the slit, then push back the soil to keep it in place. The film should be smooth but not too taut.*

3 *Cut crossed slits (about 8cm/3in long) in the film at suitable intervals for the plants.*

4 *Ease the slits apart and plant through them, laying the film back around the stem afterward.*

PROTECTED CROPPING

Greenhouses, walk-in polyethylene tunnels, garden frames, cloches and low polyethylene tunnels are all forms of 'protection'. In temperate climates, some form of protected cropping is of immense value in growing high-quality salad plants all year round.

The main value of protection is that it gives plants shelter. It is the *combination* of low temperatures and high winds that is so damaging. When protected from the elements, plants can withstand lower temperatures than they would in the open. In addition, their yield and quality is improved enormously, especially in the colder months of the year.

The use of *heated* greenhouses, tunnels and frames is outside the scope of this book, though where facilities are available, they can be turned to excellent use, especially for raising very early and very late crops. Frames are relatively easily heated with electric soil-warming cables. However, in my experience, except in extremely cold areas, heated greenhouses are not essential for maintaining a winter supply of salad crops as so many are hardy and can be grown satisfactorily in unheated forms of protection.

Unheated glass and polyethylene structures cannot provide immunity from frost. This can only be guaranteed by using artificial heating. In winter, temperatures under cover will be only marginally higher than those in the open. (Incidentally, where plants are affected by frost, either shade them, or spray them with water the following morning before the sun is on them. This helps them to thaw out slowly and may prevent serious damage.)

Protection also helps to extend the growing season. Most plants start to grow only when soil temperatures rise above 6°C/43°F in spring, and stop growing when soil temperatures fall below that point in autumn. The number of days between these two points is termed 'growing days', and varies enormously from one region to another, determining which crops can be grown successfully in any area. If the soil is protected with glass or polyethylene, it warms up sooner and remains warm later (so, of course, does the air inside the protective cover), extending the growing season by at least three weeks or 21 'growing days' at either end of the season.

This means that earlier sowings can be made of most vegetables to get an earlier crop, and also that tender, warmth-loving crops (such as tomatoes, green beans and peppers, which are borderline in regions with a short growing season) can be grown successfully. In spring, vegetables can be sown under cover to give them an early start, so that they are ready for planting outside as soon as temperatures have risen sufficiently; similarly, hardy crops can be sown outdoors in summer and transplanted under cover in early autumn for winter and spring use.

In hot weather, temperatures under cover can soar, so with greenhouses, tunnels and frames adequate ventilation is of prime importance to prevent a buildup of pests and diseases. In high temperatures, moisture evaporates rapidly from the soil, and weeds germinate and flourish, so the case for mulching is stronger than usual.

Any form of protected cropping is an investment, deserving special treatment, and should be used as intensively as possible. Make the soil very fertile by working in plenty of well-rotted organic matter. Don't use fresh farmyard manure in a permanent greenhouse, as pests such as symphilids may be introduced and can bring almost intractable problems.

The various types of protection are discussed below:

Greenhouses

Greenhouses are permanent but expensive structures. They provide excellent growing conditions for plants, as glass both transmits light well during the day and traps heat efficiently at night. There is enough height in a greenhouse to grow tall crops such as tomatoes and cucumbers, and plants can be grown either directly in the ground or in containers on the staging. Windows are easily built into the structure, so ventilation is a simple matter. In hot weather, however, it is advisable to 'damp down' frequently – that is, to sprinkle the plants and the floor with water in order to lower the temperature and create a humid atmosphere. This also helps to keep down pests such as red spider mite.

The main drawback of greenhouses is that if plants such as tomatoes and cucumbers are grown in the same soil every year, a serious buildup of soil pests and diseases, known as 'soil sickness', is likely. The soil then either has to be sterilized or replaced – both laborious procedures – or the plants must be grown in uncontaminated soil in pots, or growing bags, or by some soil-less system such as 'ring culture'.

Remember that with greenhouses and tunnels, water-

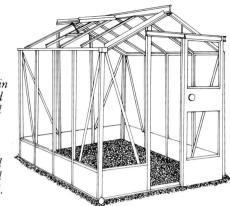

Greenhouse
A typical modern aluminum framed greenhouse on concrete foundations. Plants are either grown in the soil, in containers on the ground or on the staging. In cold areas greenhouses are mainly used in summer for tender crops such as tomatoes; their potential for growing winter salad plants is still unexploited.

ing usually has to be done by hand, unless an automatic irrigation system is installed.

In summer, greenhouses are used mainly for the more tender salad crops such as tomatoes, cucumbers and peppers, but many lie empty or under-utilized in winter. This is when they should come into their own for a wide range of salad crops, such as Chinese cabbage, endive, chicory, winter lettuce, claytonia, Japanese mustards, corn salad, land cress and Mediterranean rocket, as well as overwintered herbs. Seedling crops can be sown in the ground or in deep boxes in autumn and early spring to provide exceptionally welcome winter 'salading'.

Walk-in polyethylene tunnels

Walk-in polyethylene tunnels, used by commercial growers for some time, have only recently become available to the gardening public. They are made of polyethylene film drawn over a framework of tubular galvanized steel hoops about 2m/6ft high. The polyethylene is anchored into the ground by digging a trench about 30cm/12in deep and 45cm/18in wide around the base of the tunnel, laying the edges of the film in it and covering them with soil. No foundations are needed, as would be the case with a greenhouse. Polyethylene film can often be fitted to the framework of an existing greenhouse, if required.

The same range of crops can be grown in a tunnel as in a greenhouse, and the enthusiastic salad grower will find them excellent value.

They are less sophisticated than greenhouses but are a fraction of the cost. Their great advantage over greenhouses is that if the soil becomes diseased, they can be dismantled relatively easily and erected on a fresh site.

However, they are more difficult to ventilate. In summer, very high temperatures can build up and in winter the high humidity is conducive to disease.

The answer is to build in as much ventilation as possible. In a 6m/20ft long tunnel, have a door at each end with a permanent ventilation panel in the top half of each door. In summer, ventilation 'portholes' about 30cm/12in in diameter can be cut along the sides about 45cm/18in above ground level. Spare pieces of film can be taped over the holes in winter.

Depending on the climate, polyethylene lasts about three years before it needs replacing. For maximum life, use heavy- (500- to 600-) gauge film, treated with ultraviolet inhibitors. It must be fitted tightly over the framework, so put it up on a warm day, when the film is limp and can be pulled taut. It always wears where there is friction, so pad parts of the structure in contact with it.

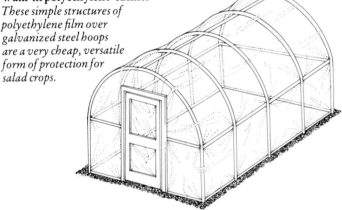

Walk-in polyethylene tunnel
These simple structures of polyethylene film over galvanized steel hoops are a very cheap, versatile form of protection for salad crops.

Garden frames

A frame is perhaps best described as a miniature greenhouse, generally covering little more than a couple of square yards of ground. Traditional frames are permanent structures with solid sides of brick or wood and a glass 'lid' or 'light', but most modern frames are portable, made of aluminum and glass, or plastic. Freestanding and lean-to frames can be made very easily from wood and polyethylene film.

The height of the frame will determine what can be grown in it. A clearance of about 23cm/9in is adequate for lettuce, endive and low-growing salad plants; a height of about 45cm/18in would be necessary for horizontally

trained cucumbers, and celery, fennel, bush tomatoes or peppers; upright tomatoes could only be grown in a lean-to frame. However, when plants are maturing the lights can be removed to give them more room.

In the absence of a greenhouse or tunnel, frames are very useful for raising seeds and for hardening off plants, as ventilation can easily be adjusted by raising or removing the lights. In winter, they are useful for forcing chicory, for lettuce, and for overwintering seedlings; in spring, they are handy for cut-and-come-again seedling crops, and for the first crops of lettuce, carrot and radish.

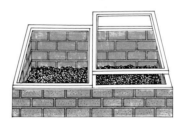

Modern garden frame (below)
Portable aluminum and glass frame with removable lights.

Traditional garden frame (above)
Permanent brick-sided frame with glass lights.

Cloches and low polyethylene tunnels

These are a convenient form of crop protection. Cloches are made from a wide range of materials including glass, fiberglass, rigid and semirigid plastics and polyethylene film. They vary in size from low, classical 'tent' cloches, suitable only for low-growing salads, to the taller 'barn' cloches, which can accommodate larger plants like tomatoes, dwarf beans, peppers and so on, at least in the early stages of growth. Cloches can either be used over single plants or placed end-to-end to cover a row.

Their main asset is their mobility. With the exception of glass cloches, they are small and light and can easily be moved around the garden to whichever crop is most in need of protection. To some extent, this is also their drawback. They need a lot of handling and have to be moved for cultivation, watering and so on. To minimize handling, try and plan the garden so they need only to be moved between adjacent strips of land, a technique known as strip cropping.

When choosing cloches from the many types on the market, the following factors should be considered:

SIZE Choose the largest size available. Apart from giving

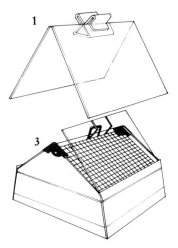

Types of cloche
Glass 'tent' cloche (1); rigid plastic cloche (2); corrugated plastic 'barn' cloche with 'anti-bird' netting (3). All cloches must have end pieces to prevent through draughts.

MATERIALS Glass cloches provide the best growing conditions but are expensive. Plastic materials are perfectly adequate; the opaque corrugated plastics create a diffuse light which is excellent for summer crops and in winter for protecting mature crops, though growing plants such as seedlings tend to become drawn. But plastic materials break down and discolor with exposure to sunlight and should be stored away when not in use.

Low polyethylene tunnels are the cheapest form of protection, consisting of lightweight polyethylene film stretched over wire hoops. The film is bunched up at each end and tied to stakes in the ground at a 45° angle. Along the length of the tunnel the film is generally held in place with strings over the top, tied to the hoops on each side. Polyethylene film usually lasts for no more than two seasons.

Low tunnels offer less protection than cloches, because of the thinness of the sheeting and the ease with which the sides are blown up by the wind. In winter the sides and even the ends of the film can be buried in the ground to make the tunnel more draftproof. Brush off heavy snow if the crops are in danger of being crushed. In summer the film can easily be pushed back for ventilation, watering and cultivation.

Low polyethylene tunnels are easily moved, and are used for similar purposes to cloches. Both can be used in winter *inside* greenhouses and walk-in tunnels to give an extra layer of protection for salad crops.

more ground coverage, a large cloche provides better air circulation, with less risk of pests and diseases becoming serious. Some cloches have extensions so that they can be raised over a growing crop; some have removable roof panels so that plants can continue growing after the panels are removed.

STRENGTH Cloches must be sufficiently robust to withstand constant handling. Flimsy lightweight cloches are easily blown away, and must have some form of anchorage, preferably metal pins which go into the soil.

VENTILATION Temperatures rise rapidly under cloches so removable or built-in ventilation panels are very useful. Otherwise move the cloches apart to provide ventilation, removing them completely in very hot weather. Some makes of cloche have netting fitted beneath the glass or plastic panels, providing useful protection against birds when the glass or plastic is removed. Cloches must never be left open-ended or wind will funnel through, damaging the plants. Where end pieces are not provided, improvise with pieces of glass or rigid plastic, held in place with upright canes.

Low polyethylene tunnel
The cheapest form of protection for salad crops: thin polyethylene over low wire hoops.

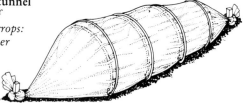

USE OF CLOCHES			
IN SPRING	**IN SUMMER**	**IN AUTUMN**	**IN WINTER**
Cloches can be used to warm up the soil, for early outdoor sowings of radishes, lettuces, corn salad, onions, carrots, seedling crops and so forth, and for hardening off.	Tender plants such as green beans, tomatoes, cucumbers, peppers and tender herbs can be planted out under cloches and, if necessary, grown under cloches the whole season.	Cloches are handy for late sowings of lettuces, endives, corn salad, radishes and many other salad crops, and also for drying off onions and ripening tomatoes.	All overwintering salad crops can be covered with cloches to improve their quality. Glass cloches stand up best to heavy winter rain.

CONTAINERS

With gardens nowadays smaller than formerly, and would-be gardeners restricted to patios, courtyards, balconies or even roof gardens and window boxes, there are many attempts to grow vegetables in containers. Tomatoes, peppers and cucumbers *have* to be grown in containers in greenhouses with a soil sickness problem, but otherwise it is best to reserve containers for fast-growing, small salad plants and herbs. Don't set your expectations too high: it takes a lot of containers to compensate for lack of garden space.

The size of the container will determine what can be grown in it. As a rough guide, seedlings and undemanding shallow-rooting herbs could be grown in a soil depth of 10cm/4in; most small salad plants like lettuce would require a depth of about 15cm/6in, while large plants like tomatoes and peppers need containers of at least 23-25cm/9-10in in diameter and depth. Tall crops are trickier to accommodate in containers, as they may become top-heavy, and will usually need some kind of support.

Provided the container is an appropriate size for the crop, most salad vegetables can be grown in containers, though the most suitable subjects are fairly fast-growing, shallow-rooting plants such as lettuce, Mediterranean rocket or purslane. Sun-loving herbs like basil, marjoram and thyme do very well in containers, as do parsley and chives, provided they have enough moisture. Rampant herbs like mint, unless confined to one deep box, should be avoided. Many of the edible flowers such as nasturtiums can be grown in containers.

Problems with containers

Three aspects of container-growing need attention:
WATERLOGGING Good drainage is essential to prevent waterlogging. Drill several, preferably slanting, 12mm/½in diameter drainage holes in the bottom of the container. Alternatively, make them an inch or so above the base in the sides. This avoids having to stand the container on chocks to keep it free-draining. Put a generous layer of drainage material (see p.32) in the bottom of the pot before adding the soil.

Window boxes and containers on balconies should have a drip-tray beneath them to prevent drainage water causing damage. Drainage is not normally a problem in growing bags filled with peat-based potting mix.

TYPES OF CONTAINER

Flower pots and plastic growing bags of peat-based mixes are often used as containers, but almost anything can be used – from discarded bathtubs, wooden barrels and plastic cans to old tea chests. The main criteria are that they should be strong enough to withstand the combined weight of damp soil and a heavy crop and, if used on balconies or roof tops, they must be lightweight.

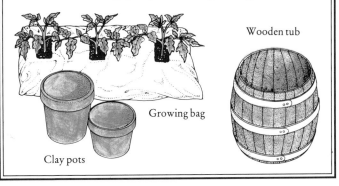

Wooden tub

Growing bag

Clay pots

DRYING OUT Containers are very vulnerable to drying out, partly because the soil is shallow and partly because they are exposed on all sides to the desiccating effects of sun and wind. They need very frequent watering. Where possible, half bury pots and growing bags in the ground to reduce their exposure. With growing bags evaporation from the soil surface can be minimized by making only slits or small holes in the plastic for each plant.

Wooden containers can be lined with plastic to help retain water, though a few drainage holes should be punched in the plastic. In hot weather, but not otherwise, the pots can be stood in pans of water: thread a piece of synthetic fabric through the drainage holes in the flower pot to enable water to be absorbed more easily. Alternatively, a semiautomatic system can be set up (see below).

It is always worth mulching containers, ideally with a

Semiautomatic watering

A good method of watering plants in pots is to make wicks about 12mm/½in wide from twisted soft material. Place one end of the wick in a bucket or dish of water and the other on the soil by the plant. Water seeps along the wick, keeping the plant moist.

couple of inches of stones or gravel. This helps to keep them from drying out.

Try to avoid putting containers in positions where they are exposed to winds. In summer, containers with leafy crops like spinach, lettuce or Mediterranean rocket can be put in light shade.

SOIL Containers should be filled with potting compost or good garden soil with some well-rotted garden compost worked into it. Compaction can be a problem, so add a handful of gravel and/or peat to help make the mixture more porous. If a few worms can be incorporated, so much the better. The soil normally needs to be changed every two years. Hungry crops like tomatoes and peppers – which, of course, *must* be planted into fresh soil every year – will need supplementary feeding during the growing season.

PESTS AND DISEASES

The better the conditions under which plants grow, the fewer problems there will be with pests and diseases. Nine times out of ten it is the overcrowded, starved or forced plants that succumb to attacks which sturdier, well-grown plants resist or outgrow: pests and diseases attack the weak. So I'm not going to dwell here on individual pests and diseases, other than those few which are most likely to occur in the salad garden. (Specialist books and leaflets can be used to identify any pests and diseases that do arise.) It is far more important to create conditions that encourage healthy growth in plants.

Although the use of chemical sprays is widespread, I am reluctant to use them. They are likely to kill beneficial as well as harmful creatures; there is always the risk to children and pets; and harmful residues can be left on plants and in the soil. Moreover, the more a particular chemical is used, the faster pests and diseases build up resistance to it and the shorter its effective life. They are also expensive.

If a pest or disease gets the upper hand and spraying seems to be the only answer, use one of the less toxic, safer products such as rotenone, pyrethrum, or a mixture of the two such as pydercite, or nicotine. These are admittedly less effective than modern insecticides, but are less damaging to the environment. Where not on general sale, sources of supply can normally be obtained through

organizations specializing in organic culture (see p.167). Whatever sprays are used, follow the manufacturer's instructions implicitly. Spray in calm, windless conditions and in the evening, when pollinating insects are no longer active.

An increasing number of non-chemical 'biological' preventive and control measures are available. These range from the use of 'collars' placed around brassica stems to deter cabbage root fly to 'biological control'. Here a pest's natural predator or parasite is introduced to

Preventing cabbage root fly
'Collars' made of flexible rubber can be placed around the stems of brassica plants, at ground level, when they are planted out. This prevents the adult cabbage root flies from laying eggs, which hatch into harmful maggots.

control it – red spider mite in greenhouses, for example, can be controlled by introducing its predator, *Phytoseiulus persimilis*. However, it is not always easy to apply biological control methods successfully under amateur gardening conditions.

Let's look at the sort of cultivation practices that will prevent pests and diseases from becoming serious:
• Encourage rapid germination by sowing in warm soil. Far better to delay sowing a week or so than to sow in cold or wet soil. If necessary, use cloches or transparent plastic film to dry out and warm up a seedbed.
• For indoor sowings, use sterilized soil or potting mix to cut down on 'damping off' disease.
• Sow thinly and thin early. Overcrowded seedlings, whether in a seedbed or in seed flats, are the most vulnerable to seedling diseases, and quickly become lanky and weak.
• Where feasible, raise plants individually – in soil blocks, for example – to encourage healthy growth.
• Harden plants off well before planting out.
• When buying in plants, choose the sturdiest and deepest colored, and examine them carefully for any signs of disease, such as clubroot swellings on the roots of brassicas.
• Choose pest and disease-resistant varieties where available and appropriate.
• Choose appropriate plants for your area. For example,

if overwintered lettuce always seems to go down with mildew, grow endives instead. They are far more tolerant of damp, wintry conditions.

• Encourage steady growth without checks, by making sure plants are never short of water or nutrients. Mulching is a great help toward achieving this. Where soil is not very fertile, supplementary feeding may be necessary.

• Grow plants 'hard' – don't force them by coddling and overfeeding. You may not have the first tomato in the neighborhood: be content with a slightly later but healthier and hardier crop.

• In summer, keep greenhouses on the cool side: over-ventilation is far healthier than under-ventilation.

• Rotate as much as possible (see p.14). Go in for mixed cropping (the norm in gardening) rather than mono-cropping. Pests and diseases are far less likely to build up if they have to travel in search of their next meal.

• Pay attention to garden hygiene. Burn any diseased plants, especially those with virus diseases. (Virused plants are usually stunted and often have mottled leaves.) Burn weeds that have gone to seed. Clear away debris, weeds and old brassica stalks, all of which harbor over-wintering pests that emerge to renew their attacks in spring. Remove thinnings; keep water tubs and tanks covered; wash pots and seed flats after use.

• Handle storage vegetables such as carrots and onions very gently. Storage rots almost invariably start with cuts and bruises, which may be invisible to the naked eye.

• Inspect plants regularly for signs of trouble. It is easy to dispose of a clutch of newly hatched caterpillars, but far harder to track them down once they are tunnelling energetically into the heart of a plant.

• Improve the drainage if your ground is waterlogged (see p.11).

• Make soil fertility your number one priority – working in bulky organic matter whenever possible.

Common pests and diseases

BIRDS Small birds like sparrows often attack seedlings and young plants of succulent vegetables like lettuce, spinach and beet. They can be deterred with a single strand of strong black thread stretched about 5cm/2in above the row. Upturned glass bottles stuck in the ground also seem to have a deterrent effect, perhaps because of the light reflected off them. In some areas, large birds such as pigeons cause serious damage to peas and brassicas,

Deterring birds
Upturned bottles can deter birds, perhaps on account of the light glinting on the glass.

especially in winter and spring. Bird-scarers may have some effect if moved around fairly frequently, otherwise erect temporary netting over the crops, fitted over hoops used for low polyethylene tunnels.

SLUGS AND SNAILS Slugs can be very damaging to salad crops. They are night feeders and, tedious though it is, the best method of control is to go out at night with a torch, collecting them up and destroying them. Conventional slug-killing baits are harmful to birds and other animal life but effective biological slug baits are sometimes obtainable. Snails can be equally damaging and can be treated similarly.

SOIL PESTS A number of soil pests such as wireworm, cutworm and soil weevils, attack plant roots and stems, often nipping plants off at ground level. They are generally more active in spring, and some, like wireworm, are worst in freshly cultivated ground but tend to disappear in time. Like slugs, many are night feeders and can be caught at night by torchlight. If young plants wilt un-expectedly, dig them up and examine the roots for soil weevils or wireworms. Kill any found.

CATERPILLARS The most common offenders are the various caterpillars that attack the cabbage family. Pick them off by hand, or spray with rotenone, pyrethrum or nicotine. Biological control is now possible with the caterpillar parasite, *Bacillus thuringiensis*.

APHIDS Green aphids (greenfly) and black aphids (black-fly) attack a wide range of crops. Spray with rotenone, pyrethrum, nicotine or a solution of soft soap. Whitefly, which is a type of aphid, is often a problem on tomatoes, peppers and eggplants in greenhouses. It can be kept to manageable proportions by interplanting the crops with French marigolds (species of *Tagetes*) as the strong scent discourages them. A tiny wasp, *Encarsia formosa*, is used as a means of biological control of whitefly in green-houses.

'DAMPING OFF' DISEASE Seedlings fail to germinate or die shortly after germination, as a result of overcrowding, or being sown in cold, wet or contaminated soil.

SALAD TECHNIQUES

This chapter looks at some of the more specialized gardening techniques which are sometimes employed in salad growing.

CUT-AND-COME-AGAIN

People tend to think of vegetables as being 'one-offs': they are picked or cut when ready, and that's that. But many leafy salad vegetables, when cut and left in the ground, will grow again, allowing two, three and occasionally more further cuts.

'Cut-and-come-again' is a useful umbrella phrase to describe this happy ability to resprout, which saves the gardener so much time, space and effort. Depending on the plant, cutting can be carried out at the seedling stage, when the plants are half-grown, or when they are mature.

Seedling crops

A seedling crop is one where the seeds are sown relatively thickly and the very young leaves cut and eaten, generally when they are between 2.5 and 7.5cm/1 and 3in high. At this stage they are not only very succulent and tasty, but are also highly nutritious – the seedling leaves can have twice the vitamin content of mature leaves.

The use of seedlings goes back a long way. Over 250 years ago, the English writer Richard Bradley, in his book *New Improvements of Planting and Gardening*, was already giving advice on the cultivation of seedlings, or 'small herbs cut in seed leaf' as he called them. In those days a wide range of plants was grown for their seedlings – lettuce, chicory, endive, types of cress, spinach, radish, turnip, mustard, salad rape – even the seedlings of oranges and lemons, which enjoyed such a vogue in the seventeenth and eighteenth centuries. These seedlings, often forced on hot beds of fermenting manure in frames or in greenhouses, kept the gentry supplied with fresh 'salading' during the winter and spring. (Frames heated with electric soil-warming cables could equally be used today.)

Seedlings can be grown inside or outdoors, according to the time of year. Although Bradley remarked that those grown outdoors were better flavored, those grown indoors are usually more tender, especially in winter.

Seedlings make such intensive use of the ground (cutting can take place as little as two weeks after sowing), that it is worth sowing even very small areas, say 30cm/12in square. Outdoors, they will make useful 'catch crops' on a piece of ground which is vacant while waiting for the main crop to be sown or planted. They can also be intercropped (see pp.15-17), particularly between widely spaced brassicas, and are ideal for creating decorative patchwork effects.

On the whole, seedling crops are more satisfactory in spring, early summer and autumn than in high summer, when, unless sown in slight shade, many will have a tendency to run straight to seed, becoming tough and coarse, and sometimes very hot-flavored, in the process.

Under cover, seedlings are an excellent means of utilizing greenhouses and frames from autumn to spring, when they are so often empty. A patch of, say, cress, salad rape or Mediterranean rocket, sown late in the year, may give one cutting before low winter temperatures prevent further growth. It will then lie dormant (looking terrible if it has been frosted), but as soon as there is any warmth during the day, it will burst into growth, providing fresh salad very early in the year.

Seedlings can also be sown in flats of soil, and in growing bags which have already been used for a main-

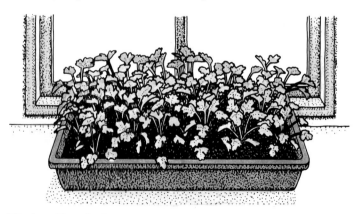

Windowsill gardening
Useful seedling crops such as coriander, above, and cress can be grown on windowsills in shallow trays of soil or potting mix.

48

A spontaneous crop of self-sown 'cut-and-come-again' claytonia seedlings being cut 20mm/¾in above ground level in autumn.

by alternating the direction of the drills: north/south in one patch; east/west in the next, and so on.

Start cutting when the seedlings are an edible size, using sharp scissors or a knife, and leaving at least 20mm/¾in of stem in the ground. Clear away any loose leaves on the surface as they tend to rot and make the seedlings beneath discolored. Keep seedling patches well watered, as they need a lot of water if they are to sustain their rapid rate of growth.

The lifespan of a seedling patch varies from a few weeks to several months, depending on growing conditions and what is required. Unless cut frequently, many will quickly outgrow the true seedling stage. But in most cases the leaves can also be eaten at a later stage. The leaves of the 'Salad Bowl' type of lettuce, for example, are useful over a period of several months.

Sometimes a patch can be thinned out to allow a few plants to grow to maturity. 'Sugar Loaf' chicory is a good example: a patch which starts life as a seedling crop in early spring can still be yielding a few good large plants the following winter. Unless the soil is very fertile, patches which have been growing for several months may need feeding, preferably with an organic liquid fertilizer.

Once growth from a seedling patch becomes tough it should be uprooted. The frequency and number of cuts that can be made will depend on the crop and the growing conditions, early spring sowings probably being the most productive. If you wish to save your own seed (see pp.23-4), a few plants can be left to run to seed after a couple of cuts have been made.

A list of salad plants which can be grown as seedlings is given below. For more detailed information on how to grow them, see pp.58-132.

crop, perhaps of tomatoes or peppers. Probably no more than one cut of seedlings could be taken without the addition of extra fertilizer, as the bags would by then be almost exhausted of nutrients. Seedlings like cress, mustard, salad rape, coriander and fenugreek can be grown in shallow seed flats on a windowsill (see left) or even on moist blotting paper or cotton wool, but in this case only one cut of small seedlings can be expected.

Sowing seedling crops

Prepare the seedbed normally (see pp.25-6), taking particular care that the soil is weed-free – weeding unwanted guests from a seedling crop is a trying task. If in doubt, prepare the seedbed first, leave it for ten days or so to allow any weeds to germinate, hoe them off, and then sow the seedling crop. In cold weather cover the ground with cloches after the initial preparation to warm the soil and make the weeds germinate faster.

Seedlings can either be broadcast (see p.27) or sown in very close drills 5-10cm/2-4in apart or in broad drills, about 10-15cm/4-6in wide. It is hard to gauge how thickly to sow: natural instinct is always to sow too thickly, so apply a moderating hand – even seedlings grow best if they stand at least 20mm/¾in clear of their neighbors. If soil conditions are dry water the drills before sowing, or, if broadcasting, cover the bed with polyethylene film after sowing to keep the surface moist, removing the film once the seedlings have germinated. Pretty effects can be created in adjacent seedling patches

SOME SUGGESTIONS FOR SEEDLING CROPS	
Abyssinian cabbage 'Karate'	Lettuce (certain varieties, see p.63)
Chervil	
Claytonia	Mediterranean rocket
Coriander	Mustard, common
Corn salad	Japanese 'Mizuna'
Cress, garden	Purslane
Dill	Radish
Endive	Salad rape
Fenugreek	Spinach
Leafy 'Pak Choi'	Turnip

Seedling mixtures

Packets of mixed salad seed, for cutting initially as seedlings, are sometimes obtainable and are rather fun to grow. Sold under various names such as *misticanza* in Italy, *mesclum* in France, and 'saladini' in England, they may contain up to ten different salad plants, which germinate in succession over a 12-month period, in rather a haphazard manner. In the early stages a mixed patch needs to be cut frequently at the seedling stage: later, it virtually thins itself out, until it eventually consists of only large, vigorous plants such as chicory and endive, which can be left to grow to maturity.

Remember that many edible weeds such as chickweed are at their best as seedlings (see pp.130-132).

Regrowth in mature plants

While many plants resprout at the juvenile stage, a few will do so even when cut at maturity – the most notable being cabbage, some varieties of lettuce and endive, 'Sugar Loaf' and red chicories, and 'Mizuna'. In some cases, if conditions are favorable, a complete second head (or heads) may even develop. For example, if, when a spring or early summer cabbage is cut, a shallow cross is made in the stump, a second crop of as many as four or five reasonably sized cabbages may have formed by the autumn. The plant must be healthy, and the soil fertile and well watered for this to succeed.

Some varieties of lettuce will also form a second head. In my experience this has happened with greenhouse overwintering varieties such as 'Kwiek', and with some of the colored varieties, including 'Marvel of Four Seasons' and 'Trotzkopf'. This is most likely to succeed in spring, when growing conditions are at their best.

A number of plants will not develop a complete second head, but after cutting the first head or mature leaf, will produce very useful secondary leaf. Endive, 'Sugar Loaf' and red chicory, Chinese cabbage and 'Mizuna' come into this category. These are all plants which are often grown for use in autumn and early winter, and, 'Mizuna' apart, are not considered very hardy. What is interesting is that, once relieved of the leafy but frost-vulnerable head, the stumps, with whatever leaf has been left, will survive very

Cut-and-come-again
A surprising number of salad plants will make further growth after the first cut. With cabbage, growth is accelerated if a shallow cut is made in the stalk. **Far left (top):** *spring cabbage 'Prospera' F_1, cut in early summer;* **far left (bottom):** *further growth six weeks later. (As many as five secondary heads can develop together on one cabbage stump.)* **Center (top):** *'Salad Bowl' lettuce, first cut in early summer;* **center (bottom):** *regrowth three weeks later.* **Left (top):** *Japanese mustard 'Mizuna', cut in mid-summer;* **left (bottom):** *further growth six weeks later. 'Mizuna' can sometimes be cut as many as five times before the plants become coarse and run to seed.*

much lower temperatures. When warm weather returns they will revive and provide very early, tender growth.

For this reason it is worth making late summer/early autumn plantings of these salad plants in unheated greenhouses, walk-in tunnels or frames; alternatively, cover with cloches or low polyethylene tunnels in autumn. In mild areas, they will very often provide pickings throughout the winter months and on into spring.

BLANCHING

Blanching – literally meaning 'to make white' – is one of the refinements of salad growing. The stems or leaves of certain vegetables are blanched (by the exclusion of light) in order to make them crisper, sweeter and more of a delicacy. Very bitter leaves, like those of some of the chicories, for example, thus become far more palatable.

Blanched leaves can often look very beautiful: the pink-tipped, white blades of 'Red Treviso' chicory, jagged white dandelion leaves tinged with yellow, and elegantly crinkled curly endive in particular, look wonderful in winter salads.

In the past blanching was a widely practiced art: our gardening forbears blanched celery, cabbage, endive, fennel, cos lettuce, cardoons, seakale, the young spring shoots or 'chards' of globe artichokes, black salsify and salsify; and even wild plants such as dandelion, alexanders and the wild chicory or succory. Nowadays, blanching has rather gone out of fashion – perhaps because we fight shy of the work involved – although it is fun to do and the end result is rewarding.

Most blanching is carried out in the cool months of autumn, winter and spring, though celery blanching (see p.91) is started in summer. Once blanching is completed, most plants deteriorate fairly rapidly: it is therefore best to blanch only a few at a time in succession during the winter months, and to use them as soon as possible.

During the blanching process, as mentioned above, light has to be excluded, and this can either be done *in situ* or by transplanting the plants into a darkened environment. Whichever method you choose, the greatest risk is of rotting, especially in damp, wintry conditions in a closed environment – it's not easy to create the ideal combination of good ventilation and darkness. To lessen this risk, therefore, always try to cover or tie the plants

Seakale is forced and blanched in spring by covering the dormant crowns with large pots, which exclude light from the young stems.

when the leaves are dry, if necessary covering them with cloches several days beforehand to dry them off. Always remove any dead or rotting leaves first.

In situ blanching methods

TYING The simplest method of blanching is to bunch up the leaves and tie them with raffia, string or rubber bands about two thirds up the plant, when the foliage is dry. The outside leaves will not, of course, be blanched, as they are exposed to light, but the central leaves will be crisp and pale within 10 to 15 days. This method, carried out on mature plants, is a quick and simple way of blanching dandelions, endives and wild chicories.

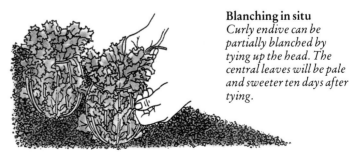

Blanching in situ
Curly endive can be partially blanched by tying up the head. The central leaves will be pale and sweeter ten days after tying.

COVERING In this method, light is excluded by covering the whole plant. A variety of things can be used for the purpose, but it's best to choose something on the large side, to avoid creating too close an atmosphere. Single plants can be covered with upturned flower pots (block the drainage holes with stones or a slate), wooden boxes, black plastic over cloches, or black polyethylene cloches. In France, I've seen what looked like purpose-built miniature wooden coffins over a row of endives. Whatever is used, it is best to tie up the leaves of the plant first, to keep them off the ground.

Plants can also be blanched by covering them with a 15-20cm/6-8in layer of straw or hay, held in place with hoops, sticks or wire netting.

Loose soil or sand can also be used, though this method is probably best reserved for strong-leaved plants. Where soil is used, it can be spaded over the plants from either side of a row, but in this case rows will have to be about 60cm/24in apart to allow room for maneuver. Plants which die back in winter, such as black salsify and salsify, or which have been trimmed off once at neck level to encourage further growth, as is often the case with red chicory, can be covered in the autumn and left until spring. The young growths will then push their way through the soil or sand, being blanched in the process. Mature dandelions can be covered in the autumn, uncovered and cut about 15 days later, then covered again, so that a second crop will be ready in spring.

Transplanted blanching methods

Plants are transplanted for blanching both for protection against frost, and so that the salad plants are more accessible during the winter. They are transplanted when fully grown.

IN FRAMES Traditionally, frames have always been used for blanching, especially for endives, which are not very hardy. The mature plants are dug up with their roots intact in the autumn, before the first frosts, and planted very close together in a frame. They should be lifted when the foliage is dry, and handled very carefully, as any cuts or tears in the leaves invite rots. It is advisable to water the soil in the frame moderately beforehand, so that no further watering is necessary.

The frames can be darkened by covering them with mats, boards, black polyethylene or carpeting. Alternatively, the plants can be covered by sifting sand, soil, or even ashes between and above them, or with a thick blanket of hay or straw.

IN GREENHOUSES Plants are often forced and blanched in a greenhouse, by creating a lightproof area under the staging with boards or black polyethylene; the plants are then transplanted as into a frame.

A dark area can also be created by erecting a low

Endive can be blanched completely by covering the mature plant with a large pot to exclude light. The leaves must be dry or they may become moldy. Plants are usually ready within ten days or so.

Forcing chicory under film
One method of forcing 'Witloof' chicory and some varieties of red chicory is to plant them in a greenhouse, under low tunnel hoops covered with black polyethylene film to exclude light. The heads are usually cut back first.

polyethylene tunnel in the greenhouse, covered with black film.

Plants can also be potted up in deep pots or boxes, and covered with an inverted pot or box of the same size, covering any holes or cracks to exclude light. These can be brought into a greenhouse or, alternatively, put into a warm room or cupboard indoors for convenience.

IN BASEMENTS In countries where basements are the norm, these are regularly used for blanching. Plants potted up in flats or pots are simply placed in a dark basement without any further cover. Where there is no basement, use cool indoor rooms instead.

Plants can also be blanched in a heap of soil. A layer of soil about 10cm/4in thick and 30cm/12in wide is built up against a basement wall. The roots of the plants are then laid close together on the soil, with their necks protruding over the edge, and covered with another 10cm/4in deep layer of soil, then a further layer of roots, more soil and so on. The blanched leaves are cut when ready, and the roots left in the heap of soil. During the course of the winter they will make further useful growth, though this will not, of course, be as vigorous as the initial growth.

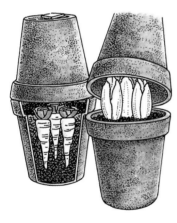

Forcing chicory in pots
The roots of 'Witloof' chicory are lifted in late autumn and trimmed to within an inch of the crown. They can be forced indoors by potting up as many as five or six roots in a large flower pot, covered with an inverted pot of the same size, with the drainage hole blocked to exclude light. If kept at about 10°C/50°F, the white chicons will be ready in about three weeks. The same method can be used for some varieties of red chicory.

Forcing

Although blanching can be done in summer, the best results are obtained at low temperatures. However, plants are sometimes forced into earlier growth in the dark by being kept at higher temperatures, either in heated greenhouses or by bringing them indoors. This method is quite often adopted with 'Witloof' chicory (see p.69). Blanched plants have more flavor and are sweeter if allowed to develop slowly at low temperatures.

SEED SPROUTING

Seed sprouting is a highly intensive form of food production. It is quite possible to sow on Monday and 'harvest' on Wednesday. And no soil or garden is required – just the simplest equipment and a windowsill or somewhere fairly warm to keep the seeds.

Sprouted seeds can be used raw or cooked in salads, and also in many other dishes, such as soups, breads, stews, and omelets. One word of caution is necessary about eating *raw* legume sprouts, such as beans, peas, alfalfa and fenugreek. They contain toxic substances which could be damaging if eaten regularly in large quantities. So use them in moderation or cook them. (Soya and mung beans are the least toxic of the legumes.)

A very wide range of seeds can be sprouted for use in salads – for example, many kinds of beans (the best known of which is the Chinese mung bean, *Phaseolus aureus*) and other legumes, including fenugreek, alfalfa, buckwheat and whole lentils; brassicas such as cabbage, kale, cauliflower and the closely related radish; and cereals such as oats, rye, rice and wheat and many more beside (see p.56).

The best sources of supply are health food shops and seed firms, but be sure that any seeds you buy for sprouting are actually intended for consumption and have not been treated with any chemicals, as might be the case if they are being sold for ordinary garden use. Remember that seeds for sprouting are viable seeds, and must be treated as such: keep them in dry, cool conditions until required for sprouting (see pp.23-4).

If you like sprouted radish seed, which has a very pleasant piquant flavor, it is easy to produce your own seeds. Just allow a few plants to run to seed in early spring or summer, and collect the pods when dry (see p.23). Seed from the large winter radishes is especially good for sprouting.

What, in fact, are sprouted seeds? They are seeds which have been germinated and allowed to grow for a few days, until the 'sprouts' are between 6-12mm/¼-½in long, depending on the species. Up to this point they are drawing on their own internal resources: in order to develop further they would need to be sown or planted in the ground.

In the germination process, the fats and starches stored in the seed are converted into vitamins, sugars, minerals and proteins. Sprouted seeds are therefore exceptionally nutritious, being particularly rich in vitamins and minerals. They are also very tasty, and most have a crisp, crunchy texture. However, they develop rapidly and soon reach and pass the optimum point, both as regards nutritional value and flavor. Once this stage is reached, they may become bitter; it is therefore advisable to sprout small quantities at regular intervals.

The useful life of sprouted seeds can be prolonged by keeping them in a refrigerator for a few days, either in a bowl of water or in a plastic bag, and rinsing them daily to keep them fresh. Some, such as bean sprouts and sprouted lentils, can be frozen, although I normally find that some-thing of the distinctive flavor they have when fresh is lost in the process.

How to sprout seeds

There are many ways of sprouting seeds, and my advice is to experiment, both with the different methods and the various seeds available, and then settle for what suits you best. It is essential to keep the seeds moist and warm so that they germinate easily, but not in too close an atmos-phere or they will go moldy. Always use clean con-tainers. Seeds must be kept fresh by regular rinsing in cold water night and morning. Rinsing is, perhaps, the secret of success: if the seeds are not rinsed, they soon become

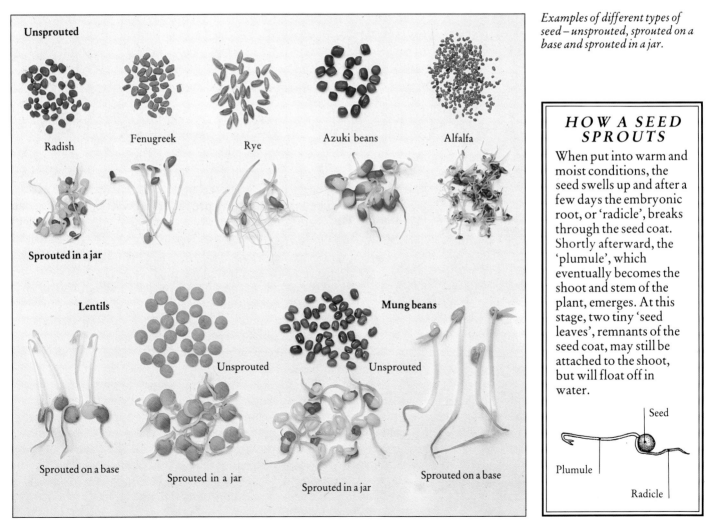

Unsprouted

Radish Fenugreek Rye Azuki beans Alfalfa

Sprouted in a jar

Lentils Mung beans

Unsprouted Unsprouted

Sprouted on a base

Sprouted in a jar Sprouted in a jar Sprouted on a base

Examples of different types of seed – unsprouted, sprouted on a base and sprouted in a jar.

HOW A SEED SPROUTS

When put into warm and moist conditions, the seed swells up and after a few days the embryonic root, or 'radicle', breaks through the seed coat. Shortly afterward, the 'plumule', which eventually becomes the shoot and stem of the plant, emerges. At this stage, two tiny 'seed leaves', remnants of the seed coat, may still be attached to the shoot, but will float off in water.

Seed

Plumule

Radicle

stagnant and sour. Apart from this main consideration, however, several other factors must be borne in mind:

CONTAINERS Seeds can be sprouted in any kind of container, in glass jars, bowls, dishes, plastic boxes or one of the many patented sprouters on the market (see right). My own preference is for wide rather than deep containers, as they will allow the seeds to sprout a great deal more evenly.

TEMPERATURE Within reason, the higher the temperature, the faster seeds will germinate, and it is better for them to germinate fairly rapidly rather than 'linger' in a moist state which will invite disease. They naturally sprout faster in summer than in winter, though it is in winter that they are most valuable as they can so easily be grown indoors. Most seeds germinate at temperatures between 13° and 21°C/55° and 70°F, though temperatures up to 24°C/75°F can be used. They can be germinated in ordinary rooms, in warm cupboards, or on a windowsill, but avoid windowsills in full sunlight, where seeds will dry out rapidly or overheat.

METHODS OF RINSING Patented sprouters usually incorporate a method of pouring water in and out of the sprouter without removing the seeds. My own method is to tip the sprouting seeds into a household strainer, then to hold this under the tap, running fresh water through them, and allowing them to drain before returning them carefully to the container. Another popular method is to cover the jar or container with cheesecloth held with a rubber band. Water is then poured in and out through the cheesecloth. In my experience, the cheesecloth tends to get clogged up, but many people do use this method, or some variation of it, quite successfully.

SEED SPROUTERS

There are many types of seed sprouting kits now on the market. Some, like the model shown here, have several tiers so that different types of seed can be sprouted at the same time. In most of them there is some means of pouring water in and out of the sprouter without removing the seeds, so that rinsing is quick and easy.

LIGHT OR DARKNESS? This is again a question of preference. Sprouts grown in the dark are whiter and crisper (the traditional Chinese bean sprouts, for example, are grown in the dark), while sprouts developed in the light are softer and greener. If you want to grow them in the dark, and are using jars as containers, you can darken them by covering them with aluminum foil or black polyethylene, or by putting them inside a cereal packet. Dishes can be darkened by covering them with foil, wrapped loosely around the dish.

The basic sprouting procedure in containers is to soak the seeds overnight first, then to drain and rinse them before putting them in a container, and subsequently to rinse twice daily. The seeds will expand tremendously when growing, and it may be necessary later to divide them between two containers if they outgrow the first.

How to sprout seeds

The illustrations show a simple method of seed sprouting using ordinary domestic equipment. Seeds can be sprouted in lidded polyethylene boxes, in jars, or any dishes which can be covered in some way so they don't dry out. The most important thing is to rinse the seeds night and morning. Put them somewhere warm to sprout, though temperatures should not exceed 24°C/75°F. Most will be ready within a few days.

1 Rinse the seeds thoroughly in a strainer, removing any that are cracked, broken or discolored.

2 Leave seeds to soak overnight in cold water. This allows them to swell up, and speeds the sprouting process. Run cold water through them again and allow them to drain.

3 Place them in a dish in a layer no more than 20mm/¾in deep, with enough headroom for them to expand to about four times their volume. Cover them and put them somewhere warm to sprout.

Sprouting on a base

Some seeds can be grown on an inert moist base such as blotting paper, flannel, cotton wool or peat – the traditional way of growing mustard and cress. The seeds soon root into the base and will thus grow larger and stand upright, making an attractive-looking dish. This method of sprouting is most suitable for mung beans and lentils, both of which can be eaten at an advanced stage of sprouting. When ready for use, the seeds will have to be cut off from the base, and there is therefore a certain amount of wastage compared with the container method.

The seeds are presoaked, then spread evenly in a single layer over the base, and either covered or put somewhere dark to germinate. They must then be rinsed daily by running cool water over them, holding the seeds in place with the back of a spoon until they have become embedded in the base.

Growing small seedlings on a base

Mustard, cress, salad rape, coriander, alfalfa and fenugreek can also be grown in this way and used when they are one stage beyond 'sprouting', that is when they are small green seedlings about an inch or so high. In this case it is not necessary to presoak the seeds. They should be spread evenly in one layer over a moist base. Grow them in the light, or start them off in the dark and then move them into the light on germination. If the base is very clean, the seedlings can be pulled up by the roots and eaten whole; otherwise, cut them off at the base. If kept

Mung beans sprouted on a moist cotton wool base, covered with tinfoil to exclude light. The top dish is ready for use.

moist and cool, seedlings will last well for two weeks.

Growing seedlings in soil

Seeds can also be sown in a seed flat of finely sifted soil or potting mix. Two or three cuttings of seedlings can then be made, making a useful windowsill 'harvest'.

SUITABLE SEEDS FOR SPROUTING

COMMON NAME	LATIN NAME	AVERAGE TIME (DAYS)	LENGTH OF SPROUT WHEN EDIBLE
Beans			
Azuki	*Phaseolus angularis*	4-5	12-25mm/½-1in
Lima	*Phaseolus lunatus*	3-5	12-38mm/ ½-1½in
Mung	*Phaseolus aureus*	3-8	12-75mm/½-3in
Other legumes			
Alfalfa	*Medicago sativa*	1-2	Very tiny and 2.5-5cm/1-2in
Clover	*Melilotus altissima*	1-2	Very tiny and 2.5-5cm/1-2in
Fenugreek	*Trigonella foenum-graecum*	3-4	12mm/½in
Lentil	*Lens esculenta*	3-4	6-20mm/¼-¾in
Brassicas			
Kale	*Brassica oleracea 'Acephala'*	3-5	12-25mm/½-1in
Brussels sprouts	*Brassica oleracea 'Gemmifera'*	3-5	12-25mm/½-1in
Cabbage	*Brassica oleracea 'Capitata'*	3-5	12-25mm/½-1in
Cauliflower	*Brassica oleracea 'Botrytis'*	3-5	12-25mm/½-1in
Radish	*Raphanus sativus*	2-4	12-25mm/½-1in
Grains			
Barley	*Hordeum vulgare*	3-5	Very tiny
Rice, brown unpolished	*Oryza sativa*	3-5	12mm/½in
Rye	*Secale cereale*	3-5	Very tiny or 2.5-5cm/1-2in
Wheat	*Triticum vulgare*	4-5	Very tiny
Buckwheat	*Fagopyrum esculentum*	2-4	20-25mm/¾-1in

*NB: the seeds given in this chart can all be sprouted and used raw, although the beans and legumes should never be eaten raw in large quantities. Seeds which require rinsing more than twice a day, or which **must** be cooked before being eaten, have been omitted.*

SALAD
PLANTS

LEAFY SALAD PLANTS

A huge range of leafy plants can be used in salads. Some of them, such as lettuce, cabbage and chicory, are used in large quantities and make up the bulk of the salad: others, such as spinach, sorrel and many of the less well-known salad plants, are used in small quantities to add special character and variety.

LETTUCE
(Lactuca sativa)

Lettuce is certainly one of the most worthwhile salad crops to grow. Not only is the quality and flavor of fresh homegrown lettuce far superior to anything one can purchase, but many of the pretty, colorful and unusual varieties which are superb in salads are never found in supermarkets.

Lettuces can be divided roughly into hearting and non-hearting types. In the hearting group the main types are the tall cos or 'romaine' lettuce, and the flat 'cabbage' lettuce. Nonhearting types include the loose-leaf 'Salad Bowl' varieties and stem lettuce. As well as the green lettuces, there are also some very decorative red and bronze forms.

Even in small gardens, space can always be found for lettuce. The pretty loose-leaf 'Salad Bowl' types make excellent edges to vegetable and flower beds; small hearting types, such as 'Tom Thumb' and 'Little Gem', are ideal for intercropping; and patches of seedling lettuce and 'leaf lettuce' (see p.63) can be worked into very small areas.

In most temperate climates it is possible to grow lettuces all year round, using varieties suited to the different seasons. However, lettuce doesn't do well in very hot climates, and in very cold regions some kind of protection is required, artificial heating being necessary to ensure a continuous winter supply.

If greenhouse space is limited in winter, it may be better to devote it to endives and chicories, which are far more tolerant than lettuces of low winter light levels and damp chilly weather. Quite a number of the colored varieties are hardy and can be overwintered: in fact, their colors are deepest in cold weather and become paler in hot weather unless grown in a slightly shaded position.

Lettuce types

COS (ROMAINE) These large lettuces have long, crisp-textured, distinctly flavored leaves. They take longer to mature than other types, but stand hot and dry conditions well without going to seed. Several varieties are hardy and can be overwintered. 'Winter Density' is a typical cos variety. The small variety 'Little Gem', which is very sweet, crisp and attractive, and probably the best flavored of all lettuces, is a type of cos lettuce.

CABBAGE HEAD These are flat or rounded and are sub-divided into 'crispheads' and 'butterheads' (or bibbs). The crispheads have crisp leaves – 'Webb's Wonderful' and the American 'Iceberg' types are typical. They take about ten days longer than butterheads to mature but stand up to hot weather better without bolting. Butter-heads are softer textured, and rather bland in flavor. They are better adapted to growth in short days than most lettuces, and many of the winter varieties of lettuce come into this group.

LOOSE-LEAF These are the so-called 'gathering' or 'cutting' lettuces, often loosely referred to as 'Salad Bowl' types. The leaves can be picked individually as required, or the head cut about 2.5cm/1in above the stem; in both cases, there will be regrowth. Loose-leaf lettuces are slower to run to seed than other types, and are reasonably hardy, so are useful over a long period. Many, such as the 'oak-leaved' varieties, have very indented foliage; others have deeply curled leaves, for example the beautiful red and green Italian 'Lollo' or bronze 'Prizehead' varieties. The very useful reddish variety 'Marvel of Four Seasons' is a type of loose-leaf lettuce. Most of this group can be grown as a seedling crop.

CELTUCE Known in the West as stem or asparagus lettuce, this is an oriental type of lettuce which develops a very long edible stem. Both the young leaves and the

SUMMER LETTUCE *Colorful varieties photographed in summer: 'Marmer' and 'Rouge d'Hiver', normally grown as cool season lettuce, were sown in early spring and, due to exceptionally cold weather, matured happily, although out of turn, in summer.*

Green oak-leaved 'Salad Bowl' type

Red oak-leaved 'Salad Bowl' type

'Rossa Friulana' seedling

Green 'Lollo' 'Salad Bowl' type

'Rouge d'Hiver' cos type

'Marmer' crisphead type

Red 'Lollo' 'Salad Bowl' type

stem, which is peeled and sliced, are edible raw or cooked. It is grown like summer lettuce but usually requires fertile conditions and plenty of moisture to do well. Plants should be spaced 25-30cm/10-12in apart.

Cultivation

SOIL AND SITE Lettuces normally need an open situation, but in the height of summer or in hot climates can be grown in light shade. They can also be intercropped between taller plants, provided they have adequate light and are not cramped. Like all leafy vegetables, they do best grown fast in fertile soil with plenty of moisture. The usual advice of preparing the ground well by digging in plenty of organic matter is especially important for lettuce.

Lettuces can be grown successfully in most containers provided they are kept well watered. The 'Salad Bowl' types are the best for this purpose, as they can be picked over a long period. They can look very effective and colorful planted in growing bags (see opposite).

SOWING Lettuce can be sown either *in situ* where it will be grown, or in a seedbed, or raised indoors in seed flats

'Marvel of Four Seasons'
'Salad Bowl' type

'Little Gem'
semicos type

'Winter Density'
cos type

'Magnet'
butterhead type

'Trotzkopf'
butterhead type

OVERWINTERED LETTUCE
Photographed in late spring, these were all sown in early autumn. They were planted out in an unheated polyethylene tunnel in late autumn and very early spring to give the first cuttings of lettuce the following season.

or soil blocks. Sowing *in situ* is used principally for seedling 'cut-and-come-again' crops (see p.48), for leaf lettuce (see p.63) and for midsummer crops where transplanting would be unsuccessful unless plants had been raised in individual pots or soil blocks. It is a quick method of sowing. The main drawback is that germination and early growth may be poor if soil and weather conditions are bad, and that thinning is essential for hearted lettuce, though not, of course, for seedling and leaf lettuce crops. All too often, in practice, thinning is neglected until too late, resulting in poor lettuces. Start thinning lettuce as early as possible, using the thinnings in salads. The final spacing used will depend on the variety, and will range from 13-15cm/5-6in apart for small varieties such as 'Tom Thumb' and 'Little Gem', to 23-30cm/9-12in apart for most cabbage head lettuces, and about 35cm/14in apart for the cos and 'Iceberg' types.

Lettuce is sown in a seedbed outdoors either where there are no facilities for raising plants indoors, or where no ground is available for direct sowing. Good plants *can* be raised in seedbeds, but there is no doubt that, on the whole, better plants are raised by sowing indoors and transplanting, especially if soil blocks or some similar system is used.

Sowing indoors both enables good-quality plants to be raised, and allows more flexibility over planting. Seedlings can be planted out under cloches, in a frame, in a greenhouse or in the open as and when ground is available. They can also be overwintered in seed flats or soil blocks in frames or unheated greenhouses for planting out very early in spring.

The seedlings will generally be ready for transplanting at the four- to five-leaf stage. Most types of lettuce should be planted shallowly with the 'seed leaves' just above soil level, though cos lettuces can be planted a little deeper. Plant with equidistant spacing (see p.15).

GERMINATION Lettuce germinates at surprisingly low temperatures (it will even germinate on ice) but some of the butterheads, and my favorite 'Little Gem', germinate very poorly when soil temperatures rise above 25°C/77°F – a phenomenon known as 'high temperature dormancy'. These soil temperatures are often reached in late spring and summer. Various measures can be taken to overcome the problem:

● Use crisphead varieties, which germinate at soil temperatures of up to 29°C/85°F.

The red and green oak-leaved types of 'Salad Bowl' lettuce are ideal subjects for containers such as growing bags. They look pretty and provide pickings over a very long season.

● Sow between two and four in the afternoon. The most critical germination phase will then coincide with cooler night temperatures.
● Put the seed flat in a cold room or basement, or in shade, covering with moist matting or newspaper to keep the temperature low until germination.
● If sowing outdoors, water the seedbed before sowing to lower the temperature or cover it with white reflective material after sowing.

WATERING Common lettuce problems, such as bitterness, bolting and incidence of disease, are exacerbated by slow growth, often caused by lack of water. In the absence of rain, summer crops should be watered at the rate of up to 18 liters per sq m/4 gallons per sq yd per week. But if regular watering is difficult, concentrate on one really heavy watering about seven to ten days before harvesting. Autumn-planted lettuce should be watered well when planted, but watering should be avoided, if possible, during the winter months as it heightens the likelihood of disease. Lettuce always benefits from being mulched.

Sowing program

For a more or less continuous supply of lettuce, several sowings will have to be made throughout the year. Precisely when to sow will vary according to locality, but the main options are given below. (For varieties, see p.63.)

SUMMER SUPPLIES Make the first sowings under cover in very early spring, transplanting outside as soon as soil conditions are suitable. Alternatively, make sowings in succession throughout the summer, either sowing *in situ* or raising plants for transplanting. In the height of summer, however, transplanting should only be attempted with plants raised in individual soil blocks.

One of the problems in maintaining a steady supply of hearting lettuce in summer is that lettuce matures at different rates during the season, varying from as little as six-and-a-half weeks to as much as 13 weeks. This depends partly on the variety, but also on unpredictable factors such as soil and air temperatures and speed of germination. Moreover, in hot weather hearting lettuce tends to run to seed soon after maturing, though here again some varieties last better than others. Regular sowings at 10- to 14-day intervals, as is often advocated, do not guarantee a regular supply, since early sowings may well catch up with later ones, leading to gluts and gaps. A useful 'rule of thumb' to try and iron out any fluctuations is to make staggered sowings, making the 'next' sowing when the seedlings from the last sowing have just emerged.

With the 'Salad Bowl' types of lettuce, which last over several months, one or possibly two sowings will be enough to ensure a supply throughout the summer.

AUTUMN SUPPLIES Sow outdoors from mid- to late summer *in situ* or indoors for transplanting into the garden when the seedlings are ready. In areas prone to damp autumn weather, which encourages downy mildew (see p.64), use varieties with mildew resistance. If the weather starts to deteriorate, cover the lettuces with cloches in late autumn to improve their quality. They can be planted directly into frames or unheated greenhouses, if space is available.

WINTER SUPPLIES For lettuce production in unheated greenhouses or frames, or under cloches in winter, sow winter hearting varieties in seed flats, in late summer and early autumn, for transplanting into frames or cold greenhouses in late autumn.

If planted late or if the weather is exceptionally severe, the lettuces may not be ready for use until early in the year. They will, of course, crop earlier if the greenhouse is slightly heated.

The winter and very early spring crops are not the easiest to grow as they are prone to fungus diseases, especially gray mold and downy mildew (see p.64). Avoid overcrowding and keep them well ventilated.

SPRING SUPPLIES Hardy varieties can be sown in autumn to overwinter as seedlings, outdoors in mild areas, elsewhere in cold frames, under cloches or in unheated greenhouses. They can also be sown *in situ* in late summer, in frames, under cloches or in unheated greenhouses, thinning to about 8cm/3in apart in early autumn, and thinning to their final spacing in spring. For a slightly later crop, they can be sown a week or two later, in soil blocks

Above *A patch of 'Rossa Friulana' seedling lettuce, showing how red lettuce tends to lose its color when temperatures rise. The greener strip on the right had been covered with a cloche for a few days so had become much paler. Patches like this can normally be cut several times.*

Left *Celtuce (or stem lettuce) is an oriental type of lettuce grown mainly for its edible stem, though the very young leaves can also be eaten. Like many of the oriental vegetables, it grows fast in fertile soil provided it has plenty of moisture.*

or flats, or pricked out into seed flats, and overwintered as seedlings for planting out under cover very early in the following year.

Although hardy varieties can withstand several degrees of frost in the open, their quality is undoubtedly improved if they are protected, at least with cloches, during the winter. There is always an element of risk with these overwintered crops, due to the vagaries of winter weather, but they can provide very early lettuce.

Seedling crop

Several lettuce varieties are suited to sowing in patches, thick rows or wide drills for cutting as seedlings (see p.48). In the past these lettuces were commonly sown in heated frames during the winter months for winter 'salading'. This method is still very useful for early sowings in unheated frames or greenhouses, as a crop is then ready far sooner than a hearting lettuce would be. It is also recommended for spring and early summer sowings outdoors, as a patch may be productive over several months. Generally two or three cuttings can be made before the plants become tough or run to seed.

When lettuce was widely grown as a seedling crop, certain traditional varieties were specially sold for the purpose. However, it is always worth experimenting with any packets of leftover seed.

Leaf lettuce

When certain varieties of cos lettuce are grown in close proximity, they grow upright, without forming hearts. After the first cut, they regrow to provide a second crop within four to six weeks. This high-yielding method of production was developed by the National Vegetable Research Station in the UK, as an adaptation of an old method of growing seedling lettuce. The purpose was to produce a crop of single lettuce leaves for caterers, to save them the necessity of tearing apart the heart.

The method is easily adapted for use in the salad garden. An average family of four could be kept in lettuce all summer by cultivating a total area of approximately 5 sq m/6 sq yd, making sowings of about 80 sq cm/1 sq yd each time, at approximately weekly intervals. Each crop would be cut twice.

CULTIVATION The ground must be fertile and weed-free. Prepare the seedbed carefully so that germination is good. Seed can either be broadcast, thinning to about 5cm/2in apart, or sown thinly in rows about 13cm/5in apart, thinning to about 3cm/1½in apart. It is very important to ensure that the plants have plenty of moisture throughout growth.

The first sowings can be made in early spring, the first cut being made about seven weeks later, and a second cut a further seven to eight weeks after that. Later sowings, which can continue until late summer, will mature more rapidly, allowing the first cut to be made after about three weeks, and the second four weeks or so after the first.

Cut the leaves when 8-13cm/3-5in high, about 20mm/¾in above ground level.

Varieties

FOR SUMMER SUPPLIES Early sowings: most cos varieties such as 'Dark Green Cos', 'Little Gem', 'Parris Island Cos'; loose-leaf varieties: 'Black Seeded Simpson', 'Grand Rapids', 'Prizehead'; butterheads: 'Hilde', 'Tom Thumb'; Boston and bibb varieties such as 'Buttercrunch'; crispheads: 'Ithaca'; successive sowings: (heat-resistant varieties) loose-leaf: 'Grand Rapids', 'Green Ice', 'Oak-leaved Salad Bowl'; butterheads: 'Buttercrunch', 'Kagran Summer'; crispheads: 'Empire', 'Great Lakes', 'Ithaca', 'King Crown'.

FOR AUTUMN SUPPLIES Most cos varieties; butterheads: 'Tom Thumb'; crispheads: 'Ithaca', 'Minetto'; cos varieties; mildew-resistant varieties; butterheads: 'Tania'; cos: 'Valmaine'.

FOR WINTER SUPPLIES (in unheated greenhouses) Butterheads: 'Amanda Plus', 'Dandie', 'Delta', 'Kloek', 'Kwiek' and 'Magnet'.

FOR SPRING SUPPLIES (varieties that can be overwintered outdoors in the open or under cover) Cos: 'Little Gem', 'Rouge d'Hiver', 'Winter Density'; butterhead: 'Brune d'Hiver', 'North Pole', 'Trotzkopf'; loose-leaf: 'Marvel of Four Seasons'; crisphead: 'Marmer'.

FOR SEEDLING LETTUCE Most 'Salad Bowl' varieties, and curly-leaved cutting lettuce, smooth-leaved cutting lettuce and the reddish-leaved 'Rossa Friulana'.

FOR LEAF LETTUCE 'Dark Green Cos', 'Erthel Crisp Mint', 'Paris White Cos' and 'Valmaine'.

Pests and diseases

BIRDS Young seedlings are most vulnerable, though mature plants are also attacked from time to time. (For protective measures, see p.47.)

SLUGS Feeding both above and below ground, slugs can damage lettuce at almost any stage, especially in damp weather and on heavy soils. (For control measures, see p.47.)

SOIL PESTS Wireworm, cutworm and soil weevils can cause fatalities, especially in spring. (For control measures, see p.47.)

ROOT APHIDS They attack lettuce roots in hot summer weather, forming white waxy colonies on the roots which cause the plant to wilt and die. Rotate lettuce, and where root aphids are a problem try growing varieties with some resistance.

LEAF APHIDS (greenfly) Attacks are most likely in hot weather outdoors and under cover in spring. (For control measures, see p.47.)

SEEDLING 'DAMPING OFF' DISEASE This is commonest in early spring and autumn. (For preventive measures, see p.47.)

DOWNY MILDEW (*Bremia lactucae*) Probably the most serious lettuce disease, it occurs in damp weather, especially in early spring, autumn, and in winter crops under cover. Pale angular patches appear on older leaves which eventually rot and die; white spores are seen on the undersides of the leaves. Wet plants are particularly vulnerable. Preventive measures include: keeping leaves as dry as possible; watering the soil around the plants rather than the plants themselves and avoiding watering in the evening; ventilating greenhouses well to minimize condensation on leaves; removing all infected leaves with a sharp knife and burning them; burning old lettuce plants and debris which might harbor disease spores; rotation; and the use of mildew-resistant varieties. Transplanted crops are less susceptible to mildew than direct sown crops.

GRAY MOLD (*Botrytis cinerea*) This causes plants to rot off at the stem, and is most serious in cold damp winter conditions. Avoid overcrowding and deep planting, and take the same preventive measures as for downy mildew, though there are no varieties of lettuce with resistance at present.

MOSAIC VIRUS A seed-borne disease which causes stunted growth and pale yellow crinkled leaves. Burn all infected plants; spray against aphids to help control the spread of the disease; use seed with guaranteed low levels of mosaic infection (less than one per cent) and grow resistant varieties where available.

CHICORY
(*Cichorium intybus*)

The chicories are a wonderfully diverse group of mostly perennial plants with a long history of cultivation for human, animal and medicinal use. The classical Roman writers often referred to the use of chicory as a cooked vegetable and for salads. Modern Italy, it seems, has inherited the mantle of chicory appreciation. An enormous range of chicories is grown in Italy (the Italian name for chicory is 'radicchio'), many of them virtually unknown further afield, although there is no valid reason why this should be so.

Since 'discovering' this treasure trove of salad plants in Italy we have experimented with many of them in our own garden. With very few exceptions they have flourished, indicating that they can probably be grown successfully in any temperate climate.

The chicories have many merits. Apart from being naturally robust, fairly easily grown and more or less pest- and disease-free, their main season of usefulness is from autumn to spring – the period when salad material is most scarce. Many are sown or planted after summer crops are cleared, and so make excellent use of ground which would otherwise be idle in winter – both in the open and under cover.

Types of chicory

There are several very distinct kinds of chicory, but they divide principally into the several types used for their leaves, and those grown for their roots.

The most dramatic of the former are the red-leaved Italian chicories, which develop deep red and beautifully variegated leaves and hearts in autumn and winter. There are also several types of green-leaved chicory. One of the best known is the 'Sugar Loaf' type, which can be used either as seedlings, or when the crisp 'loaf-like' head has developed.

Among the various other forms of leafy chicory are the rosetted and extraordinarily hardy 'Grumolo' chicory and the various narrow- and serrated-leaved chicories, which are forms of wild chicory.

RED AND GREEN CHICORY *Photographed in early spring, all the types can be overwintered outdoors in mild climates, though their quality is improved if given protection, for example by being grown in an unheated greenhouse or under cloches.*

'Red Verona'

'Red Treviso' (blanched)

'Variegated Castelfranco'

'Variegated Sottomarina'

'Red Verona Flamba'

'Grumolo'

'Red Verona Flamba' showing root

'Sugar Loaf' seedling

'Sugar Loaf' mature head

Some of the chicories grown for their edible roots are used much like winter radishes. With others, such as 'Witloof' (or Belgian) chicory, the roots are forced in the dark to produce tender white, bud-like shoots known as chicons. Some red varieties can also be forced, the leaves then taking on an exquisitely delicate pale rose hue. The beautiful pale blue chicory flowers can be used in salads, fresh or pickled.

All chicories have a very characteristic flavor, with a slightly bitter edge to it. It's addictive to those who acquire the taste, but less popular with the sweet-toothed. The bitterness can be modified by blanching, by shredding exceptionally bitter leaves, by mixing chicory leaves with milder plants (see 'saladini', p.136) and, with red chicories and 'Witloof' varieties, by braising. The bitterness also varies with the plant, the variety and the stage of growth. Seedling leaves, for example, are less bitter than mature leaves, the inner leaves of 'Sugar Loaf' chicories are less bitter than the outer leaves, and the red chicories become far less bitter after exposure to cold weather.

Chicories are deep-rooting, unfussy plants. They need an open situation, but otherwise seem able to adapt to a wide range of soils, from light sands to heavy clay, and even to wet, dry and exposed situations. Although most are perennials and will reseed themselves if not uprooted, for salad purposes it is best to treat them as annuals, resowing every year.

Obtaining seed
It is not always easy to obtain chicory seed, although an increasing number of specialist seedsmen are now stocking it (see p.167) and plant breeders are beginning to develop new improved varieties.

However, it is fairly easy to save chicory seed oneself. Chicories are almost completely self-pollinating, so plants can be left to run to seed in spring and will breed true to type.

RED-LEAVED CHICORIES
The red chicories have two curious, chameleon-like characteristics. First, they start life green, but with the advent of cooler night temperatures in autumn, their color changes. Depending on the variety they become deep red, or develop bronze, yellow, red, pink and green variegations. Secondly, the actual form and shape of the plant can change. Again, with the onset of cold weather

the upright leaves of most varieties (an exception is 'Red Treviso') become rounded, close in and form a tight 'heart' at ground level.

CULTIVATION Red chicories are sown from early to midsummer. They can be sown in rows, broadcast in patches, or sown in seed flats for transplanting. Germination can be erratic if sown in hot weather, so in such circumstances water the drills well before sowing, or, if broadcasting, keep the seedbed covered with polyethylene film until the seeds have germinated.

The young green leaves can be cut when 5-8cm/2-3in high and used in salads – they are quite mild at this stage. In late summer start thinning in stages, until the plants are approximately 13cm/5in apart; they can then be left to heart up.

The chicories are ready from late autumn onward, less hardy varieties being ready first. The size of the chicory heart or head will vary, but after making the first cut in autumn or winter, leave the stump in the ground. Further flushes of leaf will be produced until late spring or early summer. Winter cultivation should be geared toward preventing rotting, and protecting plants from the elements, so that the leaves are tender and large, well-colored hearts can develop.

It is hard to be dogmatic about the best way to do this: much depends on the season, the locality, and the varieties grown. On the whole, prolonged, wet, muggy weather seems to cause more problems than crisp, cold weather – leaves, and indeed whole plants, may rot in wet winters. To minimize the spread of rots, avoid overcrowding, keep plants weed-free, and remove any rotted leaves. If plants are grown under cover, keep them well ventilated.

On the other hand, protection both from severe frost and from the searing, toughening effects of winter winds and rain is beneficial. Plants can be cloched, or transplanted into frames for protection. On the whole, low polyethylene tunnels should be avoided, as they create humidity. The disadvantage of straw and other coverings is that they attract mice – and sometimes even rats in severe winters.

After several years of experimenting with red chicories in an area where winter rainfall is variable but not remarkably heavy, and lowest temperatures on average between −6°C/21°F and −12°C/10°F, the best chicories have been obtained by sowing in midsummer, and transplanting into a large, 'walk-in' well-ventilated but unheated poly-ethylene tunnel in late summer.

FORCING AND BLANCHING Certain varieties of red chicory, such as 'Red Verona' and 'Red Treviso', can be forced indoors, in the dark, like 'Witloof' chicory. In *extremely* cold areas, this may be the only means of obtaining a winter crop as the plants would be killed if left outside.

Chicory can also be blanched *in situ* outdoors to produce very tender leaf. One method is to cut back the foliage in early winter, and to cover the stumps with an 18-20cm/7-8in depth of soil or ashes. The chicons will push their way into the material in early spring, when they can be uncovered and cut. This is slower than forcing and blanching indoors, but the flavor is generally thought to be better.

Chicory can also be blanched *in situ* by covering it for a few weeks with a black polyethylene cloche. When being blanched in this way, the 'Red Verona' chicories are cut back to within an inch or so of the stump (see p.52) so the new growths are blanched; with 'Red Treviso' chicory, however, the leaves are simply tied together, and will become blanched in a few days (see p.51).

VARIETIES Where chicory is popular, grow varieties recommended for the area. Where chicory is still relatively unknown, you will have to experiment with whatever varieties you can obtain and see which perform best. If possible, try some in the open and some under cover.

Popular varieties are 'Red Treviso', 'Red Verona' (in fact several 'Red Verona' varieties are now available), 'Variegated Castelfranco' and 'Variegated Chioggia'.

GREEN-LEAVED CHICORIES

There are several types, of which the following are the most popular:

'SUGAR LOAF' CHICORY When fully mature 'Sugar Loaf' chicory forms large, conical heads, not unlike a cos lettuce in appearance, with very densely packed, crisp, distinctly flavored leaves. The inner leaves are naturally blanched through lack of exposure to light and are therefore sweeter than the outer leaves, though the 'sweetness' is only relative. The plants can tolerate a few degrees of frost, some varieties being hardier than others. If kept cut back during the winter, they withstand much lower temperatures.

Seedlings of 'Variegated Castelfranco' red chicory photographed in summer when still green. When it gets colder the plants become hearted and the leaves turn a deep red (see p.65).

In winter, 'Sugar Loaf' chicory needs protection, and should be covered with cloches or grown under cover. To do well, it requires fertile, moisture-retentive soil.

It can be grown either for a seedling crop, or as a heading crop. Both the seedling and the heading crop can be cut and allowed to resprout as a 'cut-and-come-again' crop. In fact, the plant is extraordinarily versatile and productive, and can be cut at almost any stage.

CULTIVATION For a seedling crop, 'Sugar Loaf' can be sown from early spring to midautumn, either in rows or broadcast thinly. Seeds need be no closer than 20mm/¾in apart (see p.49). Once they have germinated, growth is rapid, and leaves can be cut just above ground level when between 5 and 7.5cm/2 and 3in high. Under good growing conditions, further cuts can be made at approximately 15-day intervals, sometimes over several months, provided there is plenty of moisture and the soil is fertile. It may be necessary to feed with a liquid fertilizer to sustain the rapid rate of growth. As the very young leaves are the most tender in salads, several successive sowings can be made, if preferred.

After several months the plants can be dug up if the ground is required, or they can be thinned out to about 15cm/6in apart and left to develop mature heads.

'Sugar Loaf' chicory is one of the most productive seedlings crops under cover. Particularly useful sowings can be made very early in spring, as soon as soil temperatures have risen above about 5°C/41°F, or in late autumn. These last sowings remain as seedlings during the winter (they survive lower temperatures than the mature plants), and start into growth very early in the year.

For a heading crop, sow in midsummer, either *in situ* or for transplanting, spacing plants 15-20cm/6-8in apart. They will head up in the autumn. If covered with cloches or straw for extra protection, they often last well into winter. Late summer sowings can be transplanted under cover in early autumn, treated initially as a cut-and-come-again seedling crop, and then left to head up in the spring. The whole plant is occasionally blanched (see p.52).

Like the red-leaved types, 'Sugar Loaf' chicory is prone to rot in cold, wet winter conditions. Remove any rotten leaves, but leave the stumps – even 'hopeless cases' may regenerate in spring.

Popular varieties are 'Bianca di Milano', 'Bionda di Triestino' (this variety is mainly used for a seedling crop, though it will form small heads), 'Crystal Head' and 'Gradina'.

'GRUMOLO' CHICORY This is a rugged chicory from the Piedmont region of Italy, and will withstand poor soil conditions and extremely low temperatures without protection. It has upright leaves during the summer months, but in autumn rosettes start to form. In midwinter the plants more or less die back, but very early in spring, when conditions are still extremely wintry, jade-green, ground-hugging rosettes of perfectly shaped leaves suddenly appear, even pushing their way through competitive weeds and grass. They can be covered with cloches to bring them on earlier.

The leaves are rather bitter in flavor, but blend well into mixed salads of the 'saladini' type (see p.136).
CULTIVATION 'Grumolo' chicory can be sown from spring to autumn, but the most useful sowings are in midsummer, for autumn to spring supplies. It lends itself to being broadcast thinly in patches (see Red-leaved chicories, earlier), but can also be sown thinly in rows. During the summer, the young leaves can be cut when 5-7.5cm/2-3in high. In autumn, leave the plants to form rosettes. Patches will not normally need thinning, unless the plants are very close, in which case they should be thinned to about 5-7.5cm/2-3in apart. In spring, or when freshly sown, you may find that the patches may need protection from birds.

Cut the rosettes in spring, leaving the plants to re-sprout. The subsequent growth is never as prettily shaped and tends to become coarse, but may fill a gap in spring salad supplies.

'Grumolo' chicory can also be grown as a perennial, by sowing a patch in an out-of-the-way place and letting it perpetuate itself. The tall spikes of blue flowers make a striking summer feature in the garden.

'SPADONA' CHICORY This variety is very similar to 'Grumolo' in its hardiness, but retains narrow-bladed leaves all year, never forming a rosette. Cultivate and use it like 'Grumolo' chicory.

'CATALOGNA' CHICORY Also known as asparagus chicory, this tall-growing chicory has several forms. The long leaves are sometimes narrow-bladed, sometimes very serrated, with long, white leaf stalks. Some forms are grown mainly for the chunky *puntarelle* or flowering shoots which develop in spring and have a much-prized flavor, raw or cooked. Less hardy than the 'Grumolo' and 'Spadona' chicories, these are mainly sown in summer, *in situ*, or in seedbeds for transplanting when very small, spacing plants about 30cm/12in apart, for use in autumn and early winter.

WILD CHICORY Capucin's beard or *barbe de Capucin* is the name given to the wild chicory, the jagged leaves of which are very similar to dandelion. The young leaves can be eaten green (generally shredded), but the mature plants are blanched to develop the unique flavor. Like many bitter and blanched plants, it is excellent *aux lardons*. The main sowing period is in late spring and early summer, sowing *in situ* or in seedbeds for transplanting, spacing plants about 15cm/6in apart. They can either be blanched *in situ* or under cover (see pp.51-3). The top of the root is also eaten.

'WITLOOF' CHICORY
Also known as Belgian chicory, this chicory was 'discovered' when a Belgian farmer threw some large wild chicory roots into a warm dark stable. The whitened shoots which developed from this accidental form of blanching laid the foundations for the modern 'Witloof' chicory industry. Contrary to popular belief, 'Witloof' chicory is surprisingly easy to grow.

CULTIVATION Sow the seed in early summer, either in soil blocks for transplanting or *in situ*, spacing plants eventually about 15cm/6in apart. Keep them weed-free, but otherwise leave them until late autumn before digging up the roots for forcing. Wait until night temperatures are nearing freezing, as the roots need a spell of low temperatures before they can be forced successfully.

Reject any fanged or very thin roots (ideally they should be at least 4cm/1½in in diameter at the neck), trim off the tips of the roots, and cut off the foliage a good inch above the neck. It is best to force a few at a time to maintain a continuous supply during winter; so store them until required in a cool shed, lying flat in boxes of moist sand, peat or ashes to prevent the roots from drying out.

FORCING AND BLANCHING The roots should be forced in total darkness, with just a little warmth. Transplant them into frames, greenhouses, basements, or into pots or flats brought indoors, and blanch them by any of the methods described on pp.51-3.

In ordinary domestic circumstances, however, the simplest method is to pot up three to five roots, in garden soil, in a 23cm/9in flower pot, covered with another pot of the same size with the drainage hole blocked to exclude light (see p.53). At temperatures of about 10°C/50°F the chicons will be ready in about three weeks – temperatures much higher than this are not advisable.

'Witloof' chicory can also be forced *in situ* by earthing up the stumps (see p.52). However, these chicons take much longer to develop than those that have been forced indoors.

On the whole, tighter chicons are obtained by methods which involve covering with soil, ashes or some solid material, though chicons obtained simply by planting in dark conditions, as in the 'flower pot' method (see p.53), are quite satisfactory for home use. The recently introduced F_1 hybrids, 'Normato' and 'Zoom', form exceptionally tight chicons in the absence of any solid covering.

Once the chicons are ready they should be used fairly soon or they deteriorate. Cut them 2.5cm/1in above the root, and keep them wrapped in aluminum foil or in a refrigerator, as they will become green and bitter on exposure to light. The root can be replaced or replanted in the dark - it will normally resprout to give a second, though less vigorous, crop.

Wild chicory

'Witloof' root before forcing

'Witloof' chicon

'Soncino'

CHICORIES GROWN FOR ROOTS *The 'Witloof' chicory root is forced for its chicons; 'Soncino' is a typical edible rooted chicory; the top part of the wild chicory root is edible raw.*

ROOT CHICORIES

Some chicory varieties have large edible roots, which are white and surprisingly tender. They are used raw, chopped or grated in salad, or else cooked first and eaten when cold. They are a very useful standby in severe winters. These chicories are usually sown in spring or early summer, either broadcast or in rows, or in soil blocks for transplanting, spacing plants eventually about 10cm/4in apart. The roots can be lifted during winter as required.

VARIETIES 'Chiavari', 'Geneva' and 'Soncino'.

ENDIVE
(Cichorium endivia)

The endives are a useful and attractive group of salad plants, belonging to the chicory family. They are more resistant to pests and diseases than lettuce and, provided appropriate varieties are used, are less likely to bolt in hot summer weather; they also withstand damp, cold autumn and winter conditions better. Their piquant, somewhat bitter flavor is not to all tastes, but they can easily be blanched to make them milder flavored (see pp.51-3), if preferred.

There are two main types: curly-leaved endives (*Chicorée frisée*) are flat, low-growing plants with narrowish curled, fringed or indented leaves; broad-leaved, 'Batavian' endives (also known as *escarole, scarole* or *chicorée scarole*), are larger, taller and have broader leaves, rather twisted at the base. There is considerable overlap between the two groups and several intermediate types exist.

In general, the broad-leaved endives are much hardier and more suitable for autumn, winter and, where they have been overwintered, for early spring crops. The curly-leaved endives have a tendency to rot in damp, cold weather but are more tolerant of heat, so are used mainly from late spring to autumn.

Cultivation

Endives like an open situation and fertile, moisture-retentive soil, with plenty of well-rotted compost worked in beforehand. Very acid soils should be limed.

They can be sown *in situ* and thinned out, or in seed-beds or indoors and transplanted. (Transplanted crops grow faster and are less likely to become bitter.) They will germinate at very low temperatures, but problems may be encountered when soil temperatures are high. Where germination is slow, plants are more likely to bolt. So, if sowing in midsummer, water the drills heavily beforehand to lower the temperature or sow somewhere cool indoors, keeping them shaded until the seeds have germinated.

The plants should be spaced 25-38cm/10-15in apart, depending on the variety; the curly-leaved varieties generally need less space than the broad-leaved. Thinnings can be used in salads or transplanted to maintain continuity.

Most endives will withstand a few degrees of frost, but crops remaining in the open in autumn should be covered. The curly-leaved varieties rot easily if subjected to prolonged dampness. Winter supplies should be grown under cover in frames or under cloches, or in unheated greenhouses.

Although endives are slow growing (on average they take about three months to mature), they are naturally vigorous and lend themselves to cut-and-come-again techniques (see pp.48-50). Often several successive cuts can be made. Very hardy varieties such as 'Cornet de Bordeaux' are invaluable for this purpose when grown under cover in winter. If kept cropped in cold weather, they will start growing rapidly in any warm spell, producing fresh crisp leaf very early in spring. Curly-leaved endive can also be used for seedling patches in spring, under cover or in the open.

BLANCHING Whether you find it necessary to blanch endives is largely a matter of taste.

The broad-leaved endives 'Batavian Full Heart', 'Cornet d'Anjou', 'Cornet de Bordeaux' and 'Golda' generally require little blanching as the central leaves are naturally crisp and pale-colored. The curly types need blanching in hot weather, when at their most bitter.

Blanching is carried out when the plants are mature. It takes from one to three weeks, depending on the time of the year, but is slower in winter. Since plants deteriorate soon after blanching, blanch only a few at a time, in succession. In general, *in situ* methods are more practical in summer, while transplanted methods are more appropriate in winter.

Quite often 'partial' blanching suffices. The flat, curly-leaved endives can be blanched by laying a plate on the head of the plant, or by covering one endive with an uprooted one, head to head. Blanch broad-leaved endives by tying the leaves together (see p.51).

Sowing program

FOR EARLY SUMMER SUPPLIES Sow very early in spring under cover, transplanting outdoors as soon as soil conditions allow; follow with successive outdoor sowings. Use any curly endives, and broad-leaved varieties such as 'Golda' and 'Grosse Bouclée'. There is some risk of bolting from very early sowings. Seedling crops of curly endives can also be sown at this period.

FOR MAIN SUMMER TO AUTUMN SUPPLIES OUTDOORS Sow from early- to midsummer, using curly-leaved and broad-leaved types. These are very useful sowings as they mature later in the year.

FOR AUTUMN AND WINTER SUPPLIES UNDER COVER Sow midsummer to early autumn, transplanting under cover in autumn. Use mainly broad-leaved varieties.

FOR SPRING SUPPLIES Sow the variety 'Golda' under cover from late autumn until spring, to overwinter as seedlings. Plant out as early as soil conditions allow under cover or in the open.

Varieties

CURLY-LEAVED ENDIVE **Mainly for summer use:** 'Fine d'Été' ('Fine d'Italie'), 'Frisée d'Été à Coeur Jaune'; **for summer and winter use:** 'Frisée de Louviers', 'Frisée Fine de Rouen' ('Corne de Cerf'); **hardier varieties for autumn and early winter use:** 'Frisée de Ruffec', 'Frisée Reine d'Hiver', 'Pancalière', 'Wallonne'.

BROAD-LEAVED ENDIVE **For spring and summer use:** 'Géante Maraîchère Samy', 'Golda', 'Grosse Bouclée'; **hardy varieties for autumn and winter use:** 'Batavian Full Heart', 'Cornet d'Anjou', 'Cornet de Bordeaux', 'Ronde Verte à Coeur Plein' ('Fullheart').

'Cornet de Bordeaux'

'Frisée de Ruffec'

'Ronde Verte à Coeur Plein'

HARDY ENDIVES *These were photographed in early spring, after overwintering outdoors under low polyethylene tunnels. 'Frisée de Ruffec' is curly-leaved; the others are broad-leaved.*

CABBAGE
(Brassica oleracea 'Capitata')

There are cabbages for every season. Small pointed cabbages and loose-headed 'spring greens' or collards are used in spring and larger round-headed red and green types in summer. The Dutch white types are stored for use in winter, while hardy and ornamental cabbages are used fresh. Although almost any type of cabbage can be eaten raw if shredded finely, the dark-leaved spring and summer varieties may be bitter. Most popular for salads are the white winter varieties, and the colorful red and ornamental varieties.

Cultivation

Cabbages belong to the brassica group, and should be rotated around the garden (see p.14), if possible on a three- or four-year cycle, to avoid the buildup of soil pests and diseases, particularly clubroot (see p.75). They need to be grown in well-drained, fertile, slightly acid soil. Very acid soil should be limed to help prevent clubroot. Try to avoid growing cabbages on freshly manured soil, or growth will be lush and soft, making the plants prone to disease and liable to topple over in windy conditions.

A year-round supply can be maintained by sowing different varieties at appropriate times (see pp.72-3). Cabbages are usually raised in a seedbed and transplanted, or sown indoors, in seed flats or soil blocks. The block method produces fewer, better-quality plants, and is therefore particularly suitable for cabbages. Plant them into their permanent positions when quite small, at the three- or four-leaf stage, planting firmly with the lower leaves just above the soil. Cabbages can be planted into cleaned but undug soil to give them firm anchorage.

The size of the cabbage head can be controlled by the spacing adopted – from 35cm/14in apart for small heads to 45cm/18in for large ones. Where they have been widely spaced, cabbages can be intercropped when planted (see pp.15-17).

The stems can be earthed up as the plants grow to make them more stable. On very light soils and windy sites, where the 'toppling over' problem is acute, plant cabbages in furrows about 10cm/4in deep, which should be filled in as the plants grow. Very large plants may need to be staked.

Cabbages need plenty of moisture during their growth, and, in the absence of rain, will benefit from weekly watering at the rate of 9-14 liters per sq m/2-3 gallons per sq yd. Failing this, try to give them at least one very heavy watering two or three weeks before harvesting. If growth seems slow in midseason, give them a liquid feed with a seaweed-based fertilizer, or a topdressing with a nitrogenous fertilizer.

Cabbages can also be cultivated as a cut-and-come-again crop: early maturing cabbage heads can be cut so as to give a second crop late in the season (see p.50).

Storage

The white winter cabbages, often called 'Dutch winter whites' as many originated in Holland, should be lifted for storage in late autumn before the first heavy frosts. Handling them very gently, cut the heads with a couple of inches of stalk attached, to serve as a handle. Remove any loose outer leaves by rolling them off with the hand. The cabbages should be stored somewhere ventilated, cool and dry. They can be kept for several months.

Where very low temperatures are expected they can be built up in a pile on a shed floor with a thick layer of straw between each head; otherwise, suspend them in nets or place them on racks so that air can circulate around them. Where outdoor frames are used, keep them off the ground on raised wooden decks. In very severe weather cover the frames with extra matting or sacking. Remove the lights on sunny days for ventilation.

Most red cabbages can be stored for a few months. All stored cabbages should be inspected regularly during the winter and any rotten leaves removed.

Sowing program

As with lettuces, several sowings will have to be made to maintain a continuous supply.

FOR SPRING SUPPLIES In areas where winter temperatures do not normally fall below about −6°C/20°F, sow in late summer, either *in situ*, or in seedbeds, transplanting seedlings into their permanent positions in early autumn. They will mature in late spring. For headed cabbages, space them 30cm/12in apart; for unhearted spring greens, 10cm/4in apart. They should be earthed up during the winter.

Varieties: 'Avoncrest', 'Offenham' selections, 'Prospera' F_1, 'Spring Hero' F_1.

For a succession to follow this very early crop, make sowings in frames, seed flats or seed blocks in autumn, to overwinter under cover as seedlings. Plant these out as early in spring as soil conditions allow.

Varieties: Those listed above and red varieties, such as 'Langedijk Red Early Preko', 'Red Acre', 'Ruby Ball', 'Ruby Perfection'.

FOR SUMMER SUPPLIES Make the first sowings in gentle heat under cover early in the year, planting out as soon as soil conditions allow. Subsequent sowings can then be made in frames or unheated greenhouses, followed by sowings in the open – planting in succession in their permanent position when ready. Plant between 35cm/14in and 45cm/18in apart, depending on the size of cabbage required.

Varieties: Traditional varieties of summer cabbage had a tendency to bolt rapidly when mature but newer, improved varieties, such as the F_1 hybrids 'Minicole' and 'Stonehead', are valuable because they stand much longer.

Also the red varieties listed above. Those particularly suitable for salads are 'Danish Ballhead', 'Hispi' F_1, 'Minicole' F_1, 'Stonehead' F_1.

FOR EARLY WINTER AND STORAGE SUPPLIES Sow in spring, planting out in early summer 45cm/18in apart.

Varieties: 'Hidena' F_1, 'Holland Winter White Extra Late', 'Polinius' F_1 and 'Premium Late Flat Dutch'.

FOR WINTER SUPPLIES These will not survive very low winter temperatures so be guided by what can be grown in your area. Sow outside in late spring, planting in early summer about 45cm/18in apart each way.

Varieties: In order of maturity and hardiness these are: 'January King' types such as 'Hardy Late Stock 3'; savoy x Dutch white hybrids such as 'Celtic' F_1; and savoys such as 'Blue Max' and 'Savoy Ace'.

ORNAMENTAL CABBAGES AND KALES

The ornamental cabbages and kales are at their brightest and best in the winter months: they only start to develop

SPRING AND EARLY SUMMER CABBAGE 'Prospera' F_1 is a good new spring cabbage suitable for sowing in autumn. The round-headed early summer cabbage was bought in a market so the variety is unknown.

Spring cabbage 'Prospera' F_1

Round-headed summer cabbage

their vivid deep colors when night temperatures reach about 10°C/50°F. Their prettily shaped leaves, which are rounded, frilly, or deeply serrated, depending on the variety, in combinations of pink, purple, white and gray-green, can be used to create stunning effects both in the garden and in the salad bowl.

Although grown mainly for their ornamental rather than edible qualities, these cabbages and kales are quite palatable, especially after frost has been on them. They are reasonably hardy (the kales tend to be hardier than the cabbages), but will not survive very severe winters.

They vary in height from about 30 to 60cm/12 to 24in, again depending on the variety.

CULTIVATION Most varieties are raised like late summer cabbages, being sown in spring and planted out in early summer. Some of the new Japanese F_1 hybrids, however, are faster growing and will mature in about three months. These will benefit from frequent transplanting. The

'Minicole' F_1 Dutch winter white type

'Savoy King' F_1 savoy type

'Langedijk Red Early Preko' red type

CABBAGES FOR WINTER USE *Red and Dutch winter white cabbages need to be lifted and stored; savoys and ornamental cabbages are hardier.*

'Osaka Red' F_1 ornamental type

'Osaka White' F_1 ornamental type

'Ragged Jack' is one of the old-fashioned ornamental kales, the leaves of which look very attractive in a salad. Unfortunately, unlike most kales, it will not withstand very low temperatures.

Pests and diseases

BIRDS Can be serious on seedlings and mature plants, especially in winter. (For preventive measures, see p.47.)

SLUGS AND SNAILS Can be serious on seedlings and mature plants, especially in wet weather. (For remedies, see p.47.)

CABBAGE ROOT FLY Often a serious pest: white maggots attack the roots, causing the plants to die. The adults can be prevented from laying their eggs by protecting the plant with a disk of flexible material when it is planted out (see p.46). Alternatively, use a plastic drinking cup with the bottom removed, slipping it over the plant and lightly pressing it into the soil.

FLEA BEETLE Tiny blue-black beetles nibble holes in seedling leaves of all members of the cabbage family. Spray or dust with rotenone and/or pyrethrum.

CATERPILLARS Very common, especially in late summer. Spray with rotenone and/or pyrethrum (see also p.47).

MEALY APHIDS The gray aphids appear on the undersides of leaves in late summer and can be very destructive, causing the plants to die. Squash colonies by hand, move ladybirds to the plants if possible, and spray with appropriate chemicals as a last resort. Clear overwintered brassicas by late spring, to destroy the adult aphids.

CLUBROOT A very serious soilborne disease of brassicas, causing swollen galls on the roots, which eventually result in the plant wilting and dying. It is worst in poorly drained acid soils. So where it is a problem, improve the drainage, lime the soil, rotate over a three- or four-year cycle, and raise plants in sterile soil blocks for transplanting; all the transplants can also be dipped in calomel or some appropriate chemical before planting.

'DAMPING OFF' DISEASE This affects seedlings sown in unsuitable conditions. (For prevention, see p.47.)

recommended procedure is to sow them in early summer, in temperatures of about 20°C/68°F, either singly in soil blocks, or in seed flats, thinning soon after germination to about 5cm/2in apart. About a month later they should be transplanted about 15cm/6in apart, and, when space is available, they can be planted into their permanent positions 35-40cm/14-16in apart, the ground having been prepared with plenty of organic matter. A month or so afterward, about ten of the outer leaves can be removed, to improve air circulation between the plants which encourages the development of top-quality plants later in the season.

VARIETIES Japanese F_1 hybrids, 'Osaka Red' and 'Osaka White'.

CULINARY KALES

Although there are many types of culinary kale, most are considered too coarse for use in salads. Young leaves of the dwarf, curly-leaved types, however, can be used, such as 'Dwarf Blue Curled Vates' and 'Frosty'. They grow about 30cm/12in tall, and are very hardy and attractive to look at. Sow them in late spring and plant about 30cm/12in apart. The old-fashioned dwarf variety 'Ragged Jack', which has prettily serrated purple and blue-green leaves, is less hardy, but very decorative.

ORIENTAL BRASSICAS

A whole range of exciting oriental brassicas is gradually becoming available to gardeners in the West. Their subtle, interesting flavors when raw, their crisp texture and their high nutritive value make them valuable additions to the salad garden. The majority are in their prime in autumn and early winter and, being very fast growing, lend themselves to the cut-and-come-again technique and to use in gardens where space is at a premium.

There is tremendous confusion over the names of the different species. So for practical purposes I have simply divided the oriental brassicas into four categories: the **solid-headed Chinese cabbages**; the **leafy brassicas**, including leafy 'Pak Choi' (celery mustard) varieties; the **leafy mustards** and the **flowering mustards**. Any adventurous salad lovers should certainly experiment with any new varieties which appear in Western seed catalogs: the odds are that they will prove worth growing for use raw in salads, as well as cooked.

SOLID-HEADED CHINESE CABBAGES

The typical Chinese cabbage is conical – though some are rounded – with closely folded, densely packed leaves. What makes it quite distinct from Western cabbage is the crinkled texture of the leaves, the broad-based white midribs, and the prominent white venation; sometimes they look almost marbled. The flavor is delicate and quite different from Western cabbage.

CULTIVATION Chinese cabbages are semitropical marshy plants in origin, and remarkably fast-growing brassicas – they can reach a weight of several pounds within six to ten weeks after sowing. Rotate Chinese cabbages like other brassicas as they are very susceptible to clubroot. They must be grown in fertile, neutral to alkaline soil, rich in organic matter. (Very acid soil should be limed.)

Chinese cabbages are short-day plants, maturing naturally in late summer and autumn. They have a tendency, therefore, to run to seed without hearting up if sown early in the year or if checked, say, by a sudden drop in temperature. Some recently introduced varieties, however, such as the F_1 hybrids 'Tip Top' and 'Two Seasons', are better adapted to earlier sowings.

Chinese cabbage is at its most useful as a late summer/early autumn crop outdoors (often following early potatoes, peas or green beans), or for an autumn and winter crop under cover. Although it will not normally stand more than light frosts, if treated as a cut-and-come-again crop in an unheated greenhouse or cold frame, it often survives through winter into early spring, producing useful leaf during much of the winter (see p.50). In my garden, they have survived temperatures of −10°C/14°F under cover, when grown as a cut-and-come-again crop.

Spring sowings for an early summer crop of Chinese cabbage should only be made *if a 'bolt-resistant' variety is used, and, if temperatures can be kept above 10°C/50°F, during the period between germination and planting out.* Otherwise, sow from early to midsummer for the late summer and autumn outdoor crop, and in late summer and early autumn for the winter crop.

Chinese cabbages do not transplant well, so should either be sown *in situ* or raised in soil blocks or individual pots, so they can be planted out with minimum root disturbance. Plant out at the two- to three-leaf stage, spacing plants about 30cm/12in apart each way. The autumn crop, in particular, should not be overcrowded, as leaves are apt to rot in damp wet weather.

Chinese cabbage is a very thirsty crop: a single plant may need as much as 22 liters/5 gallons of water during its growing period. Moreover, the plants are shallow-rooted and cannot utilize water reserves deep in the soil. So water regularly, and keep the ground well mulched so that it never dries out.

When the heads are ready, cut them off just above ground level, leaving the stumps to resprout. The heads can be stored for several weeks in a refrigerator, or hung in nets in a cold place.

When Chinese cabbages are planted in very late autumn into an unheated greenhouse they are unlikely to heart up. They can therefore be planted about 13cm/5in apart; the young leaves which develop can be cut for use in salads when they are about 8-10cm/3-4in high. In spring, the plants will run to seed, and the flowering shoots, which are very tender and tasty, can be used in salads.

VARIETIES Reliable varieties are 'Chiko' F_1, 'Nagoda' F_1, 'Serrated Santo', 'Tip Top' F_1 and 'Two Seasons' F_1.

PESTS AND DISEASES **Slugs:** by far and away the most serious pest: they adore Chinese cabbages. (For control measures, see p.47.) **Flea beetle, caterpillars, cabbage root fly** and **clubroot** are other common problems. (For control measures, see p.75.)

LEAFY BRASSICAS

'PAK CHOI' (*Brassica chinensis*) These leafy brassicas generally have bright green, rounded, glossy leaves and prominent white swollen stalks and leaf midribs, all of which are edible. They are mild flavored and very succulent.

They need much the same growing conditions as Chinese cabbages and are robust plants, relatively pest-

'Tip Top' F₁

'Serrated Santo'

'Two Seasons' F₁

'Chiko' F₁

CHINESE CABBAGE *Several varieties of Chinese cabbage photographed in autumn when they are at their peak. Although not normally considered frost-hardy, Chinese cabbage can withstand several degrees of frost when treated as a cut-and-come-again crop. If planted in unheated greenhouses in autumn, it can prove a very useful salad vegetable in winter and early spring. Improved F₁ varieties are constantly becoming available.*

and disease-free. They grow rapidly, often being ready for cutting within five or six weeks of sowing.

Those listed here are most suitable for summer sowing, either for late summer and early autumn crops outdoors, or for winter crops under cover. They can be sown direct in the ground or transplanted, and can be used at the seedling stage, as young plants, or as mature plants; finally, the flowering shoots can be eaten, provided they are picked when still tender.

CULTIVATION Space plants between 20cm/8in and 30cm/12in apart, depending on the size of plant required. One method of growing 'Pak Choi' varieties is to sow them *in situ*, thinning in stages to the final distance apart (the thinnings can be used in salads). The hardier varieties are excellent winter crops in unheated greenhouses or frames. Although they stop growing in midwinter, they start growing again very early in the year, especially in warm spells, providing useful pickings. Virtually all respond to cut-and-come-again treatment. Outdoor plants can be cloched in late autumn to prolong their season of usefulness and improve their quality.

VARIETIES Those suitable for salads are: 'Chinese Pak Choi', 'Shanghai Pak Choi' and 'Japanese White Celery Mustard' (the hardiest of the three).

LEAFY MUSTARDS

These are rougher leaved and sharper flavored than the 'Pak Choi', sometimes becoming very hot flavored when about to run to seed. However, they are more flexible in their sowing dates. Those listed below are exceptionally hardy, and are most valuable in the winter months, in the open in mild areas (cloched as suggested for 'Pak Choi'), or under cover where several degrees of frost are expected in winter.

They can be sown *in situ* or transplanted, but are less fussy about soil conditions than 'Pak Choi'. The small young leaves can be used in salads while the larger, mature leaves are best cooked. Again, the flowering shoots, which appear in early spring, can be used in salads before they become tough. The following are useful varieties.

JAPANESE 'MIZUNA' *(Brassica juncea* 'Japonica') This plant (also known as Japanese greens or 'Kyona') has very beautiful, dark green, deeply dissected, fern-like leaves. It makes a compact plant about 15-20cm/6-8in high and up to 30cm/12in across on maturity, and can look very effective in a flower bed or patch-cropping design. It is useful for intercropping, and grows very well under sweetcorn.

It can be sown from very early spring to late autumn, thinning or planting to about 23cm/9in apart; thinnings can be used in salads. It can also be grown as a seedling crop (see pp.48-9). Either cut individual leaves as required, or cut the whole head just above ground level, leaving it to resprout, which it will do up to five times.

MUSTARD SPINACH 'TENDERGREEN' *(Brassica rapa)* This is another very hardy species, with rounded, dark green leaves; an excellent, fast-growing winter crop. Use the smaller leaves whole in salads; the large leaves will need to be shredded. The flavor is relatively mild. Sow in summer for a winter crop, spacing the plants about 30cm/12in apart.

'GREEN IN THE SNOW' *(Brassica juncea)* Another exceptionally vigorous, extremely hardy winter mustard, which is only suitable for sowing in summer and autumn for an autumn and winter crop. Space plants 15-20cm/6-8in apart. They will grow up to 45cm/20in tall, but are best harvested for salads when very young before the leaves become too hot.

Several oriental brassicas including, top left, Japanese mustard 'Mizuna', a versatile, pretty plant; top right, 'Shanghai Pak Choi', a hardy leafy mustard; above left, the flowering mustard 'Hon Tsai Tai'; above right, the mustard spinach 'Tendergreen' which, like many oriental brassicas, is grown for its leaves but has flowering shoots that can be used in salads.

'MIIKE GIANT' *(Brassica juncea)* This is a very hardy, giant-sized mustard; its huge leaves have very striking purple veins. The leaves are sometimes peppery, so use them sparingly in salads, preferably shredded. Sow in late summer for autumn and winter use, spacing plants about 35cm/14in apart.

FLOWERING MUSTARDS

The two varieties below are grown primarily for their flowers. Like all the 'Pak Choi' varieties, they need fertile, moist soil.

FLOWERING PURPLE 'PAK CHOI – HON TSAI TAI' *(Brassica campestris* 'Purpurea') This pretty plant has purplish leaves and leaf stalks and yellow flowers. The flowering stalks are eaten when about 20-25cm/8-10in long. In areas with cool summers it can be sown in spring for use in summer; otherwise, sow in summer for use in autumn and early winter. It will survive two or three degrees of frost. Plants should be spaced about 40cm/16in apart, kept well watered, and given a liquid feed just before flowering to encourage growth.

FLOWERING 'PAK CHOI – CHINESE TSAI SHIM' (*Brassica chinensis* 'Parachinensis') This plant has thicker, more succulent flowering shoots than 'Hon Tsai Tai', and is slightly less hardy. Nevertheless, it is excellent in late summer and autumn salads. Grow it like 'Hon Tsai Tai', spacing the plants about 25cm/10in apart. It is ready for use 40 to 60 days after sowing.

SPINACHES

Several plants in the spinach family, and closely related families, though generally used cooked, are very good value in salads. The younger, smaller leaves are the best for salads.

SPINACH (*Spinacea oleracea*) AND CHARD (*Beta vulgaris*)

Spinach and chard (the latter is also known as leaf beet, Swiss chard and seakale beet) are very similar vegetables. True spinach is rather refined compared to chard: it has smoother, paler leaves, and does not grow as tall or as vigorously. An annual plant, most varieties unfortunately run to seed very rapidly in hot and dry conditions. For this reason it is mainly grown in spring and autumn, and has a relatively short season of usefulness. The plants stand only a few degrees of frost. However, they have that very characteristic 'spinachy' flavor.

The chards belong to the beet family, but in their case the leaves rather than the roots have developed. The glossy, dark green, handsome leaves have very prominent white leaf stalks and midribs which are used as a cooked vegetable. For salad purposes the type of chard known as spinach beet, perpetual spinach or cutting chard (*poirée à couper* in France) is used. The chards, being biennials, do not run to seed until their second season, and so are useful over a much longer period than spinach. They are also much hardier and much more tolerant of hot and dry conditions, but have the disadvantage that they are coarse textured and less finely flavored.

CULTIVATION Spinach and chard need fertile, well-drained, moisture-retentive soil, rich in organic matter. The summer crops can be grown in light shade, provided they have adequate moisture. Both can be treated as cut-and-come-again crops (see p.50).

For the main summer supply, spinach is sown in spring, generally *in situ*. If large plants are required, thin in stages to 15cm/6in apart, using the thinnings in salads. However, if the intention is to make frequent pickings, thin them to only 7.5-10cm/3-4in apart. The main problem with these sowings is that the spinach is likely to run to seed as soon as the weather begins to warm up.

For autumn to spring supplies, sow spinach in late summer. In cold areas these plants should be cloched in winter or covered with protective litter. They will push their way through again in spring. They can also be sown under cover.

Spinach beet is also sown in spring or summer; the spring-sown plants may last until the following spring, and the summer-sown until the following summer. A very useful crop is obtained by sowing in soil blocks in late summer and early autumn for transplanting into an unheated greenhouse during winter. This gives tender pickings very early in the year. Space plants at least 25cm/10in apart. The quality of spinach beet is improved if it is protected with cloches in winter.

SORREL (*Rumex spp.*)

The sorrels are very hardy perennial plants, often found growing wild; there are several varieties. The so-called 'garden' or 'common' sorrel, *Rumex acetosa*, has narrowish, arrow-shaped leaves, while buckler-leaved or French sorrel, *Rumex scutatus*, has shield-shaped leaves which are wider at the base.

Sorrel has a delicious, sharp, lemony flavor. It is only necessary to use a few leaves at a time in a salad, preferably mixed with something blander.

CULTIVATION The plants are not fussy about soil, but produce more lush growth in fertile, moist conditions. They do quite well in light shade. To establish a patch, sow in spring or autumn, either *in situ* – thinning to about 25cm/10in apart – or in seed flats for transplanting. When they are large enough to use, the outer leaves should be picked first, leaving the 'heart' intact to produce fresh leaf. Cut off the seedheads to conserve the plant's energy.

The plants should be renewed every three or four years. To avoid resowing, a good plant can be left to run to seed, and the seedlings transplanted in spring or autumn. Sorrel can also be resown every year in spring, thinning to about 10cm/4in apart, when using only young leaves.

One of the great merits of sorrel is that it is among the last plants to die back in autumn and the first to reappear in spring; in mild areas it remains evergreen all winter. Plants can be covered with cloches in winter to improve their quality and extend their season. Where winters are severe a few plants can be lifted in late summer and transplanted into frames or an unheated greenhouse.
VARIETIES 'Blond de Lyon' and 'Large de Belleville'.

PATIENCE DOCK (*Rumex patientia*)
Sometimes known as spinach dock, this is a perennial plant closely related to sorrel and is cultivated like sorrel.

It can grow over 2m/6ft high, is extremely hardy, and comes into growth even earlier in the year. The flavor is milder than that of sorrel.

GOOD KING HENRY (*Chenopodium bonus-henricus*)
This old-fashioned hardy perennial plant has a taste very similar to that of spinach. Like sorrel it is ready very early in the year. Both the very tender flowering shoots and the young leaves can be used in salads, though it is best not to pick the shoots until the plants are in their second season.

It does best in moist, humus-rich soil, and will tolerate some shade. To establish a clump, either divide an old plant or sow seed in spring, spacing plants about 30cm/12in apart. Plants can be covered with litter or bracken in early spring to bring them into growth sooner. They generally need renewing every five years or so.

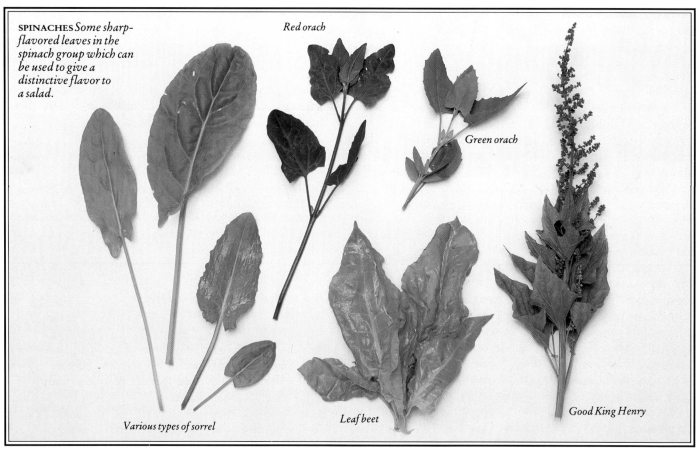

SPINACHES *Some sharp-flavored leaves in the spinach group which can be used to give a distinctive flavor to a salad.*

Red orach

Green orach

Various types of sorrel

Leaf beet

Good King Henry

ORACH (*Atriplex hortensis*)
The orachs (also known as mountain spinach) are tall, rather decorative annuals, growing up to 2m/6ft high. They are sometimes used as spinach substitutes, as they are somewhat slower to run to seed in hot weather. Being mild-flavored, they are often cooked with stronger-flavored leaves such as sorrel or spinach. There are green and red forms.

Sow in spring and early summer, *in situ*, in rich, moisture-retentive soil, thinning to about 20cm/8in apart. To keep the plants bushy and dwarf, pick the leaves regularly, and cut off the flowering spikes as they start to form. A few selected plants can be allowed to flower and seed themselves for future use.

LEAF AMARANTHUS (*Amaranthus spp.*)
There are many edible species of these mainly tropical plants. The majority are green-leaved although some have beautiful red or reddish tints. With their mild, spinachy flavor, they are useful spinach substitutes in hot climates, growing fast on fertile, light sandy soils.

Sow in spring, either indoors for transplanting, or outdoors after all danger of frost is past. Thin plants to about 10-15cm/4-6in apart. Pick the young leaves regularly.

MILD-FLAVORED LEAVES

The following are easily grown salad plants which are on the whole mild in flavor. Most of them can be worked into mixed salads to offset sharper-flavored plants.

ABYSSINIAN CABBAGE 'Karate' (*Brassica carinata*)
This brassica has only recently been introduced into Europe from Africa: 'Karate', the name by which it has become known, is the variety currently available. It is very nutritious, tolerant of fairly low temperatures and, most important, one of the faster-growing brassicas. It has a pleasant fresh taste, halfway between cabbage and mustard.

In good growing conditions a seedling crop can be ready three weeks after sowing; a mature crop two weeks later. It will grow up to 60cm/24in high, but can be used at various stages. At the seedling stage, from about 8 to 13cm/3 to 5in high, it can be cut an inch above ground level and treated as a cut-and-come-again crop (see p.48). Up to the 'spring greens' or 'collards' stage, 25-30cm/10-12in high, the smaller, more tender leaves and young stems can be eaten raw, but the larger leaves and stems will require cooking.

CULTIVATION 'Karate' grows in any reasonable soil. Sow outdoors from spring to late summer, starting as soon as the soil is workable. It is very useful as a catch crop on a vacant patch of ground or for intercropping. If a seedling crop is required either broadcast thinly or sow in rows about 15cm/6in apart, thinning to about 5cm/2in apart. If larger plants are wanted thin to 25-30cm/10-12in apart.

'Karate' grown under cover is exceptionally tender, and very useful sowings can be made in frames and unheated greenhouses in late autumn and early spring.

PESTS AND DISEASES 'Karate' is subject to the normal range of cabbage pests and diseases (see p.75).

ALFALFA (*Medicago sativa*)
This pretty, evergreen, perennial plant, also known as lucerne, is a member of the clover family, and has attractive blue and violet flowers. The plants are very deep-rooted, so withstand dry conditions well. They can grow up to 90cm/36in high.

Alfalfa can be grown in decorative patches (see pp.20-21) or as a small hedge, but cut the plants back hard after flowering to renew their vigor.

CULTIVATION Sow in spring or autumn, *in situ* outdoors, either broadcast or in rows a few inches apart. Seed sold for seed sprouting (see p.53) can be used. Germination is usually rapid, and the young growths can be used in salads when between 2.5 and 5cm/1 and 2in long. Pickings can be made throughout the growing season, but the leaf texture becomes tougher as the plants mature.

CORN SALAD (*Valerianella locusta*)
This humble-looking, low-growing annual, also known as lamb's lettuce or fetticus, has been cultivated for centuries and is found growing wild in much of the Northern Hemisphere. It is a very hardy little plant, and for this reason is most useful for winter and early spring salads, when mild-flavored leaves are at a premium.

CULTIVATION Corn salad is an easily grown plant, tolerating a wide range of soils and conditions. It can be used at the seedling stage as a cut-and-come-again crop (see p.48) or, when mature, individual leaves can be picked or the whole head cut an inch above ground level: fresh growth will then be made. It can be sown *in situ*, either broadcast or in rows, or sown in containers for transplanting. The mature plants need to be thinned to about 10cm/4in apart. Being small, corn salad can be used for intercropping – for example, grown between winter brassicas.

The main sowings are made from early to late summer, for the autumn and winter crop outdoors. The seed is hard and may not germinate well in hot weather, so water the drills well before sowing, or keep the seedbed covered until germination. Corn salad is surprisingly slow-growing: plants may take up to three months to reach their full size.

Further sowings can be made in autumn for transplanting under cover in late autumn or early winter. This will give a very useful crop during the winter and again in early spring, when rapid new growth is made. It is also worth sowing early in spring, either indoors for transplanting outdoors, or *in situ* outdoors. This can provide a useful heading crop in spring and early summer, though it may run to seed rapidly in hot weather.

Crops left in the open in winter survive surprisingly low temperatures, but their quality will be improved if they are protected with cloches.

VARIETIES There are many varieties of corn salad. **For summer sowings:** 'large-seeded' types such as 'Dutch', 'Large-leaved English', and 'Valgros'; **for later sowings:** 'green' varieties, such as 'Coquille de Louviers', 'Verte de Cambrai' and 'Verte d'Etampes', are generally hardier.

ICEPLANT *(Mesembryanthemum crystallinum)*

Iceplant is a sprawling plant with thick, fleshy leaves and thick stems, both covered with tiny membranous bladders which sparkle in the sun like ice crystals – hence its name. In South Africa and the Mediterranean, where it grows wild, it is a perennial, but in cooler climates it must be treated as an annual.

In hot climates it is grown as a substitute for spinach in summer, but it is far better as a salad plant. The succulent juicy leaves have an interesting taste with a hint of saltiness about them. They normally keep fresh for several days after picking.

CULTIVATION A sun-loving plant, iceplant grows best on fertile soil, but tolerates poorer soil. It can be grown beneath sweetcorn or full-grown 'Karate' plants.

One of the hardier corn salad varieties, 'Verte de Cambrai', and self-sown hairy bitter cress, photographed in early spring.

Sow indoors in late spring, transplanting outdoors after any risk of frost is over, spacing the plants about 30cm/12in apart. Within a month the first young growths can be picked for salad; from then on pick regularly to encourage further tender growths, removing any flowers which appear. The plants will survive the first touch of frost, and often put on a surprising burst in the autumn. At this stage they can be covered with cloches to extend the season a couple of weeks.

PESTS Iceplant is sometimes attacked by slugs in wet weather. Precautions should be taken (see p.47).

PURSLANE *(Portulaca oleracea)*

Forms of purslane grow wild in much of the temperate world and have been cultivated for centuries. It is a half-hardy plant with succulent rounded leaves and similarly succulent stems, both leaves and stems being edible raw. There are green and golden cultivated forms, the green being more vigorous, with thinner leaves and, some say, a better flavor; the golden form has thicker leaves and is more sprawling, but it is the more decorative in a salad. Purslane has a refreshing, crunchy texture but its flavor is rather bland. In the past, purslane leaves and stems were pickled for winter use.

CULTIVATION Purslane does best on light, well-drained soil in a sheltered, southfacing position. It can be grown as a seedling or cut-and-come-again crop, or alternatively as a mature plant.

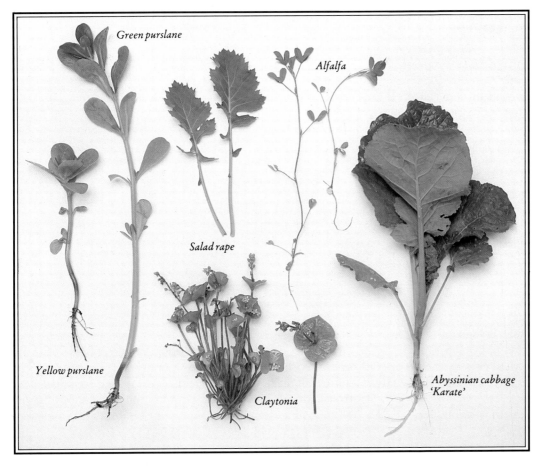

Green purslane

Alfalfa

Salad rape

Yellow purslane

Claytonia

Abyssinian cabbage 'Karate'

MILD-FLAVORED PLANTS
Examples of some lesser-known plants which are very useful in salads. Although photographed in summer, all of these with the exception of purslane can be used from spring to autumn, and even in winter in mild areas.

Sow indoors in late spring for transplanting outside after the danger of frost has passed, spacing plants about 15cm/6in apart. In cold weather, the seedlings damp off very easily (see p.47), so little is gained by premature sowing. In warm areas purslane can be sown *in situ* outdoors in spring and early summer. Very useful sowings for a seedling crop can be made in frames or unheated greenhouses both in spring and in late summer, the latter for an autumn crop.

Purslane is generally cut an inch or so above ground level, always leaving two leaves at the base for regrowth. The young growths must be picked continually or the leaves become tough; any seedheads which appear must be cut off as they are knobbly and tough to eat.

PESTS In cold, wet summers purslane is a miserable plant, prone to slug damage. Covering it with cloches can sometimes give it a new lease of life.

CLAYTONIA (*Claytonia perfoliata, Montia perfoliata*)
Also known as winter purslane, miner's lettuce and spring beauty, this is my favorite winter salad plant. A dainty-looking, hardy annual, its early leaves are borne at the end of short stalks and are triangular in shape; the later leaves are rounded and wrapped around the flowering stalk in a curious way. They look very pretty in a salad, especially when mixed with flowers, for example, and have a fresh, mild flavor.

CULTIVATION Although claytonia does best on light sandy soils, it is highly adaptable. It can be grown as a seedling cut-and-come-again crop (see p.48), or, and this is probably the more productive method, as mature plants, spaced 13-15cm/5-6in apart. It can be broadcast thinly or sown in rows, or in seed flats for planting out. If you allow plants to go to seed in early summer, the seedlings can be transplanted in autumn, but the plants are very shallow-rooted, so should be uprooted and transplanted with care.

The principal sowing is in summer for winter use, but sowings can also be made in spring for summer use. It is always worth planting a few seedlings under cover, say, into an unheated greenhouse, in autumn and winter. If the plants grow large enough, the first cuttings can be made in autumn and winter. Otherwise they remain small until early spring, when they will grow with extraordinary rapidity and be very welcome.

With mature plants, either pick individual leaves as required, or cut the whole head an inch above ground level: the leaves will resprout several times.

Plants overwintered outdoors are best protected with cloches, especially on heavy soils. Waterlogging is more likely to be fatal than cold weather, although they will not survive very severe frost. Seed left in the soil, however, will germinate in spring.

SALAD RAPE (Brassica napus)

When boxes of seedlings are sold as 'mustard' or 'cress' they are often neither, but are in fact salad rape. This is much milder flavored than mustard or cress and is rather more like cabbage in taste; it is an excellent salad vegetable.

CULTIVATION It can be grown in various ways: on a windowsill as a short-term crop, using a blotting paper base; in a seed flat of potting mix or finely sifted soil, which will allow the seedlings to grow larger and be cut more frequently; or broadcast in the ground, either indoors or outdoors, for a cut-and-come-again crop. It is less successful outdoors in very wet areas.

Salad rape seed germinates at very low temperatures. It is therefore an excellent winter crop in unheated greenhouses or frames, sown in late autumn or very early in spring. It will survive temperatures of −10°C/14°F.

The most useful outdoor sowings are made in spring and early summer, and again in late summer and early autumn. Salad rape runs to seed much more slowly than mustard or cress, so can be used over a longer period – I've known a spring-sown patch give pickings over four months. Make the first cut when the seedlings are tiny, and further cuts as the plants grow larger. Much like 'Karate', salad rape will eventually grow about 60cm/24in high, but even at this stage the large, individual leaves can still be used in salads.

<hr>

SHARP-FLAVORED LEAVES

Not all the 'sharp-flavored' salad plants in this group are to everybody's liking. But mixed into salads in small quantities, especially when blended with the mild-flavored leaves, they can be used to create unusual salads. Some, like coriander, fenugreek and Mediterranean rocket, deserve to be more widely grown.

SHUNGIKU (Chrysanthemum coronarium)

This annual chrysanthemum has fragrant, somewhat indented leaves and pretty yellow flowers. It is also known as garland chrysanthemum or crown daisy. The young growths are widely used in oriental cookery, generally lightly cooked. When used raw in salads, the leaves have a strong, aromatic taste.

CULTIVATION Though not fussy about soil, shungiku needs moist, cool conditions or it tends to become coarse and bitter. It does best in spring and autumn and can be grown in light shade in hot climates. It can grow up to about 60cm/24in high when flowering, but for salads it is best kept cut back to a maximum height of about 30cm/12in. At this height it makes pretty patches or edges in a vegetable garden. If kept cut back to 13-15cm/5-6in high, it can be used for intercropping (see pp.15-17). It is reasonably hardy and fast growing – seedlings can sometimes be cut a month after sowing.

It can be grown as a seedling crop or as individual plants, spaced about 15cm/6in apart. Sow in spring, either outside, broadcast or in rows, or indoors in seed flats for transplanting. A second sowing can be made in late summer for an autumn crop, either outdoors, or sown or transplanted under cover to prolong the season. Outdoor crops can be cloched in autumn. Shungiku will survive light frosts, but the quality, of course, will deteriorate as a result.

Seedlings can be used whole when 5-10cm/2-4in high. With older plants, pick only the tender leaves (five or six) of the young growths just before use, as shungiku wilts rapidly. Cut off all flowering shoots and never be afraid to cut the plant back: it regenerates rapidly but becomes very 'woody' if allowed to flower. Liquid feeding after cutting is beneficial.

CORIANDER *(Coriandrum sativum)*

Coriander leaves and seeds are used to flavor food all over the world. An annual plant, also known as Chinese parsley, it grows up to 60cm/24in high when flowering, but for salads the spicy-flavored bright green leaves, rather similar to broad-leaved parsley in appearance, must be cut young. Some strains of coriander are much better than others, but at present it is difficult to obtain named strains though seed sold for culinary purposes often grows quite successfully. The coriander 'seed' is enclosed in a tiny round pod, which sometimes prevents germination. If trouble is encountered, crack the pods by lightly crushing a thin layer of seeds with a rolling pin.

CULTIVATION Coriander prefers light soils and, for a continuous supply, successive sowings should be made. It grows best in cool spring and autumn weather, running to seed rapidly in hot weather.

Seeds can be broadcast or sown in close rows about 5cm/2in apart, or in wide drills or bands, 10cm/4in wide and 5cm/2in apart. Also, several seeds can be sown in a soil block and transplanted as one unit. Although generally sown outdoors, coriander can be sown under cover in early spring and late summer, and it can be grown indoors in seed flats, like cress (see p.48).

Coriander withstands light frosts, and can be overwintered outdoors in mild areas; it starts into growth very vigorously in spring. If protected with cloches, it will be ready earlier.

Leaves can be cut at any stage from about 2.5 to 15cm/1 to 6in high. Several successive cuts can be made from one sowing, but once the plants run to seed the flavor deteriorates and they should be uprooted. One word of warning: coriander can seed itself and may easily become a persistent weed.

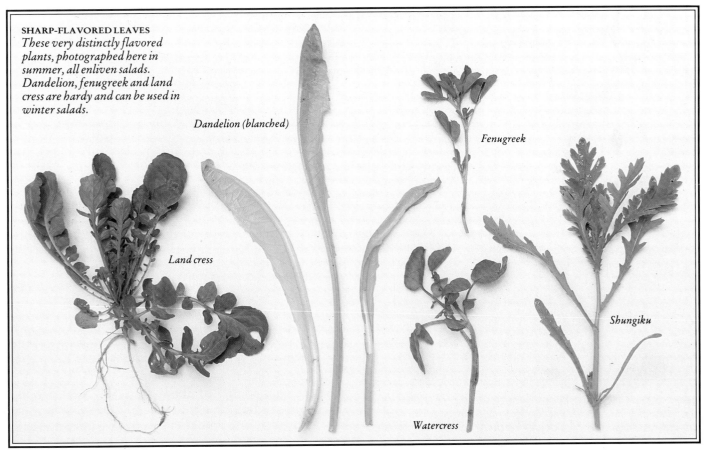

SHARP-FLAVORED LEAVES
These very distinctly flavored plants, photographed here in summer, all enliven salads. Dandelion, fenugreek and land cress are hardy and can be used in winter salads.

Dandelion (blanched)

Fenugreek

Land cress

Shungiku

Watercress

CRESSES

Many plants in the cress family have a long history of cultivation for use in salads. They all have a characteristic pungent flavor.

GARDEN CRESS (*Lepidium sativum*) For centuries this hot-flavored plant has been cultivated for salads as a cut-and-come-again seedling crop.

CULTIVATION Cress grows best in light soil with plenty of moisture. It can make a very effective dense patch of deep green in an ornamental design, and is useful for intercropping. It is grown exactly like salad rape, though

Coriander

White mustard seedlings

Garden cress

Mediterranean rocket and seedlings

SHARP-FLAVORED LEAVES *This group includes some of the most versatile and productive of salad plants. They can all be grown as a cut-and-come-again seedling crop, either from spring to autumn outdoors or in the winter months under cover.*

it runs to seed faster in hot weather and so has a shorter season of usefulness. In cool weather, however, as many as five consecutive cuts can be made from one sowing. It is easy to save seed for future sowings (see p.23). Probably the most valuable sowings are those made in late autumn or very early spring in an unheated greenhouse or frame.

LAND CRESS (*Barbarea verna, Barbarea praecox*) A very hardy, low-growing, biennial plant, land cress has dark green, shiny, deeply cut leaves which remain green all winter. Also known as early winter or Belle Isle cress, it has a hot flavor almost indistinguishable from watercress, for which it is often substituted. In hot weather it runs to seed very rapidly, the flavor then becoming unbearably hot.

CULTIVATION Land cress does best in moist humus-rich soils; hot, dry soils should be avoided. It grows well in damp corners, and slightly shaded and northfacing situations, intercropped between taller vegetables such as brassicas. It makes a neat edging during the winter months.

The main sowings are made from mid- to late summer, for plants that will crop from autumn until spring. Land cress can also be sown in early spring for a summer crop. Sow *in situ* or in seed flats for transplanting – the latter method is sometimes preferable as germination can be erratic outdoors in summer. Space the plants about 15cm/6in apart and keep them well watered until they become established.

The smallest, central leaves are the most tender. Pick them as required, or cut the whole head just above ground level: further growth will be made. Plants can be cloched during winter to improve their quality. Seedlings can also be transplanted under cover in autumn to give especially tender pickings in winter and spring.

PESTS Watch out for flea beetle attacks in the early stages (see p.75). Transplanted plants may avoid attacks.

WATERCRESS (*Nasturtium officinale*) This pungently flavored hardy perennial is also extremely nutritious. It grows naturally in springs or fresh running streams in limestone areas. It needs clean, flowing water with a constant temperature of about 10°C/50°F and dappled shade – bright light but not full sun. Obviously it is not easy to create these conditions in most gardens.

CULTIVATION If you have a stream, plant young, rooted

pieces of watercress (see below) in the soil along the edges in spring, spaced about 15cm/6in apart.

Small quantities of watercress can sometimes be grown successfully in flower pots. Put a layer of gravel or moss in the bottom of the pot to prevent the soil being washed out, and cover this with rich garden or potting soil, to which a little fresh-ground limestone has been added. Plant several young, rooted pieces in the pot. Take these from old plants, or alternatively buy shop watercress, trim off the tips, and dangle the stems in a jar of water: they will rapidly develop roots and these rooted stems can be planted. Stand the pot in a dish of cool, clean water, which should be changed daily in hot weather, less frequently in cool weather. Keep it somewhere sheltered but with good light, top-dress it from time to time with well-rotted garden compost, and nip off any flowering shoots that develop.

DANDELION (Taraxacum officinale)

The leaves and roots of dandelion have a long tradition of culinary and medicinal use. It is a perennial plant, with a great deal of natural variation in leaf size, shape and form, and is at its best from autumn until spring, though plants tend to die back in midwinter. The leaves have a distinct, tart flavor which is subtly changed by blanching, but the young leaves can often be eaten green. The tops of the roots are well flavored and may be used in salads.

CULTIVATION Dandelion does not like waterlogged conditions, but otherwise tolerates a wide range of soils and situations. Sow in spring and early summer, either *in situ* to thin out, or in seedbeds or seed flats for transplanting. Plants should be spaced about 35cm/14in apart. Seedlings can also be thinned to 5cm/2in apart, so that one pot can be used to blanch a group of seedlings.

From late summer onward, blanch a few plants at a time. In mild areas it is easiest to blanch them *in situ* (see p.51). Where winters are more severe, it is preferable to lift and blanch the plants indoors; they should be discarded after use.

FENUGREEK (Trigonella foenum-graecum)

Fenugreek, a very spicy, aromatic plant in the clover family, is nowadays grown mostly for its seeds, which are used to flavor curries. Used very sparingly, however, the fresh green leaf can give quite a kick to a salad.

CULTIVATION Fenugreek is not fussy about soil, and can be sown outdoors from spring until autumn, in much the same way as coriander. For a constant supply, small sowings should be made every three weeks or so, cutting when a couple of inches high before the stems thicken.

Fenugreek needs moisture both for germination and throughout growth, so for summer sowings water the drills well beforehand, and keep well watered during hot weather. It survives temperatures as low as $-16°C/3°F$, so sowings can be made under cover in autumn for a winter crop. It can also be sown indoors in seed flats.

MEDITERRANEAN ROCKET (Eruca vesicaria)

Rocket, or Italian cress as it is sometimes known, is one of the most versatile and worthwhile salad plants. The leaves have a delicious spiciness, though the flavoring can become overpoweringly hot in mature plants. It grows best in cool weather, tending to run to seed rapidly in summer. It is fast-growing and very useful for inter- and undercropping.

CULTIVATION Sow rocket broadcast, or in rows, or in seed flats for transplanting, or as a windowsill crop in seed flats (see p.46). It can be sown outdoors from early spring, as soon as the soil is workable, until autumn. Summer sowings must be kept moist or grown in light shade. It can be grown as a cut-and-come-again seedling crop (see p.48) – as many as five cuts can be made from one patch – or as single plants spaced about 15cm/6in apart. Rocket can withstand several degrees of frost, but crops overwintered outside should be cloched to keep them tender. An exceptionally useful sowing can be made *very* early in the year under cover: it will give continuous cutting throughout the spring. It is also worth sowing or transplanting under cover in autumn for winter supplies. Leave a few plants to run to seed in summer – you'll need plenty of seed if you want to broadcast rocket.

WHITE MUSTARD (Brassica hirta, Brassica alba)

As a salad crop, white mustard has always been partnered with cress. It is grown in exactly the same way, but it germinates faster. So, if the two are wanted together, sow white mustard three days later than cress. It has a hot flavor, and once past the seedling stage, 5-7.5cm/2-3in high, the leaves are inclined to become rather tough and bristly. Its useful life, therefore, tends to be shorter than that of cress. In areas of high rainfall, its growth is sometimes too vigorous and rampant.

STEMS, STALKS AND FRUITS

Some of the most subtle salad flavors are found in the stalks and swollen stems of fennel, kohlrabi, seakale, mitsuba, celery and celeriac. The fruits of tomatoes, cucumbers and peppers are the mainstay of summer salads.

FLORENCE FENNEL
(Foeniculum vulgare 'Azoricum')

Fennel is a lovely plant growing about 45cm/18in high, with feathery, shimmering green foliage. Florence fennel (also known as sweet fennel or *finocchio*) is the annual form, grown mainly for the greatly swollen leaf bases which form a 'bulb' at ground level. This has a crisp, celerylike texture and a delightful aniseed flavor.

Florence fennel is not always easy to grow. In areas with unpredictable summers it is likely to bolt rather than form a 'bulb' especially if sown early in the year or subjected to cold or dry spells. The stems and foliage of bolted plants can still be used in salads, but are not the same quality as the truly solid 'bulb'.

Cultivation
Florence fennel does best on light, fertile well-drained soil rich in organic matter.

For the main late-summer/autumn outdoor crop, sow in midsummer. Florence fennel germinates erratically and is best sown in seed flats and pricked out a few days after germination into small pots, or soil blocks. Alternatively, sow in soil blocks, thinning to one seedling per block. Plant out two or three weeks later, at the stage when the seedlings have two or three real leaves. If transplanted when any larger, the plants may bolt. Plant 30cm/12in apart. If grown in good conditions, they will be ready four to six weeks later.

When ready for use, cut the 'bulbs' just above ground level rather than uprooting them completely; useful secondary growths are made which are tasty and decorative in a salad.

Florence fennel can stand fairly low temperatures, and it is worth making a second sowing in late summer or early autumn for transplanting into an unheated greenhouse or frame. This may provide at best a 'bulbed' plant, but at least some very tender 'fern' during autumn and early winter. Keep the crop well ventilated.

Some recently introduced varieties, such as 'Zefa Fino' are less likely to bolt than traditional varieties if sown in late spring and early summer for a summer crop. They are not infallible but worth a try where available.

Varieties
Standard: 'Perfection', 'Sirio'; **new:** 'Zefa Fino'.

FENNEL HERB *(Foeniculum vulgare)*
The fennel 'herb' is a much taller perennial plant growing up to 1.5m/5ft high. It does not form a 'bulb', and is far less fussy about soil conditions. The leaves are used for flavoring and garnishing.

Sow it in spring *in situ*, thinning to 45cm/18in apart. The plants will last for several years if the flower heads are removed as they form. There is a very striking, though less strongly flavored, bronze form.

KOHLRABI
(Brassica oleracea 'Gongylodes')

Kohlrabi is one of the odder-looking brassicas. An inch or so above the ground its stem swells into a graceful ball; it's a very fast-growing nutritious vegetable, often grown as a substitute for turnip as it withstands heat and drought better. Although normally cooked, it is excellent in salads, either grated, sliced or chopped. The flavor is nutty and sweet. The green varieties, sometimes called white, are sweetest, the purple varieties hardiest. Kohlrabi is one of the most nutritious vegetables, rich in protein, calcium and vitamin C.

Cultivation
Kohlrabi does best on fertile, light, moist soils – lime the soil if it is acid. Rotate kohlrabi like other brassicas. It can be ready seven weeks after sowing, so is useful for inter-cropping, say, between slow-growing brassicas.

Kohlrabi can be sown outdoors from spring until late

Florence fennel in the ground showing, right, a cut stump which is now resprouting. As with so many plants, the small resprouted shoots survive considerably lower temperatures than the large 'branches' of mature fern.

Kohlrabi 'Green Vienna'

Kohlrabi 'Purple Vienna'

Florence fennel 'Perfection'

VEGETABLES WITH SWOLLEN STEMS *Florence fennel and kohlrabi are grown for their swollen stems or 'bulbs', which have a very subtle flavor when raw. They are usually sliced or grated. Kohlrabi is an easily grown vegetable, but fennel is more temperamental.*

summer, although there is a risk of bolting with *early* spring sowings, and with midsummer sowings in hot areas. Sow *in situ*, thinning to about 23cm/9in apart. Never allow seedlings to become overcrowded. It can also be sown in seed flats or soil blocks, and planted out when at the two- or three-leaf stage. A useful crop can be obtained by sowing or planting under cover in early autumn. Always keep kohlrabi well watered so that it grows steadily.

Though reasonably hardy, kohlrabi is lifted in late autumn in very cold areas and stored in boxes of sand for winter use. The outer leaves should be trimmed off, leaving a small tuft on the crown to prevent the stem from drying out.

Varieties

Most varieties of kohlrabi must be eaten when about tennis-ball size as they become coarse and woody when larger. New F_1 hybrid varieties are being introduced which grow large without becoming coarse, are very sweet and have good resistance to heat and drought.
RECOMMENDED VARIETIES: 'Blue Danish', 'Green Vienna', 'Purple Vienna', 'Lanro' F_1, 'Karla'.

SEAKALE
(Crambe maritima)

This handsome, hardy, perennial plant, a native of the seashore, is cultivated for the deliciously flavored young leaf stalks which are eaten raw after blanching.

Cultivation

Establish a seakale bed in good, light, well-drained soil in a sunny position: the plants should last eight to ten years. They can be raised by sowing *fresh* seed in moist soil in spring, either *in situ* or in a seedbed or seed flats for transplanting. (Seakale seed loses its viability rapidly.) Alternatively, buy young plants or rooted cuttings (known as thongs) for planting in spring or autumn. Space plants 30-45cm/12-18in apart. They die right back in winter.

In its third season, seakale is forced into growth and blanched in early spring, by covering the crowns (which die right back in winter) with several inches of leaves and a lightproof box or pot at least 30cm/12in high (see Blanch-ing, p.51). The young leaves will be ready several weeks later. Cut them when about 20cm/8in long. Then leave the plants uncovered to grow normally. Feed them annually with a seaweed fertilizer.

Seakale can also be lifted and forced in warm conditions indoors but the roots have to be discarded afterwards. under but the roots have to be discarded afterward.

MITSUBA
(Cryptotaenia japonica)

This hardy, evergreen plant, also known as Japanese parsley or honewort, grows about 38cm/15in high. It has long leaf stalks and a pale green leaf divided into three leaflets. The stems and leaves are used raw in salads: their delicate flavor could be described as a blend between parsley, celery and angelica.

Cultivation

By nature a woodland plant, it thrives in moist, lightly shaded situations; it can be grown as a ground cover plant. Although a perennial, it is best treated as an annual. Sow *in situ* in spring or autumn, thinning to about 15cm/6in apart. The plants are ready for use within about two months. Successive sowings can be made for a continuous supply. It is useful to have a few plants under cover for use during the winter. Plants left in the ground will seed themselves naturally for use the following year.

CELERY
(Apium graveolens)

The celeries are marsh plants in origin, and are grown mainly for their long stems, which have a very distinct flavor and an appetizing crisp texture. The stems are often blanched to make them paler and crisper. The leaves are also strongly flavored, and are used for seasoning and garnishing, both fresh and dried. Several closely related kinds of celery, all of which are of varying hardiness, are described here.

LEAF CELERY

This bushy type of celery (also known as green or cutting celery) is very similar to wild celery, growing about 30cm/12in high, with slender, relatively short stems and shiny, healthy looking foliage. It is very hardy and is generally available all year round. Once established it perpetuates itself, as the plants eventually run to seed, their seedlings popping up everywhere. It is very strongly flavored, so must be used sparingly in salads.

CULTIVATION Sow from late spring until autumn (*in situ* or in seed flats). On the whole, celery is best sown in seed flats indoors in gentle heat. It germinates badly at high temperatures but must have light to germinate, so sow seeds on the surface, and keep the potting mix moist until they have germinated. Prick the seedlings out as soon as they are large enough to handle, and, before planting out, harden them off well. Space the plants about 13cm/5in apart. Nice clumps can be obtained by sowing in soil blocks (see p.30). Sow about eight seeds in each block, planting them out 'as one', about 20cm/8in apart.

The first cutting can generally be made within a month of planting, when plants are about 23cm/9in high; they will continue to grow over many months. Although leaf celery is very hardy, a few plants can be transplanted under cover in late summer to ensure a supply of good quality leaf for winter use.

SELF-BLANCHING CELERY

Unlike 'trench' celery (see right), self-blanching celery is not hardy, so is grown mainly for summer and autumn use. The stems are very palatable without blanching, but if light can be partly excluded when they are growing, their texture and appearance are improved.

CULTIVATION The plants have a tendency to bolt if sown too early, or subjected to dry or cold conditions, so try to grow them steadily. They need fertile soil, rich in organic matter, and plenty of moisture.

Sow in spring in gentle heat, as for leaf celery. If possible, sow in soil blocks to minimize the 'shock' of transplanting. Seedlings may bolt if subjected to temperatures below 10°C/50°F for more than 12 hours, so delay sowing if there is a risk of this occurring. Harden off carefully and plant out after risk of frost is past, when the plants are at the five- to six-leaf stage. Plant them 23-30cm/9-12in apart in a 'block' formation, so that outer plants blanch the inner. Intermediate plants can be cut when small, allowing the remainder to grow larger. Keep them well watered, and feed occasionally with a seaweed-based or high-nitrogen fertilizer. Straw can be tucked around the block and between the plants to blanch them further.

In areas with severe winters the plants are dug up with the roots intact in autumn, the leaves being tied neatly together. They are then transplanted into protected frames or pits 30cm/12in deep, and covered with dried leaves or straw and a rainproof 'lid'.

For a late crop under cover, sow in late spring and plant under cover in late summer. This will crop until affected by frost.

VARIETIES These are divided into 'green' and 'golden'. The golden are more attractive-looking, but the green are said to be better flavored.

Green varieties 'Celebrity', 'Green giant', 'Greensnap', 'Tendercrisp'; **golden varieties** 'Avonpearl', 'Golden Self-blanching', 'Lathom Self-blanching' (the least likely to run to seed).

'TRENCH' CELERY

Hardy 'trench' celery is always considered a very English crop. The long white or pink stems (depending on variety) are superbly flavored and very handsome. But they must be blanched and this, of course, does take time and effort.

CULTIVATION Trench celery needs the same soil and growing conditions as self-blanching celery and is raised in the same way, being sown in gentle heat in spring, and planted outside in early summer about 25cm/10in apart.

Blanching is carried out either by planting the celery in a trench and earthing up the stems, or by growing it on the flat and covering the stems to exclude light.

Trench method The trench should ideally be prepared the previous autumn, being dug at least 38cm/15in wide and 30cm/12in deep, with plenty of well-rotted manure or compost worked into the bottom level, leaving the surplus soil along the edge for earthing up. Plant in the bottom of the trench.

Start earthing up when the plants are about 30cm/12in high. Water the soil first, then tie the stems loosely with raffia just below the leaves, removing any suckers. Draw the soil up the stems to a height of about 10cm/4in, taking care that no soil falls between the stems. Repeat the operation twice more at approximately three-week intervals, never earthing up higher than the lower leaves of the plant.

Flat method Prepare the plants similarly, tying heavy brown paper or black polyethylene firmly around the stems in stages, covering about 10cm/4in at a time.

Celeriac

Green self-blanching
celery 'Celebrity'

Golden self-blanching celery

Leaf celery

THE CELERY FAMILY *The characteristic flavor of celery is found in the leaves of leaf (or green) celery, the stems of self-blanching celery and in the swollen stem of celeriac, an excellent winter standby.*

Trench celery is ready for cutting from early winter onward. It will not stand much frost unless covered with straw or bracken.

VARIETIES The white varieties are less hardy than the pink and are cut first. Recommended: 'Clayworth Prize Pink' ('Giant Pink'), 'Giant White'.

Pests and diseases

SLUGS Particularly damaging on the stems of self-blanching and trench celery. (For remedies, see p.47.)

CELERY FLY Tiny maggots attack the foliage in spring, causing blisters. Discard any blistered seedlings, remove blisters on mature plants by hand, spray with pyrethrum and/or rotenone, and burn infested foliage.

LEAF SPOT Brown rusty spots appear on leaves and stems. The disease is seedborne so, wherever available, use thiram-treated seed which gives some protection.

WILT Starts with outer leaves, and is caused by a fungus in the soil. Choose wilt-resistant varieties.

CELERIAC (*Apium graveolens* 'Rapaceum')

Celeriac, also known as turnip-rooted celery, is a bushy type of celery grown mainly for its stem which swells into a knobbly 'bulb' at ground level. It is an excellent winter vegetable, either cooked and cold or grated raw into salads. It has a delicious mild celery flavor. The leaves have a much stronger flavor and can be used sparingly.

Cultivation

Celeriac requires moist, rich soil and needs a long, steady growing season to develop a large 'bulb'. Sow as for stem celery, in gentle heat very early in spring. Plant out after hardening off well in late spring or early summer, 30-38cm/12-15in apart. Don't plant too deeply; the base of the stem should be at soil level. Water well and mulch after planting to help conserve soil moisture. Celeriac normally benefits from regular feeding, every two weeks, with a liquid feed. Water generously in dry weather.

Celeriac stands at least −10°C/14°F, but it is advisable to put a thick layer of straw or bracken between and around the plants in late autumn to give them protection and make them easier to lift in winter. The flavor and texture is better, however, if they are kept in the ground.

Varieties

'Blanco', 'José', 'Tellus'.

TOMATOES
(*Lycopersicon esculentum*)

The tomato is a half-hardy South American plant, introduced into Europe in the sixteenth century as an ornamental greenhouse climber. It has, deservedly, become one of the most universally grown vegetables: beautiful to look at, versatile to use both raw and cooked, and rich in vitamins. In warm sunny climates it grows like a weed, but in northern areas or where summers are cold and short, and light levels are poor, it has to be coaxed into fruiting.

Plants can be either tall, bush or dwarf. In the tall types, the main stem can grow over 4m/12ft in length in favorable conditions, the sideshoots also developing into branches several feet long. They are trained up strings or tied to supports, growth being kept within bounds by nipping out the growing point and pruning back the sideshoots. The bush types are stockier plants in which the main leader and the sideshoots develop to a limited extent, then more or less 'stop' themselves naturally. They require almost no pruning and are best grown sprawling on the ground. The dwarf types form very compact, miniature bushes.

Tomatoes display an enormous range of color, shape and size. They can be red, pink, orange, yellow, red- and orange-striped, even white. In size they range from the enormous, fleshy American beefsteak varieties, down through the large, flattish, ribbed and rather ugly 'Marmande' types (both of which have superb flavor and flesh) to standard-sized round tomatoes, boxy Italian 'canning' tomatoes, pear-shaped tomatoes and, at the smaller end of the scale, the sweet, round 'cherry' tomatoes such as 'Gardener's Delight', and the tiny 'currant' tomatoes.

If you are taking the trouble to grow tomatoes, it is well worth going all out for the colorful, fleshy, well-flavored varieties. Nothing can compare with a thick slab of a beefsteak or 'Golden Boy', sprinkled with fresh basil and black pepper, on a slice of homemade bread. There are few limitations on what can be grown except that beefsteak tomatoes require somewhat higher temperatures than the others in the early stages, pear-shaped tomatoes may not develop a true pear shape at low temperatures, and the Italian 'canning' types are slow-maturing, so need a fairly long season.

'Supermarmande' F₁ marmande type

'Dombito' F₁ beefsteak type

'Italian Plum' canning type

'Pixie' F₁ bush tomato

Striped 'Tigerella'

'Yellow currant'

'Yellow Perfection'

'Jubilee'

'Golden Boy' F₁

'Pink Pear'

'Gardener's Delight' cherry type

'Cerise' cherry type

'Pink Panther' F₁

Tomato flavor is determined in some cases by acidity, in some by sweetness. However, the flavor of the same variety can vary with the soil, with the season, at different stages of growth and according to how it is grown.

As a general rule, flavor is better if tomatoes are ripened outdoors rather than under cover in greenhouses or polyethylene tunnels; also, when fruit ripens on the plant, and when the fruit is *slightly* under-ripe (particularly with the yellow varieties). There is some evidence that varieties with more leaf have better flavor than those with less leaf. So don't remove healthy leaves unless they are shading fruit at the end of the season. Overwatering (see p.96) and overfeeding probably diminish flavor, though high potash feeds are generally believed to have a beneficial influence on it.

Cultivation

Tomatoes can be grown in a number of ways, determined largely by the climate. Be guided by local practice. The options are: **1** in the open; **2** outdoors, but under cloches or frames, using bush types; **3** outdoors but under cloches or in frames in the early stages, using bush and tall varieties (remove the cloches or frame lights when they are outgrown); **4** in unheated greenhouses, either in the ground or in containers; **5** in heated greenhouses; and **6** in containers, which can be placed indoors or out.

Growing bags and large boxes or pots are particularly useful for growing tomatoes on patios, or in greenhouses infected with soil sickness (see p.42). For additional information on the cultivation of tomatoes in heated greenhouses consult a specialist book on tomato growing.
SOIL AND SITE Except in very warm areas, outdoor tomatoes should be grown in a sheltered position – against a south-facing wall, for instance. They should be rotated (see p.14), but as they are in the *Solanaceae* (potato) family and subject to the same pests and diseases, avoid growing them near potatoes or where potatoes were grown in the previous season. Indoors, tomatoes should not normally be grown in the same soil for more than three consecutive years.

Tomatoes need fertile, well-drained soil, which should be limed if acid. Prepare the ground beforehand by

SALAD TOMATOES *A selection of varieties grown for their color, unusual shape or outstanding flavor. All those shown are grown as staked varieties except for 'Pixie' F₁, a fast-maturing bush variety, excellent for containers and window boxes.*

making a trench 30cm/12in deep and 45cm/18in wide. Work in generous quantities of well-rotted manure or compost. Cover this with 15-20cm/6-8in of good soil. If comfrey is available, line the trench with comfrey leaves; they are high in potash which suits tomatoes. Where the soil is not very fertile, apply a general fertilizer to the ground about ten days before planting.

Where tomatoes are grown in containers, use a brand name peat and perlite potting mix.
SOWING AND PLANTING Sow in gentle heat in early spring at a temperature of 16°C/60°F. Outdoor bush varieties will germinate at slightly lower temperatures. Either sow in seed flats, pricking out into small pots at the three-leaf stage or sow in soil blocks (see p.30). The blocks can be potted up later into small pots if necessary. Where only a few plants are required, sow two or three seedlings in some potting mix in small, 5-7.5cm/2-3in pots, trimming to one seedling per pot after germination. Give the plants plenty of ventilation, space and light. Although they need warmth to germinate, young plants can withstand short periods of low temperatures, provided temperatures rise during the day to compensate for the night temperatures.

They are normally ready for planting, into the ground or into containers, six to eight weeks after sowing. The best time to plant is just before the first flower truss is visible, delaying planting if the soil temperature is below 10°C/50°F or if there is any risk or frost. Harden plants off well beforehand, and, if necessary, protect them with cloches or portable windbreaks when they are first planted.

Plants can be bought ready for planting. Always select dark green, sturdy, healthy-looking plants, grown in individual pots.

INDOOR CROPS (in unheated greenhouses)

The tall varieties make best use of valuable greenhouse space. They should never be overcrowded. Plant them in single rows 45cm/18in apart, or at the same spacing in double rows with 90cm/36in between each pair of rows. I always interplant French marigolds (*Tagetes sp.*) between tomato plants, as a deterrent against whitefly.

Plants will need to be supported. Many systems are in use, but one of the simplest is to suspend heavy-duty strings from the greenhouse roof, the lower end of the string looped around the lowest leaves of the plant. Pro-

'Stopping' the tomato plant toward the end of the season, above, and nipping out the sideshoots, left, are means of concentrating the plant's energies so that fruits swell.

vided it is done carefully, the tomato plant can be twisted around the string as it grows.

Plants should be watered well and heavily mulched after planting. This will cut down the need to water subsequently. In the first few weeks, little further watering is required, but once the weather becomes warm the plants must be watered regularly enough to prevent them flagging, generally at least 9 liters/2 gallons per plant per week. One school of thought maintains that flavor is best if they are watered, at most, once a week, allowing the soil almost to dry out between waterings. Tomatoes in containers will need much more frequent watering.

All the sideshoots which appear in the axils of the leaves should be nipped out regularly as the plants grow, preferably when no more than an inch long. This is done most easily in the morning when the plants are turgid. Before the end of the growing season the plants must be 'stopped' by nipping out the growing point a couple of leaves above a fruit truss. This allows the remaining fruit to mature and ripen. It is done either in late summer or when the plants reach the roof, whichever is earlier. In an unheated greenhouse, plants may produce seven or eight trusses, and continue ripening into early winter.

Tomato growth is poor if temperatures fall below about 7°C/45°F, but on the whole the plants like well-ventilated, airy conditions. In hot weather 'damp down' by spraying the greenhouse and plants with water in the middle of the day: the extra humidity will help the fruit to set. Watering and sprinkling should always be done early enough to allow the foliage to dry before nightfall. All withered and yellowing leaves should be removed; any seriously diseased plants should be dug up and burnt.

With indoor tomatoes and tomatoes grown in containers, supplementary feeding is usually necessary to obtain high yields. Start feeding after the first truss has set fruit, feeding weekly with a high-potash tomato fertilizer, liquid seaweed extract or comfrey fertilizer.

OUTDOOR CROPS

Tall varieties can be planted about 38cm/15in apart, and bush varieties 30-45cm/12-19in apart. The closer spacing gives earlier crops, but the wider spacing gives heavier yields, and is advisable in areas of high rainfall where there is a risk of blight. Tall varieties must be tied to heavy canes or stakes, or to horizontal wires stretched between poles. It is advisable to mulch bush varieties with white film to keep the crops clean.

Tall varieties need to be sideshooted and 'stopped' in midsummer. They will produce anything from three to six trusses depending on the area. In dry weather they will need heavy watering (see above). Supplementary feeding should not normally be necessary.

Toward the end of the season, plants with unripened fruit can be cut down from the canes without uprooting them, laid on a bed of straw and covered with cloches to encourage further ripening. Alternatively, the plants can be uprooted and hung indoors for further ripening.

Varieties

All varieties suitable for culture in unheated greenhouses can equally well be grown outdoors, and *vice versa*.
AMERICAN BEEFSTEAKS: 'Beefmaster' F_1, 'Dombito' F_1
MARMANDE: 'Furet' F_1, 'Supermarmande' F_1 (some new 'Marmande' varieties are smoother in appearance but have less flavor than the old: be warned!)
'ORDINARY' TALL TYPES: 'Ailsa Craig', 'Alicante', 'Ronoclave' F_1, 'Tigerella' (striped)
BUSH TYPE: 'Pixie' F_1, 'Sleaford Abundance' F_1
CHERRY TYPE: 'Gardener's Delight' ('Sugarlump'), 'Sweet 100' F_1
ITALIAN CANNING: 'Napoli', 'Royal Chico', 'San Marzano'
YELLOW AND ORANGE: 'Golden Boy' F_1, 'Jubilee', 'Yellow Currant', 'Yellow Pear', 'Yellow Perfection'
PINK: 'Pink Panther' F_1, 'Ponderosa Pink'

Pests and diseases

INDOOR TOMATOES In unheated greenhouses, the majority of disorders and diseases can be avoided simply by growing plants well – in good soil, with sensible watering and good ventilation and by avoiding overcrowding. The most serious pest is whitefly which can be deterred by interplanting with French marigolds.

OUTDOOR TOMATOES Potato blight can be very serious in wet summers. It is first seen as brown areas on the leaves, then as unpleasant brown patches on the fruits, which eventually rot. In blight-prone areas, spray with a copper fungicide in early summer.

CUCUMBERS
(Cucumis sativus)

Cucumbers are by nature climbing and sprawling tropical plants. Three main types are cultivated: the high-quality, long, smooth-skinned 'greenhouse' cucumber, often over 30cm/12in long (though the new 'minicucs' are fully mature when only 10-15cm/4-6in long); the shorter, prickly skinned 'outdoor' or 'ridge' cucumber (so called because it was originally grown on ridges); and the prickly skinned pickling cucumber (a type of ridge cucumber), grown for pickling. There is also a crisp, round, ridge cucumber which is attractive in salads. The modern Japanese and 'Burpee' hybrid ridge cucumbers are approaching greenhouse cucumbers in both length and quality.

Cultivation

Cucumbers cannot stand even a hint of frost. The true greenhouse varieties need almost tropical conditions: warm soil, warm air, high humidity and, in midsummer, shade from direct sunshine. Outdoor cucumbers are more hardy, but in cold areas should be grown on a sheltered site – sunny but not baked dry. In warm areas they can be grown in light shade.

Most varieties throw out long vines. Indoors, they can be trained to a network of strings or wires. Make a grid with wires running horizontally across the greenhouse about a foot apart, intersected with strings or wires running from the roof to the lower wire, these also about a foot apart. Outdoors, allow the plants to climb up trellises or strong supports: they may need to be tied to the supports in the early stages. Although plants can be left to sprawl on the ground, they are healthier, and the cucumbers straighter and cleaner, where trained off the ground. The two exceptions are pickling cucumbers, which are more suited to sprawling, and the compact new American 'bush' varieties of ridge cucumber.

Cucumber roots need to romp freely through humus-rich, well-prepared, moisture-retentive soil. Prepare the ground by making trenches or individual holes about 30cm/12in deep and 45cm/18in wide for each plant, working rotted manure or garden compost in well. The ground can be mounded up to ensure good drainage.

INDOOR CUCUMBERS

In the Northern Hemisphere greenhouse varieties are grown in *heated* greenhouses for an early summer crop – a crop requiring considerable skill. (For specialist books, see p.167.) Late summer crops can be grown in *unheated* greenhouses and garden frames, using the more adaptable of the greenhouse varieties and, in areas with shorter, colder summers, the hybrid ridge cucumbers, which will grow indoors or out.

Sow in spring in a heated propagator, at soil temperatures of at least 15°C/65°F. Note that *hybrid greenhouse varieties* need a temperature of 21°C/70°F to germinate. Cucumbers dislike being transplanted, so are best sown in potting mix in small pots or soil blocks. Sow two or three seeds per pot, thinning to one per pot later. Sow them on their edge, covered by about a quarter of an inch of moist mix. Try to avoid watering until they have germinated, as they are susceptible to 'damping off'.

Keep temperatures as high as possible, and plant out at the three- or four-leaf stage, normally four or five weeks after sowing. Allow 45cm/18in between each plant, taking care not to bury the stem.

As the stem grows, tie it to the supports. Nip off the growing point when it reaches the top of the supports, and train the sideshoots along the horizontal wires. Nip off their tips when they reach the neighboring plant. When grown in frames, the plants can be trained flat over a horizontal support raised just above ground.

New roots appear at the base of the stem during the season. Cover them with potting mix or compost as an extra source of nutrients. Water the plants regularly, particularly once they start to bear fruit, combining watering with a weak liquid feed.

In sunny weather the greenhouse and the plants should be 'damped down' by spraying once or twice daily. This helps to create a humid atmosphere, which is the best defence against red spider mite, a serious cucumber pest under cover. If the greenhouse is kept mulched with a thick layer of straw, it is much easier to maintain the necessary humidity; the mulch also helps to keep the roots cool. Keep greenhouses well ventilated in hot weather: a southfacing roof may need to be shaded in summer.

Cucumbers set fruit without being pollinated. However, if they *are* pollinated the true greenhouse varieties become swollen at the ends, coarse and bitter. So the male flowers, which often appear first, should be removed: they are easily distinguished from the female, the latter having an embryonic fruit visible behind the petals (see below). 'All-female' varieties have recently been intro-duced. Although these produce the occasional male flower (which should be removed), they are highly recommended. It is not necessary to remove the male flowers on ridge cucumbers.

Keep picking fruits regularly to encourage further fruiting. In mature fruits the ends are rounded rather than pointed, and the sides are nearly parallel.

OUTDOOR CUCUMBERS

Only the ridge types of cucumbers can be grown out-doors, but they cannot be planted outside until all risk of frost is past. Either sow indoors in late spring, as for indoor cucumbers, planting out after hardening off care-fully, or sow outdoors in early summer when soil temperatures have reached about 13°C/55°F. In the latter case, sow two or three seeds per station, spaced 45cm/ 18in apart if being trained upward, or 90cm/36in apart if

Greenhouse or frame cucumber

Ridge cucumber

Pickling cucumbers

'Minicucs'

Above *Cucumber flowers (male, right; female, left, with the embryonic fruit visible behind the petals). On greenhouse varieties male flowers have to be removed to prevent pollination.*

Types of cucumber *Traditional greenhouse cucumbers and the new small 'minicucs' are smoother skinned than ridge and pickling cucumbers, though these can be grown at lower temperatures.*

trailing on the ground. They can be sown under jam jars, which will act as minicloches. Remove all but the strongest seedlings after germination. The plants can be cloched in their early stages, but will soon outgrow them. Little training is necessary, other than nipping out the growing points if the supports are outgrown. Mulch, water, feed and harvest as for indoor cucumbers. Pick pickling cucumbers before they become over-ripe.

Varieties

FOR UNHEATED GREENHOUSES ONLY Traditional greenhouse varieties: 'Butcher's', 'Conqueror', 'Resisting', 'Telegraph'; **'All female' greenhouse varieties:** 'Femdan' F_1, 'Pepinex 69' F_1, 'Petita' F_1 ('minicuc').
FOR UNHEATED GREENHOUSES AND OUTDOORS **Traditional ridge varieties:** 'Marketer', 'Straight Light'; **rounded ridge variety:** 'Crystal Apple'; **Japanese and Burpee varieties:** 'Burpee Hybrid' F_1, 'Burpless Tasty Green' F_1, 'Kyoto', 'Tokyo Slicer' F_1; **Pickling cucumbers:** 'Burpee Pickler', 'Northern Pickling'.

Pests and diseases

Cucumbers are prone to many pests and diseases, perhaps because they are being 'forced' outside their natural climatic range. Grow them as healthily as possible. For example, plant only strong seedlings and avoid planting in cold soil and cold weather; uproot any diseased plants, and cut off and burn diseased foliage; keep plants well watered, but never waterlogged. Several modern varieties have good disease resistance, and these should be grown wherever available. Remember that soil sickness builds up if cucumbers are grown continually in the same soil.
SLUGS Take usual precautions (see p.47).
APHIDS Colonies on the underside of leaves cause stunted and puckered growth. (For remedies, see p.47.)
RED SPIDER MITE (A problem found mainly indoors.) Maintain a humid atmosphere, spray with rotenone, or use biological control by introducing the parasite Phytoseiulus persimilis.
CUCUMBER MOSAIC VIRUS This causes mottling, yellowing, and distortion of the leaves, and the plants may become stunted and die. Remove and destroy infected plants. Controlling aphids may help to prevent its spread.
POWDERY MILDEW White powdery patches occur on the leaves in hot weather. Spray with a fungicide.

PEPPERS
(Capsicum spp.)

Peppers are tender tropical plants producing very varied, beautiful fruits.

Also known as green peppers or capsicums, **sweet peppers** (Capsicum annuum) are annuals, and although most of them are green when immature, they become red, yellow, orange or a deep purple-black when fully ripe. They also vary tremendously in shape. They can be square, boxy or 'blocky' (in fact almost rectangular), bell-shaped, or squat as is the 'bonnet-' or 'tomato-shaped' pepper. The more tapered varieties can be narrow or broad, while some have twisted ends like goat horns.

Sweet peppers are often used in salads, either raw, or cooked and cooled. They retain their vivid skin colors when cooked, and wonderful decorative effects can be created by mixing variously colored peppers in a dish. Their flavor changes subtly as they mature, and when cooked or blanched. Mature peppers are sweeter and richer in vitamins than immature fruit.

Hot peppers (Capsicum frutescens), also known as red or cayenne peppers and chillies, are mostly perennials, and although the archetypal 'hot' pepper is long, thin and bright red, neither shape nor color is a reliable guide to how hot they are. Yellow, green, broad, tapered, chunky and round peppers can all be extremely hot. The flavor runs the gamut from mild to almost unbearably hot – and they become hotter as they mature. Use them cautiously in salads, and beware of the seeds, which are often the hottest part of all.

Cultivation

The warmer the climate, the happier the pepper plant will be. Broadly speaking, wherever tomatoes can be grown, so can sweet peppers, but they need slightly warmer conditions and high light intensity to perform really well. Hot peppers require a longer season and slightly warmer conditions than sweet peppers, but otherwise the cultivation is similar.

The various options for growing peppers are the same as for tomatoes (see p.95). Very good crops can be grown in unheated greenhouses, heated greenhouses being necessary only for an out-of-season crop. Where peppers are grown outdoors they should be sited in a sunny, sheltered position. If possible, plant them in frames or

Bonnet-shaped types

'Hot Gold Spike'

Long types

Immature
red chillies

Red chilli

'Blocky' types

Bell-shaped types

under tall cloches; they can easily be kept to a height of about 45cm/18in. Peppers can also be grown very satisfactorily in containers such as growing bags, large pots or flats.

The newer, thin-walled sweet pepper hybrids require lower temperatures and lower light levels than the thick-walled 'Bell Boy' types, so are recommended in areas with unreliable summers.

Peppers need to be grown in reasonably fertile, but not over-rich soil. Prepare the ground beforehand by working in well-rotted manure or garden compost: fresh manure leads to overlush growth. Where grown in containers, use a similar soil mixture as for tomatoes. Sweet peppers seem less prone to disease than tomatoes, but it is still advisable to rotate them.

Plants should be sown like tomatoes (see p.95); a minimum soil temperature of 15°C/60°F, and preferably a higher temperature, is necessary for germination. It is important to raise strong, sturdy plants by growing them steadily without checks. Move them into small 5-7.5cm/ 2-3in pots at the three- to four-leaf stage. When about 10-12cm/4-5in high, with the first flower truss just showing, plant them into their final position, 38-45cm/15-18in apart, either in the ground or in a container. It normally takes about eight to ten weeks from sowing to planting.

Plant outside only after all risk of frost is past, hardening off well beforehand.

Indoors, whitefly can be a serious problem so it is well worth planting a dwarf French marigold plant between each pepper as a deterrent. Pepper stems are brittle and the plants can become top-heavy, so staking may be necessary. Either tie the plants to individual canes, or run wires or string about 30-45cm/12-18in high horizontally either side of the row, attached to posts at either end. (The stems can also be earthed up to support the plants.)

Peppers should never be allowed to dry out, so it is best to keep the ground mulched to conserve soil moisture. Water requirements are highest once fruiting has started.

Strong bushy growth should be encouraged. If growth is spindly, nip out the growing point, or the first small 'king' fruit at the top of the plant, when the plants are 30-38cm/12-15in high. This will stimulate the development of strong side branches.

Once the fruits start to swell, plants grown in containers and any weak-looking plants can be fed with a tomato fertilizer on a weekly or two-weekly basis. Otherwise supplementary feeding is unnecessary.

The indoor crop must be kept well ventilated, and should be sprayed regularly with water in hot weather, both to create the humidity which helps fruit to set and to discourage red spider mite. Start picking as soon as some fruits are tennis-ball size so that others will develop. Leave the later fruits to color up, though this will only happen in warm areas.

At the end of the season plants can be uprooted and the whole plant hung indoors. Hang sweet peppers somewhere cool but frost-free: the peppers should keep in reasonable condition for several weeks or months. Hang hot peppers in the warmth – in the kitchen, for example. Although they will shrivel up, they will remain usable for two or three years.

Varieties
For cooler areas: F$_1$ hybrids: 'Ace', 'Canape', 'Early Prolific', 'Gypsy'. **For warmer areas:** any varieties.

Pests and diseases
The outdoor crop is relatively free of pests and diseases: bad weather is the worst enemy. The indoor crop is subject to whitefly and red spider mite (see above) and greenfly (for remedies, see p.47).

TYPES OF PEPPER *The hot peppers illustrated are labelled; all the others are sweet varieties. As As the bonnet types show, peppers change color as they mature.*

Above *Peppers interplanted with dwarf French marigold,* Tagetes patula, *as a deterrent against whitefly, which can be a very serious problem in greenhouses.*

BULBS, ROOTS AND TUBERS

Although the term 'salad' conjures up leafy green plants, many of the vegetables grown for their edible bulbs, roots and tubers can also be used in salads, especially during the winter months when leafy plants are in short supply.

ONIONS
(Allium spp.)

Several plants have the very characteristic onion flavor and are used in salads. Large bulbing onions – some of which are mild flavored, others far stronger – are generally sliced or chopped into salads. Small bulbing onions and shallots are mainly used for pickling. Scallions, which have a slightly swollen bulb and plenty of appetizing green shank, are eaten whole or chopped, while various other green onions including chives, a herb with its own distinctive flavor, are chopped for seasoning and garnishing. The red-skinned, pink-fleshed onions are very attractive in salads.

There is a wide choice of onions for summer use, and a family can be kept supplied with bulbing onions all year round if storage onions and shallots are grown for use from winter to early summer. Moreover, in all but the most severe climates, the Welsh and everlasting onions remain green all year round.

Onions need an open position and fertile, well-drained, weed-free, firm soil, which should be limed if it is acid. Rotate them on at least a three-year cycle. The ground should be manured and prepared several months before sowing or planting.

BULBING ONIONS (Allium cepa)
Some varieties of bulbing onion are grown for use fresh, others for storage. They are raised from seed or from 'sets', which are small, specially grown bulbs. Bulbing onions need a long growing season if they are to grow large, so should be sown or planted as early as possible. Raising them from sets is easier than from seed, especially in areas with short summers or where spring sowing conditions are likely to be difficult. Moreover, sets mature earlier than seed and largely avoid the problem of onion fly (see p.104). However, only a few onion varieties are available as sets and in some seasons sets bolt without forming bulbs. Very small sets and those which have been 'heat treated' are less likely to bolt.

GROWING FROM SETS Plant ordinary sets as soon as the ground is workable in spring. (Heat-treated sets should be planted later, according to the supplier's instructions.) Plant the sets about 8cm/3in apart in shallow drills with the tips protruding just above the soil. Space rows 23cm/9in apart to allow weeding and, where necessary, protect the plants against birds (see p.47). 'Unwins First Early', a recently introduced variety, is at present unique in that the sets can be planted in autumn and so are ready very early in summer.

GROWING FROM SEED: Seed can be sown early in the year or in autumn, depending on the variety.

Early sowings The very first sowings can be made in gentle heat indoors from Christmas onward. Either sow in seed flats and prick out, or sow in soil blocks, thinning to one per block. Harden seedlings off well before planting out in spring as soon as soil conditions allow. Space the plants 4cm/1½in apart for medium-sized bulbs and up to 10cm/4in apart if larger bulbs are required.

Space can be saved by 'multiseeded' sowing in soil blocks. Sow up to eight seeds per block, planting them out 'as one' at least 25cm/10in apart. They can be intercropped in the early stages (see pp.15-19).

Sowings can be made *in situ* outdoors as soon as the soil is workable, but never sow in poorly drained or cold soils. Thin in stages to the required distance apart, using the thinnings in salads.

Always keep onions well weeded as the leaves are too thin to form a weed-suppressing 'canopy'. Otherwise, they require little attention.

Although bulbing onions can be used at any stage of development, those sown in spring will not be fully mature until late summer.

Autumn sowing Onions will mature earlier if they can be sown the previous autumn. In mild areas, certain traditional varieties are used for the purpose, but they are unreliable and fail in unexpectedly cold winters. In recent years, several hardier Japanese overwintering varieties,

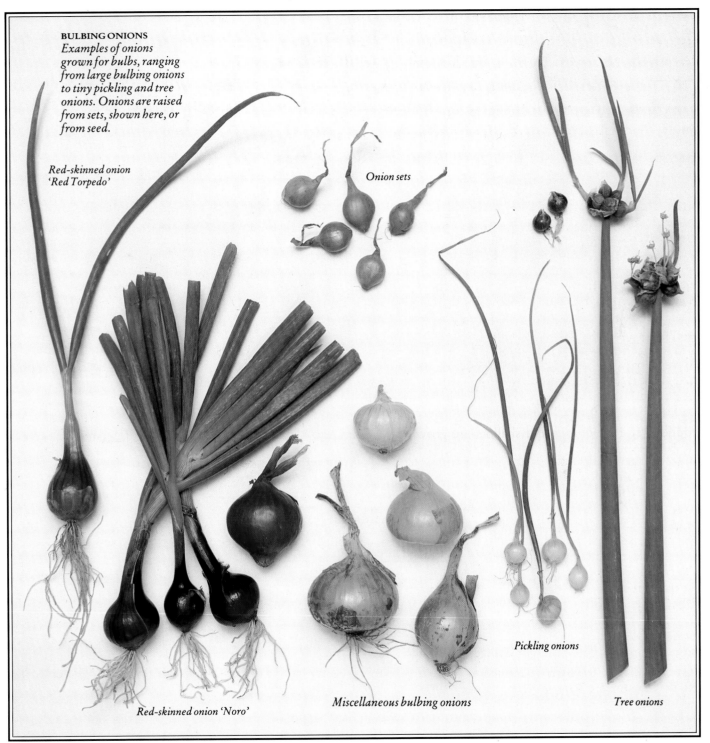

BULBING ONIONS
Examples of onions grown for bulbs, ranging from large bulbing onions to tiny pickling and tree onions. Onions are raised from sets, shown here, or from seed.

Red-skinned onion
'Red Torpedo'

Onion sets

Red-skinned onion 'Noro'

Miscellaneous bulbing onions

Pickling onions

Tree onions

which mature very early in summer, have been introduced. However, the sowing date for these is critical and varies from one area to another: consult your supplier for the correct time in your area. The Japanese onions may be superceded by autumn-planted sets, if these become widely available.

HARVESTING AND STORAGE Bulbing onions needed for storage are not usually lifted until the leaves have died back naturally. Don't bend the tops over, as this shortens the storage life of the bulbs. Lift the onions carefully and dry them in the open, as fast and as thoroughly as possible, raised off the ground on upturned boxes. If the weather is wet, bring them indoors to dry off somewhere warm. Handle them very carefully as storage rots always start with cuts and bruises. Store them hanging in nets, or in plaited ropes, or flat in seed flats, in a well-ventilated, cool, dry, frost-free place.

VARIETIES **For storage:** 'Early Yellow Globe', 'Orbit', 'Sentinel'; **for use fresh:** 'Ailsa Craig', 'Ringmaker', 'Riverside', 'Sweet Spanish'; **red-skinned:** 'Noro', 'Red Torpedo', 'Ruby', 'Southport Red Globe'; **Japanese overwintering:** 'Express Yellow' F_1, 'Senshyu Semi-Globe Yellow'.

PESTS AND DISEASES **Onion fly** Tiny maggots attack the base of the bulb causing seedlings to die. Remove and burn all infected plants. Where the problem recurs, rake bromophos into the soil before sowing and planting.
Rots and mildews Onions are susceptible to several fungus diseases which are largely avoided by sowing in warm soil, thinning early and removing thinnings, and rotation. Burn all infected plants.

SHALLOTS (*Allium cepa* 'Aggregatum')
Shallots are compact, medium-sized bulbs with a strong, distinct flavor. They multiply into a cluster of bulbs. There are red-, brown- or yellow-skinned varieties. Easily grown, they mature rapidly and will keep longer than bulbing onions, often remaining sound until the following summer. They are very good pickled.
CULTIVATION Shallots need the same soil type and soil preparation as bulbing onions. Plant single shallots very early in spring or, in mild areas, in late autumn. Space them about 20cm/8in apart each way, pressing them into the ground so that they are half buried. (Don't plant very large shallots: these are more liable to bolt than smaller ones.) Protect them against birds with black thread.

Keep the shallots weed-free and lift, dry and store them like bulbing onions. Since they are not always easily available, it pays to save a few of the healthiest, firmest-looking bulbs to plant the following season. Start again with reliable bought stock every few years, as shallots can become infected with virus disease.

PICKLING ONIONS (*Allium cepa*)
These are very small onions which are suitable for pickling because they don't develop papery outer skins. They will grow in poorer, drier and less fertile soil than the larger bulbing onions, but should be in full sun.
CULTIVATION Seed is sown *in situ* in spring, usually in broad, flat drills or bands about 12mm/½in deep and 13cm/5in wide. Space seeds about 12mm/½in apart. If grown at this high density, they keep small and need no further thinning.

They can be lifted for pickling when they reach an appropriate size. Don't leave them in the soil after they mature or they are apt to resprout.

TREE ONIONS (*Allium cepa* 'Proliferum')
These onions, also known as Egyptian onions, produce clusters of tiny aerial bulbils not unlike hazelnuts instead of flowers. These, in turn, sprout on the plant and develop further clusters, so the plant eventually becomes two-, sometimes three-tiered. In due course, the stems bend over to ground level where the bulbils root, the plant thus perpetuating itself. Its main merit, apart from being a picturesque curiosity, is that it is extremely hardy. The bulbils can be picked 'midair' in midwinter.
CULTIVATION Tree onions will grow in most soils in a sunny spot, but prefer fertile, well-drained soil. Plant either single bulbils or a cluster, about 25cm/10in apart, in spring or autumn. The plants will keep going for several years, but should be thinned out periodically.

SCALLIONS (*Allium cepa*)
The refreshing flavor and color of these onions, also known as spring, salad or bunching onions, are a treat, especially early in the year. Several varieties are used as scallions, some having almost straight shanks, others with the stem swollen into a small bulb.
CULTIVATION Scallions need the same soil conditions as bulbing onions. The first sowings can be made in frames or under cloches very early in the year, followed

'Giant chives'   Welsh onion

Everlasting onion

Chives

Chinese chives   Scallion

GREEN ONIONS *These plants with onion or garlic flavored leaf are widely used in salad dishes. Welsh and everlasting onion are very hardy, and in many areas provide greenery all winter long.*

by outdoor sowings as soon as the soil is workable. For a regular supply from early summer to autumn, make small successive sowings at three-week intervals. They will be ready in about eight weeks.

Sow in rows about 10cm/4in apart, or in bands about 8cm/3in wide with 23cm/9in between bands, spacing seeds 12-25mm/½-1in apart.

Where winters are not too severe, hardier varieties can be sown in autumn, preferably under cloches. The first pullings can be made the following spring.

VARIETIES **Spring sowing:** 'White Lisbon'; **autumn sowing:** 'White Lisbon', 'Winter Hardy White Lisbon'.
PESTS AND DISEASES see Bulbing onions, p.104.

WELSH ONIONS *(Allium fistulosum)*
These perennial onions, also known as ciboule, grow in clumps about 60cm/24in high. The coarse, hollow leaves are strongly flavored and thicken at the base into a flattened bulb. They normally remain green all winter and make a useful edging to vegetable beds.

CULTIVATION Welsh onions need a sunny position and do best in fertile, well-prepared soil.

Plants can be raised either from seed, or by the division of old clumps, replanting the younger parts from the outside of the clump. Clumps should always be lifted and divided every two or three years and planted somewhere new, or they will deteriorate. Seed can be sown *in situ* in spring or late summer; thin in stages to 20cm/8in apart.

Where winters are severe, Welsh onions are treated as an annual or biennial and raised from seed.

EVERLASTING ONIONS *(Allium perutile)*
These hardy perennial onions form clumps at most 30cm/12in high. The leaves are finer in texture and milder flavored than those of Welsh onions, but are grown and used in very much the same way. However, they do not produce seed, so must be propagated by division.

CHIVES *(Allium schoenoprasum)*
Among the most universally grown herbs, chives make a lovely edge in the vegetable garden. Grown well, they form vigorous clumps up to about 30cm/12in high; 'Giant Chives', a handsome larger form, grow several inches taller.

Chives tolerate light shade and their natural habitat is in damp meadows. Therefore, they amply repay being grown in fertile soils and kept moist throughout their growing season.
CULTIVATION Chives can be raised either by dividing old plants or from seed – in both cases in spring or autumn. Old clumps should be lifted and divided every three years or so, clusters of three or four small plants being taken from the outer edges of the clump. Treating each cluster as one group, replant about 23cm/9in apart. Seed can be sown *in situ* but, as the seedlings are small and easily get lost, establishment of a clump is much faster if seed is raised indoors and the seedlings transplanted outside. The best method is to sow several seeds in a soil block, which is planted out 'as one'.

Chives can be cut back to just above ground level several times during the growing season. Unless wanted for decorative purposes, the lovely pink flower stalks should also be cut back so as not to exhaust the plant.

The foliage dies down in late winter. Cover a few plants with dry leaves and cloches, or dig them up and replant in frames or greenhouses to get very early growth.

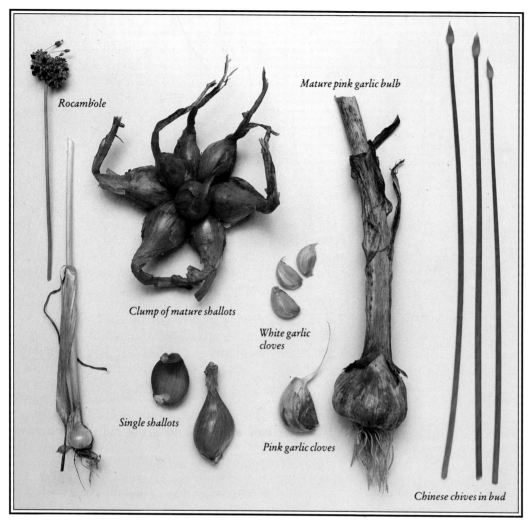

Rocambole

Mature pink garlic bulb

Clump of mature shallots

White garlic cloves

Single shallots

Pink garlic cloves

Chinese chives in bud

GARLIC AND SHALLOTS *More easily grown and useful members of the onion family, shallots keep longer in store than any other onions; rocambole, a type of garlic, produces masses of chive-like leaf very early in spring, and Chinese chives are very decorative in the garden and invaluable for salad as leaves, flower buds and flowers are all edible. Garlic, of course, is an essential plant in the salad garden.*

GARLIC *(Allium sativum)*

The strong, unique flavor of garlic is invaluable to the salad lover. A cut clove rubbed around a salad bowl imparts something very special, and the cloves have many other culinary uses. A Mediterranean plant, it has white and pink forms, the latter reputedly hardier and longer-keeping. Garlic is much hardier than often supposed.

CULTIVATION Garlic needs an open sunny position, and grows best on rich, light, well-drained soil – these last two factors are probably the key to success. The soil should be manured for the previous crop.

Garlic needs a long growing season and, where possible, should be planted in autumn; otherwise, plant the cloves early in spring as soon as the soil is workable, splitting the firm, large cloves off from the outer layer of a mature bulb (a cluster of cloves). Plant them 10cm/4in apart in drills about 4cm/1½in deep, with the neck of the clove just protruding from the soil. In very light soils the cloves can be deeper, while on heavy soils they are sometimes planted in ridges to improve the drainage, or sand or ashes are worked into the bottom of the drill before planting. Keep the plants well weeded.

Once the foliage has died down, the bulbs can be lifted very carefully, dried off thoroughly and hung indoors as with bulbing onions. If well dried, they should keep for nearly a year.

ROCAMBOLE (*Allium sativum* 'Ophioscorodon')
This unusual form of fine-leaved garlic, also known as serpent garlic, has very coiled stems. It forms a small basal bulb and a cluster of tiny bulblets in the flower head. Although the bulb can be used like garlic, rocambole is most useful for its chive-like leaves which appear suddenly in autumn and spring. They have a very delicate garlicky flavor, and can be used for seasoning and garnishing, from autumn until early summer.
CULTIVATION Rocambole seems to tolerate most soils and can be grown in light shade. Plant the bulbs or bulblets in spring, summer or autumn, about 12mm/½in deep and 5cm/2in apart. Once established, the plants seed themselves liberally and perpetuate themselves. Indeed, there is some danger of their becoming a weed, so don't hesitate to uproot surplus seedlings.

CHINESE CHIVES (*Allium tuberosum*)
These useful perennial plants, also known as garlic chives, have only recently been introduced to the West from China and Japan, where several forms are grown. They form clumps of flat-bladed leaves, crowned in summer with fragrant, star-like flowers up to 60cm/24in high when fully mature. (The dried seedheads are useful for flower arrangement.) The leaves have a very pleasant flavor, a blend between garlic and chives. The fresh leaves, blanched or otherwise, and the flower buds, heads and stalks can all be used in salads.
CULTIVATION Chinese chives tolerate a wide range of soils and climatic conditions, preferring a well-drained situation, and can also be grown in flower pots. They are raised from seed or by dividing established plants in spring or autumn. Sow in spring, either indoors or outdoors in a seedbed or *in situ*, in rows or broadcast.

Plants should eventually be spaced 15-20cm/6-8in apart. They grow slowly and start developing into a sizable clump only in their second season.

In their first season, the leaves should not be cut until they are about 15cm/6in high, nor should the plants be allowed to flower. It is always best to take just a few leaves at a time rather than cutting the clump back severely.

The leaves normally die back in midwinter. Plants can be potted up and brought indoors for use in winter.

There seems to be no reason to lift and divide clumps, other than for propagation, unless they start showing loss of vigor.

RADISHES
(*Raphanus sativus*)

Radishes are a far more varied and versatile salad crop than is commonly realized. The seed can be sprouted (see p.53) or grown as a seedling crop (see p.48). For both these purposes, a lot of seed is needed, so allow a few plants from an early sowing to run to seed. After the plants have flowered, the seed pods, while still crisp and green, are an appetizing delicacy either fresh or pickled. The small-rooted radishes are generally grown for use in the summer months, and the large-rooted varieties, which can be lifted and stored if necessary, for the winter.

SUMMER CROPS
Summer radishes are either round, up to about 2.5cm/1in in diameter, or tapered; these are usually about 5cm/2in long, though there are a few varieties, such as 'Long White Icycle' and some Japanese summer varieties, which grow to about 15cm/6in. Radishes are white inside, but the outer skin can be red, white, red and white, black or yellow, giving scope for colorful designs when sliced.
CULTIVATION Radishes do best on cool, light soils: sandy soils are ideal. The soil needs to be reasonably fertile, but should not be over-rich or the radishes will produce leaf at the expense of the root.

The secret of success is to grow radishes fast, with plenty of moisture throughout growth. In very dry conditions they develop a very hot flavor. They are normally ready three to four weeks after sowing, but most summer types deteriorate rapidly after maturing, becoming woody outside and puffy or hollow inside. So, for a continuous supply, it is advisable to make small successive sowings every few weeks.

Radishes are useful for intercropping and intersowing: they can be broadcast, for example, with early carrots; sown on the surface above early potatoes (they will be ready before the potatoes come through); and intersown between brassica plants, or between rows of carrots, beets or lettuce, for example.

Sowings can be made from very early spring until autumn. Make the first sowings under cover, in greenhouses, frames or under cloches, followed by the first outdoor sowings in a sheltered, sunny, well-drained situation. For early sowings the quick-maturing 'forcing' varieties, such as 'Saxa' ('Red Forcing') and 'Saxerre',

'Scharo'

'Sparkler'

'French Breakfast'

Japanese summer radish

'Long White Icicle'

'Rond Jaune d'Été'

Radish seed pods, used young and green or else pickled, are a delicacy. The photograph shows the flowering seed heads with pods just forming of two radish varieties and, top right, pickled pods.

SUMMER RADISHES *The photograph indicates some of the variety in shape and skin color which can be found in summer radish. The seedling leaves of radishes can also be used in salads.*

are best; any varieties can be used for later sowings.

Sow either in rows or broadcast. It is most important to sow thinly, at a shallow and even depth – otherwise the seedlings nearer the surface germinate first and take over, and the late starters don't stand a chance. Sow most varieties no more than 12mm/½in deep; very long varieties can be sown a little deeper. Space seeds at least 2.5cm/1in, preferably 5cm/2in apart. This spacing may seem absurdly generous, but radishes grow very fast, and if they once become leggy and entangled with each other, the roots never swell properly.

Radishes tend to bolt rapidly in hot weather, so midsummer sowings can be made in light shade. Water the drills very thoroughly before sowing (see p.27).

WINTER GREENHOUSE CROPS Hitherto, it has been difficult to grow the summer type of radish in unheated greenhouses in winter because of the poor light and low temperatures, and the high humidity which tends to cause mildew. However, some new Dutch-bred varieties, with less leaf than traditional ones, are much better adapted to winter conditions. These attractive round, red radishes

Japanese
winter radish

'China Rose'

Brown winter radish

Chinese
winter radish

'Long Noir de Paris'

'Violet de Gournay'

WINTER RADISHES *Some of the large hardy radishes which can either be pulled fresh all winter or in severe climates, be lifted in autumn and stored under cover. Old European varieties were widely grown in the past but now new Japanese and Chinese varieties are being introduced to the West. Some of these can be several feet in length and weigh over 20kg/44lb.*

can be grown successfully if night temperatures do not normally fall below approximately 5°C/41°F.

Sow them in late autumn, early winter and again in early spring. Sow in light soil, giving them plenty of ventilation, and extra covering if heavy frost is likely. It is only necessary to water in sudden hot spells, or if the leaves start to look very dark. These radishes take much longer than summer varieties to mature, but are very welcome in late winter and early spring.

VARIETIES **Early sowings:** 'Saxa' ('Red Forcing'), 'Saxerre'; **summer sowings:** 'Cherry Belle', 'French Breakfast', 'Long White Icicle', 'Red Prince', 'Revosa', 'Sparkler'; **winter sowings:** 'Minitas', 'Robino'; 'Rota' (very early spring sowings only).

WINTER OUTDOOR CROPS

These are much larger than the summer radishes, the common varieties being 500-1000g/1-2lb in weight while some of the giant Japanese varieties tip the scales at over 18kg/40lb. There are round and long varieties – long varieties sometimes growing a couple of feet long in light soils! Skin color can be white, red, brown, violet or black. Unlike the summer varieties they are very hardy, and will keep for several months after maturing without any deterioration.

CULTIVATION They grow best on light, fertile soils, but can be grown on heavy soil, if it is well drained and has been deeply dug. The ground should not be freshly manured.

Since they take several months to mature, sow in early summer for autumn use, and in midsummer for winter use, in situ in rows at least 38cm/15in apart, thinning early to about 20cm/8in apart. The plants develop a great deal of leaf so should never be crowded. Water them if the ground is in danger of drying out; otherwise no further attention is needed.

In most areas the radishes can be left in the ground during the winter (they survive temperatures as low as −10°C/14°F), but there is a risk of slug damage. Tuck straw or bracken around the plants to make them easier to lift in heavy frost. Where winters are very severe, lift the roots in late autumn, trim off the leaves and store the roots in sand or peat in basements or somewhere cool. They should keep sound until spring. However, roots left in the ground are probably better flavored. The roots can be used grated or sliced into salads. A partially used root, if wrapped, will normally keep in a refrigerator for several weeks.

VARIETIES Recommended varieties include: 'China Rose', 'Round Spanish', 'Long Spanish', 'Violet de Gournay'. Several white-skinned Japanese varieties are becoming available. As some of these have a tendency to bolt, I would advise making small experimental sowings before growing larger quantities of any one variety.

PESTS Both types of radish are subject to attacks of flea beetle (see p.75). The large varieties are susceptible to cabbage-root fly (see p.75) and should be rotated in the brassica group.

RADISH PODS

The seed pods of any radishes that have run to seed can be eaten in salads, but the larger the radish, the larger, the more succulent, and the tastier the pods. They can be very pleasantly spicy. Whether being used fresh or pickled, they should be picked when still young enough to snap crisply in two.

In Europe the large Bavarian radishes are grown for their pods; sown in spring, they are thinned to about 15cm/6in apart, and allowed to flower. Any of the large winter radishes can be left to run to seed in spring instead of being dug up. A single plant will produce a huge crop of pods, developing in succession over several months. In India, an exceptionally long-podded radish, the 'Rat's Tail Radish' is grown for its pods, which can apparently be anything from 25cm/10in to 60cm/24in in length.

CARROTS
(Daucus carota)

Carrots are divided rather arbitrarily into two principal groups, popularly known as 'earlies' and 'maincrop'. The earlies are smaller, faster maturing and less hardy, and are widely used raw in salads. (Raw carrots are sweet and rich in vitamin A.) The maincrop carrots are mainly grown for use as a cooked vegetable. For their cultivation, consult a standard book on vegetable growing (see p.167).

Within the early group are the 'Amsterdam Forcing' varieties which are small, slender and smooth-skinned with cylindrical, rather stumpy roots; the 'Nantes' varieties which are somewhat broader-shouldered and longer and are sometimes used as maincrop carrots, and the attractive round varieties which are suitable for growing on shallow soils.

Cultivation

Carrots do best on fertile, well-drained, light soils; the roots cannot expand in the type of soils that become compacted and hard when dry. They may become fanged if grown in freshly manured soil, so dig well-rotted manure into the ground the autumn before sowing, or follow a crop for which the ground has been well manured. Carrots are a difficult crop to weed, so the ground should be as weed-free as possible before sowing.

The early varieties can be sown throughout the year. Make the first sowings in greenhouses or frames in very early spring, waiting until soil temperatures have reached at least 7°C/45°F, as germination is poor in cold soils. Make the first outdoor sowings in a warm, well-drained site as soon as the ground is workable.

Sowings can continue throughout the summer, although in areas where carrot fly is a serious problem, early summer sowings should be avoided. The last sowings can be made under cover in late summer or early autumn, depending on the area: they need about 12 weeks to mature.

Carrots are normally sown *in situ*. Where possible, prepare the seedbed several weeks before sowing so that weed seeds can germinate and be hoed off beforehand. The seedbed should never be compacted: it should be possible to plunge your finger into the top layer of soil.

There are various methods of sowing. Carrots can be sown in rows about 10-13cm/4-5in apart, or in broad drills 15-30cm/6-12in wide, with the same distance between drills. This makes weeding easier. Thin in stages to 6-8cm/2½-3in apart. This wide spacing allows roots to develop very fast. On weed-free land, carrots can be broadcast thinly or mixed with annual flower seed.

In heavy soils, and to avoid thinning so as to minimize the likelihood of carrot fly, small quantities of carrots are sometimes sown in soil blocks and transplanted outside, thinned to one seedling per block and planted at normal spacing. The round varieties are suitable for multiseeded sowings, sowing four seeds per block and planting them out as one about 10cm/4in apart.

Weed carrots by hand in their early stages. Water only if the soil is in danger of drying out.

Varieties
'Amsterdam Forcing', 'Colora', 'Early French Frame'.

'Amsterdam' type carrot

Round type carrot

Golden beet

Red beet

COMMON ROOT VEGETABLES
Red beet are widely grown for salads, but for more colorful effects grow the gold variety shown here. The small early types of carrots are the best for use raw in salads as they are more tender and sweeter than larger roots.

Pests and diseases

Carrot fly is the most serious carrot pest, the maggots tunnelling into the roots. Adult flies are attracted by the smell of bruised carrot foliage, especially when thinning. Do everything to minimize the need for thinning. Thin in the evening (when the flies are inactive), in still weather when the scent travels less far, and water the drills beforehand, firm the stems afterward and remove all thinnings, burying them in the compost pile. Early summer sowings are most vulnerable to carrot fly attacks.

BEETS
(Beta vulgaris)

Beet, also known as beetroot, is flat, round, tapering or cylindrical in shape and deep purple, white or yellow in color. Some varieties, such as the old Italian 'Chioggia', have very prominent white rings. The yellow and white varieties are well flavored; the yellow, which do not 'bleed' like red beet, look very attractive in salad dishes.

Young beet leaves can be used in salads, either raw or lightly cooked. The root is usually cooked and used as a salad vegetable when cold, but it can be grated and used raw. Baby beets, about 4cm/1½in in diameter, are generally considered the best size for salad.

Beets are used fresh during the summer months and stored for use in winter. On the whole, round varieties are grown for fresh consumption and cylindrical varieties for storage, though some round varieties can be stored.

Cultivation

Although beets grow satisfactorily in heavier soil than carrots, they generally like much the same conditions, and the soil should be prepared in the same way. Similarly, the first sowings can be made indoors, or in a warm spot outside, once soil temperatures have risen to about 7°C/45°F.

Most beet varieties are liable to bolt if sown very early, so for the first sowings use bolt-resistant round varieties (see right). Successive sowings, using any variety of round beet, can be made from late spring to late summer; the last sowings can be cloched or made under cover. Varieties for storage should be sown in midsummer.

Sow beet in rows 20cm/8in apart, thinning to 10cm/4in apart. This spacing allows early beets to grow rapidly, and

later sowings to develop into reasonably sized but not oversized roots. For smaller pickling beets, sow in rows about 7.5cm/3in apart, thinning the plants to 9cm/3½in apart.

Early beets can also be sown in bands about 15cm/6in wide, seed being spaced evenly across the band, thinned to about 7.5cm/3in apart.

Beets also lend themselves to multiseeded sowing in soil blocks (see p.30). Sow three seeds per block, planting them 20-23cm/8-9in apart. They can be intercropped in the early stages with a fast-growing crop such as radish.

The so-called beet 'seed' is in fact a cluster of seeds, so a cluster of seedlings often germinate together, and must be thinned early to prevent overcrowding. Single-seeded or 'monogerm' varieties are sometimes available, and with these there is no problem.

Once established, beets need little attention other than protection from birds in the seedling stage (see p.47) and sufficient watering to prevent the soil from drying out. They benefit from being mulched.

Pull fresh beets when they are the size required. Beets for storage should be lifted before the first frost. Handle them very carefully to prevent bruising; twist off the tops, and store the roots in boxes of slightly damp sand in frost-proof conditions.

Varieties

ROUND VARIETIES WITH 'BOLT RESISTANCE': 'Avonearly', 'Boltardy', 'Detroit Regala'.
ROUND VARIETIES FOR MIDSEASON SOWING: 'Burpee's Golden' (golden-fleshed).
CYLINDRICAL STORAGE VARIETIES: 'Cheltenham Green Top', 'Cheltenham Mono', 'Cylindra'.

HARDY ROOT CROPS

The hardy root crops are a neglected and undervalued group of nutritious vegetables, mostly sweet flavored. They are at their most useful during the winter months, when there are fewer green vegetables and salad plants. The majority can be grated or sliced raw into salads, but their flavor is usually best if cooked and allowed to cool. The more knobbly roots can be difficult to peel when raw. If so, scrub them and then boil or steam them for a few minutes, after which the skins can be removed easily.

Cultivation

Most root crops grow best on deep, light soils, with plenty of well-rotted manure or compost worked in several months before sowing. They require little attention other than weeding, and watering when the soil is in danger of drying out. They are relatively free from pests and diseases.

Harvesting and storage

The roots described here normally survive temperatures of −10° to −15°C/14° to 5°F. They taste best and keep firmest if left in the soil, lifted during winter as required. The leaves die down in winter, so mark the ends of the rows to enable them to be found in snow, and cover the stumps with straw or bracken to make them easier to lift in frosty weather.

Where winters are very severe or where the soil is so heavy and wet that digging is difficult in winter, lift them in late autumn. They can be stored in piles covered with soil and straw, either outdoors or in a shed.

CHINESE ARTICHOKES (Stachys affinis)

These tiny white knobbly tubers are rarely more than 4cm/1½in long and 20mm/¾in wide. Scrubbed and used raw in salads, they have a lovely nutty flavor and crisp texture. The plants, which have leaves very like spearmint, grow about 45cm/18in high.

Plant the tubers in spring in a sunny position in fairly light soil about 5cm/2in deep and 25cm/10in apart. They will be ready from late autumn onward. Being so small, they shrivel up fairly rapidly once lifted. Keep a few of the largest tubers to plant the following spring. Be warned: even tiny tubers left in the ground will resprout and can become invasive.

JERUSALEM ARTICHOKES (Helianthus tuberosus)

These very knobbly tubers, roughly the size of a large hen's egg, are a marvellous winter standby. They have a distinctive sweet flavor and are excellent raw or cooked. Closely related to sunflowers, they grow over 3m/10ft high, and so can be used as windbreaks or screens. They do best in rich soil but tolerate a wide range of soils: their fibrous root systems are useful for breaking up heavy ground.

CULTIVATION Buy firm tubers from the supermarket, and plant them 13cm/5in deep and 30cm/12in apart in spring. To increase the plant's stability, earth up the stems when they are about 30cm/12in high, and cut the tops back to about 1.5m/5ft in late summer. The tubers are best overwintered in the soil as they tend to dry out once lifted. For convenience, however, they can be clamped for a few weeks. Lift even tiny tubers, as they can become very invasive, and save a few of the smoothest for planting next year's crop.

PARSNIP (Pastinaca sativa)

Parsnips have large, sweetly flavored roots up to 25cm/10in long and 10cm/4in in diameter at the crown. Use the shorter varieties on shallow soil.

CULTIVATION Parsnips can be grown in lightly shaded soils but germinate badly in cold wet soils, so delay sowing outdoors until the soil has warmed up. Seed can be started indoors, in soil blocks (see p.28) to minimize root disturbance when transplanting. Plant them out when the seedlings are still small. Always use fresh parsnip seed, as it loses its viability rapidly.

For average-sized roots, grow parsnips in rows about 25cm/10in apart thinning in stages to 13cm/5in apart. Parsnips germinate and grow slowly, so can be station-sown (see p.26), and intersown with radishes or small varieties of lettuce. Weed carefully in the early stages.

PESTS AND DISEASES In some areas canker, which causes the crowns to rot, is a serious disease. If so, grow canker-resistant varieties such as 'Avonresister'.

TURNIP-ROOTED PARSLEY (Petroselinum crispum 'Tuberosum')

This type of parsley, also known as Hamburg or Berlin parsley, has a large root. The dark green foliage is of the broad-leaved parsley type, and is a very useful substitute for parsley in winter, remaining green under much more severe conditions. Young leaves can be used whole or chopped in salads, or for garnishing and seasoning. It is grown and used in the same way as parsnip (see above), and is also quite tolerant of light shade.

SALSIFY (Tragopogon porrifolius)

Salsify, also known as the oyster plant or vegetable oyster, is a biennial plant with long, brown-skinned, tapering roots, narrow leaves and purple daisylike flowers. Although normally grown for the delicately flavored roots, the chards (young shoots), flower buds

HARDY ROOT VEGETABLES *These vegetables come into their own in the winter months when greenery is scarce. They are exceptionally well flavored when cooked and cold, though the artichokes and horseradish can also be used raw.*

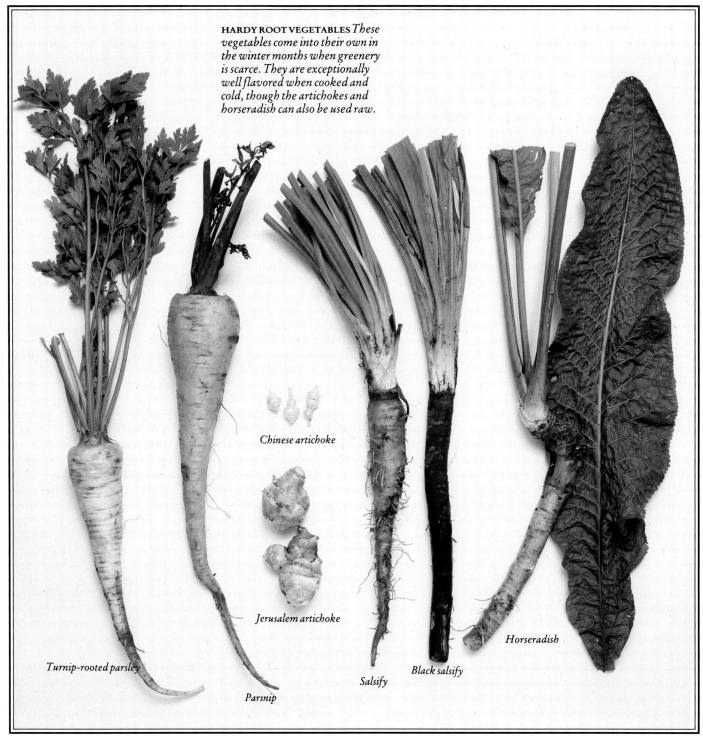

Chinese artichoke

Jerusalem artichoke

Turnip-rooted parsley

Parsnip

Salsify

Black salsify

Horseradish

and flowers, all of which develop in the second season, can also be used in salads. It is hard to grow roots of a worthwhile size in very heavy soil, but in rich light soil they can be over 45cm/18in long.

CULTIVATION Sow in spring (using fresh seed) *in situ* outdoors in warm soil, spacing rows 25cm/10in apart. If grown for roots, thin in stages to about 10cm/4in apart. Lift and use the roots in early winter; they may become rather coarse later. The plants develop slowly and can be station-sown and intercropped in the early stages.

Where grown for the flowering shoots, the plants should be thinned to about 8cm/3in apart, or two to three seeds should be sown together in groups about 15cm/6in apart and left unthinned. The flowering shoots will be ready early the following summer or the fat flower buds can be picked just before they open, and used raw or lightly cooked and cooled – they taste almost like asparagus. (For flowers, see p.129.)

For chard production, cut back the withering stems just above ground level in autumn, and earth up the roots with about 13cm/5in of soil. Alternatively, cover the rows in spring with a 15cm/6in thick layer of straw. The chards push through, and will be lightly blanched. Cut them when 10-15cm/4-6in long.

BLACK SALSIFY (*Scorzonera hispanica*)

Black salsify, sometimes known as viper's grass, is a perennial plant very similar to salsify, except that it has broader leaves, a black-skinned root and yellow flowers. The roots, chards, flower buds and flowers can all be used in salads and have a distinct, interesting flavor. It is grown like salsify, except that it can also be sown in summer. If the first roots lifted in winter seem only pencil-thin, leave them to thicken up for the following year. As the plant is a perennial, they will do so without becoming coarse.

HORSERADISH (*Armoracia rusticana*)

This vigorous perennial plant, with leaves up to 60cm/24in long, has stout roots that are used to make the strongly flavored relish. The roots can also be grated into a salad to add a piquant touch. When about 5cm/2in long, the young leaves have a very pleasant flavor and can be used in salads.

CULTIVATION Grow horseradish in well-manured ground where there is plenty of moisture. It is usually

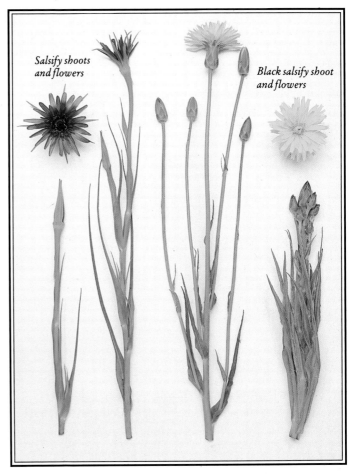

Salsify shoots and flowers

Black salsify shoot and flowers

FLOWERING BUDS OF SCORZONERA AND SALSIFY *These are an excellent salad vegetable, best when cooked and cold. The flowers can be used fresh or pickled, as they were in the past.*

raised from root cuttings – pieces of roots about 12mm/½in thick and 20cm/8in long, taken from a mature plant. Plant these in early spring, by making holes at an angle to the soil surface, and pushing in the roots so that the tops are 5cm/2in below the soil level. Space them at least 30cm/12in apart. Alternatively, you could start by buying a plant.

Plants should be discarded after three years or so, or the roots become tough and fanged. Fresh plants can be grown in the same spot, if plenty of well-rotted manure is dug into the ground. If planted in a new site, remove as much root as possible from the original site, as horseradish can become a *very* invasive weed.

COOKED AND COLD

This section looks at some of the remaining vegetables which, though not primarily considered 'salad' vegetables, can be used in salads, generally cooked and cold. Lack of space prevents us from covering them fully. For methods of cultivation, see a general book on vegetable growing recommended in the appendix.

LEGUMES

Several different types of peas and beans are among the legumes which can be used in salads.

GARDEN PEAS (Pisum sativum)
Many people enjoy eating ordinary 'garden' or 'green' peas raw when they are very young and tender or very small. Otherwise, peas can be cooked and used in salads.

The young leafy shoot tips and tendrils of peas are edible raw and have a good distinctive flavor.

SUGAR PEAS (Pisum sativum 'Macrocarpon')
These are the peas with edible pods which are eaten before the peas are fully mature. They have a superb sweet flavor and are excellent in salads, raw or lightly cooked. They are hardier than is realized and in many districts can be sown in autumn outdoors or in unheated greenhouses for a very early crop. There are many different types, some very flat-podded, some round-podded: all are well worth growing. The recently introduced variety 'Sugar Snap' is highly recommended.

ASPARAGUS PEAS (Psophocarpus tetragonolobus)
These ornamental plants, growing about 45cm/18in high, have delicate cloverlike foliage, pretty scarlet-brown flowers, and odd-looking triangular pods which can be eaten raw when very small. When a little larger cook them and eat them cold in salads. Never allow the pods to grow larger than about 4cm/1½in long or they will be tough.

BROAD OR FAVA BEANS (Vicia faba)
These large, very hardy beans must be shelled and cooked before eating, on account of the toxic substances in all raw beans. Although fresh and dried broad beans can be used cooked and cold in salad, the fresh beans have a far more interesting flavor. The red-seeded variety 'Red Epicure' is especially well flavored, but not easily obtained.

GREEN BEANS (Phaseolus vulgaris)
Green beans are eaten in their three stages: the immature pods as 'green beans'; the half-ripened bean seeds as 'flageolets'; the mature, ripened beans as dry 'navy' beans, which are usually stored for winter. All forms can be used in salads, but must be cooked first. There are climbing and dwarf forms. Of the many varieties, each is more suited to one of the above purposes, and choice should be made accordingly. The podded varieties can be green, purple or golden. Experts argue, but for quality of flavor I always grow purple varieties and golden 'wax pod' varieties.

A variety recommended as flageolets is 'Chevrier Vert'; 'Dutch Brown' is an excellent variety for use dried. There is an enormous range of colors and forms in dry beans.

RUNNER BEANS (Phaseolus coccineus)
These climbing beans with beautiful flowers have a distinct flavor of their own. The cooked runner beans make excellent salads when cold; the dried and half-ripe beans are probably less flavored than the green type. A dwarf variety, 'Hammond's Dwarf Scarlet' has recently been reintroduced.

POTATOES
(Solanum tuberosum)

Potatoes are normally cheap to buy and occupy a lot of ground for a long period, so fewer are grown today for home use. However, where potatoes are wanted for salads, freshness, flavor and texture count for a great deal so it really is worth growing your own if space can be found in the garden. Here we look at factors which influence the choice of variety for salads. For the general cultivation of potatoes, consult standard books on vegetable growing (see p.167).

What makes a 'salad' variety?

After cooking, potatoes tend to become moist and 'waxy' or dry and 'floury' in texture. It is the waxy types, which stay in firm cubes when diced and/or mixed with dressings, that are best for salads. The difficulty, given the scant information available when seed potatoes are sold, lies in identifying the waxy varieties – but there are a few simple clues.

For practical purposes, potatoes are divided into three groups – 'earlies', 'mid-season' and 'maincrop' – on the basis of the number of days they take to mature. Earlies take around 80-100 days and late maincrop varieties up to four weeks longer. Apart from a few notable exceptions in the maincrop potato varieties, early and mid-season varieties tend to be closer-textured, waxier and better-suited to salads. They also tend to be smaller, especially as

LEGUMES *The pods and seeds of many types of peas and beans are used in salads, raw and cooked. Highly recommended for flavor are the golden 'wax pod' varieties of dwarf green beans, such as 'Constanza', and the exceptionally sweet, edible-podded sugar peas.*

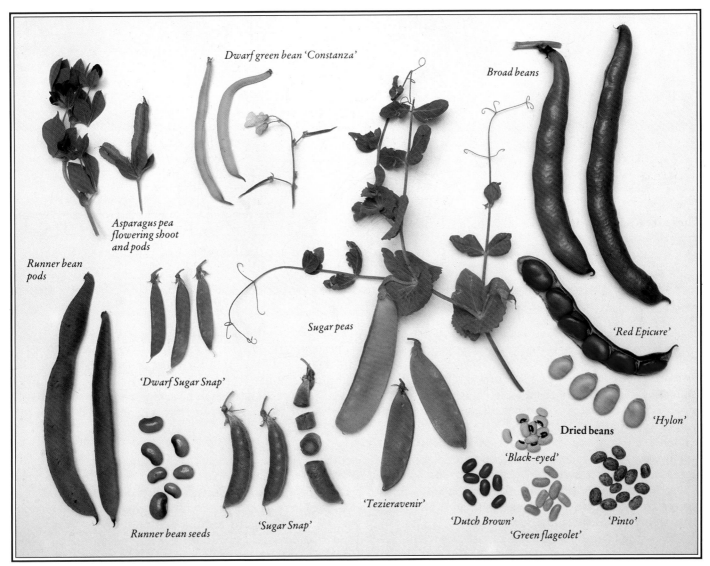

Dwarf green bean 'Constanza'

Broad beans

Asparagus pea flowering shoot and pods

Runner bean pods

Sugar peas

'Red Epicure'

'Dwarf Sugar Snap'

Dried beans

'Hylon'

'Black-eyed'

Runner bean seeds

'Sugar Snap'

'Tezieravenir'

'Dutch Brown'

'Pinto'

'Green flageolet'

'Pink Fir Apple'

'Maris Peer'

'Aura'

Solanum ajanhuri

'Kipfler'

'Red Craig's Royal'

SALAD POTATOES *Some of the varieties which, on account of their waxy texture and good flavor, are particularly suitable for salads. Unfortunately, some of the more unusual salad varieties are not easy to obtain, other than from specialist suppliers.*

they are often lifted young as 'new' potatoes. Small, young, 'new' potatoes of good varieties are superb, hot or cold. Unfortunately, *some* modern varieties are noticeably lacking in flavor.

Earlies and mid-season varieties are normally planted first because they are fast maturing, but later plantings can be made of these varieties to get a succession of small tubers for salads. A few tubers planted in mid- or late summer may provide 'new' potatoes in autumn or even, in very mild areas, in midwinter.

Among the maincrop varieties suitable for salads are a group of mainly long, irregularly shaped potatoes, mostly

European in origin, with a distinctive nutty flavor. Some are yellow-fleshed with a close-grained texture, making them ideal for salads. Occasionally, one can obtain blue-fleshed varieties. They are reasonably flavored and certainly have novelty value. (For further information, see the list of suppliers on p.167.)

Potato varieties come and go with astonishing speed, and unfortunately many of the best salad varieties are sometimes difficult to obtain other than through a specialist supplier.

Varieties
EARLIES 'Arran Comet', 'Belle de Fontenay', 'Belle de Juillet', 'Civa', 'Colmo', 'Manna', 'Ukama', 'Ulster Sceptre'.
MID-SEASON 'Estima', 'Red Craig's Royal', 'Jersey Royal', 'Maris Peer', 'Romano', 'Wilja'.
MAINCROP White-fleshed: 'Burbank Russet', 'Kennebec', 'Superior'; purple-fleshed: 'Purple Congo'; yellow-fleshed European varieties: 'Aura', 'Bintje', 'Kipfler'; white-fleshed European varieties: 'Etoile du Nord', 'Red Star', 'Eigenheimer', 'Pink Fir Apple'.

OTHER VEGETABLES

Among the vegetables that can sometimes also be used cooked and cold in salads, the following are my preferred choice. Consult a standard reference book for general cultivation information (see p.167).

ARTICHOKE, GLOBE (Cynara scolymus)
These perennial thistlelike plants with beautiful gray foliage are often grown for their ornamental value. The edible part is the heart or 'choke' at the base of the flower bud. Very small hearts can be eaten raw, but their marvelous flavor is brought out best when cooked and eaten cold.

ASPARAGUS (Asparagus officinalis)
A perennial plant, asparagus has a long life but a very short productive season (hence its high price). It is a decided luxury to grow your own asparagus: you have to wait until the third season before cutting! Very small spears can be used raw, but their flavor is far better when cooked, and eaten either hot or cold.

CALABRESE (*Brassica oleracea* 'Italica')

A type of cauliflower, also known as Italian sprouting broccoli, calabrese deserves to be more widely grown. It has an excellent flavor and in good conditions matures fast and crops heavily, as after the first central head is cut, sideshoots develop. Very young florets can be eaten raw, but otherwise they should be cooked and used cold. The purple-tinted variety 'Romanesco' has an outstanding flavor.

CARDOON (*Cynara cardunculus*)

Cardoon is closely related to globe artichoke, but grows taller and is even more striking. The 'chokes' are normally too small to use, but in the plant's first season the stems can be blanched like celery and make an unusually flavored salad, cooked and cold.

CAULIFLOWER (*Brassica oleracea* 'Botrytis')

There are many types, adapted to different climatic conditions. Grow those most suited to your area, and use in salads in the same way as calabrese.

EGGPLANT (*Solanum melongena*)

One of the marvelous-looking Mediterranean vegetables, also known as aubergine, eggplant requires much the same growing conditions and treatment as sweet peppers. The deep purple fruits are unpleasant raw, but have a most interesting flavor when used cooked and cold in salads. For fun, grow the white-fruited variety, which leaves no doubt as to why eggplant was so named.

LEEKS (*Allium porrum*)

Although used mainly as a hot vegetable, leeks have a very distinctive flavor when cooked and cooled. For this purpose, use young pencil-thin leeks: they are far better flavored than the large coarse leeks most cooks favour. The blue-leaved French variety 'Bleu de Solaise' is very colorful during the winter months.

SWEETCORN (*Zea mays* 'Saccharata')

When very fresh, and if picked slightly immature, sweetcorn is delicious raw – a good reason for growing your own. Otherwise cook it and use the cold kernels in mixed salad dishes. They are far better flavored than tinned sweetcorn. Some of the recently introduced 'extra sweet' varieties really live up to their name.

TURNIP (*Brassica rapa*)

Turnip roots are mild in flavor and can be grated raw into salads. The young seedling leaves and larger leaves can also be used raw. The leafy crop is very hardy and should be grown in the same way as salad rape (see cultivation details, p.84).

ZUCCHINI (*Cucurbita pepo*)

These are immature squashes, also known as courgettes, and although any variety of squash can be used when young, the modern hybrid varieties are best for use as zucchini. There are long and round forms, and their skin colour ranges from dark and light green to grey and yellow, with some attractive striped forms. Grow a selection for salads. Use very small courgettes raw, and the slightly older ones cooked. The flowers can also be used raw in salads, or can be fried in light batter or stuffed.

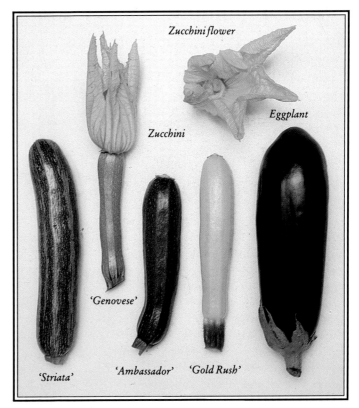

EGGPLANTS AND ZUCCHINI *These fruits have the best flavor when cooked and used cold in salads. Grow several varieties of zucchini to get a range of skin colors. The flowers are edible.*

HERBS, FLOWERS AND WILD PLANTS

Herbs, flowers and wild plants add an individual touch to salads. Since both flowers and wild plants have numerous popular names, they have been listed here under their Latin names, to avoid confusion.

HERBS

The deft use of herbs transforms an ordinary salad into something rich, memorable and unique. Add a little chopped coriander or fenugreek to evoke the orient; a few leaves of balm or lemon thyme for a hint of lemon; chervil or sweet cicely to create the subtle tones of aniseed. Or go for a more daring flavor with lovage, or a generous sprinkling of dill, or a little sage, tarragon or basil. The permutations are infinite, and the pleasure comes from experimenting with what you have to hand. Don't overlook the decorative qualities of herbs, especially the variegated and colored forms, and the delicate leaves of salad burnet, sweet cicely, and the bronze and green fennels. Add these, freshly picked, for a last-minute garnish to a salad.

In fresh simple salads, there is nothing to compare with the use of fresh herbs, but most outdoor herbs die back in winter. For the winter months, grow a little chervil or parsley under cover; or, in late summer, pot up a few plants of thyme, winter savory or one of the marjorams and keep them on a windowsill indoors.

Preserved herbs suffice for made up salad dishes and in cooking. The more succulent herbs, such as chives, parsley and basil, can be frozen either in sprigs or by chopping them into ice-cube trays and covering them with water. When the herb is required for use, simply thaw out the cube and strain it.

Most herbs can be dried for winter. Pick them in their prime – just before flowering – and dry them slowly in a very cool oven, or hang them somewhere warm indoors. Store them when completely dry in airtight jars.

Many herbs are worth growing for their ornamental qualities. Walls, patios and dry areas can be carpeted with thymes; ordinary and Chinese chives, parsley, hyssop and savory make neat edges; the fennels, angelica, chervil and lovage make handsome specimens, while many of the mints and balms are superb groundcover plants. The soft-colored sages and the variegated mints and Chinese chives are lovely for flower arranging. So, one way and another, a salad lover's garden should be romping with herbs.

Brief information is given here on some of the herbs which can be used in salads. For fuller information on cultivation and use consult specialist books (see p.167).

ALECOST, COSTMARY (*Chrysanthemum balsamita*)
A large-leaved hardy perennial herb, growing up to 1m/3ft high, alecost has a very distinctive but strong flavor with a hint of balsam about it. Use only small young leaves sparingly in salads.

Although it grows in most situations it does best in a sunny position. Start by planting a rooted piece from an old plant in spring or autumn; one plant is sufficient for most households.

ANGELICA (*Angelica archangelica*)
A beautiful vigorous hardy perennial plant growing up to 3m/10ft high when flowering. The typical angelica flavor is found in the leaves and stems; both can be used sparingly in salads when young. Angelica is valuable because it is one of the first herbs to reappear in spring.

Grow it in fairly rich moist soil where it has plenty of room. Sow fresh seed in autumn and plant out the following spring or autumn. After flowering it loses its vigor, but young seedlings can be transplanted for future use.

BALM, LEMON (*Melissa officinalis*)
This very easily grown hardy perennial plant, also known as melissa, forms sprawling clumps growing up to 60cm/24in tall. The delightful lemon-scented leaves can be chopped into many salad dishes.

It tolerates a wide range of soils and situations including rich, moist ground and light, dusty shade, and makes

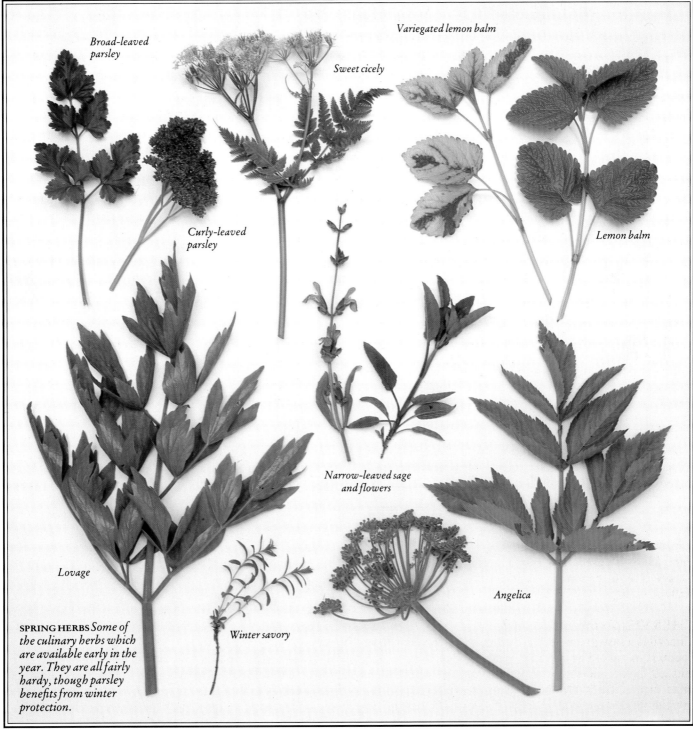

Broad-leaved
parsley

Variegated lemon balm

Sweet cicely

Curly-leaved
parsley

Lemon balm

Narrow-leaved sage
and flowers

Lovage

Angelica

Winter savory

SPRING HERBS *Some of
the culinary herbs which
are available early in the
year. They are all fairly
hardy, though parsley
benefits from winter
protection.*

121

excellent ground cover if trimmed back hard from time to time. It is easiest to raise balm by planting a rooted piece taken from an old plant; otherwise sow seed outside in spring, thinning or transplanting to about 60cm/24in apart. There are very pretty variegated and golden forms.

BASIL (Ocimum spp)

The basils are wonderful, powerfully flavored, tender annual herbs, used chopped in many salad dishes but above all with tomatoes. There are two main types. Common or sweet basil (Ocimum basilicum) has large, strongly flavored leaves, and grows 60cm/24in high depending on variety and situation. There's a beautiful red-leaved form. The dwarf or bush basils (O. minimum), also known as Greek or fine-leaved basil, have smaller, milder-flavored leaves; they are more suitable for growing in pots. A lemon-scented species (O. citriodorum) has small leaves and a delicate lemony flavour.

Basils cannot stand frost and must be grown somewhere warm and sheltered. Sow indoors in late spring, and plant outdoors, after any risk of frost is past, about 13cm/5in apart. To prolong the season, make a second sowing in midsummer or cut bush basil plants hard back in late summer, so they will resprout, and bring them indoors. They will last two or three months before the leaves finally shrivel.

BORAGE (Borago officinalis)

These beautiful blue-flowered annuals can grow up to 1.2m/4ft tall. The sweet-tasting flowers and the fresh, cucumber-flavored young leaves are used in salads, but the older leaves are rather hairy for salads.

Borage grows best in moist fertile soil, and will stand some frost. Sow in situ in spring for summer use and in summer for autumn use, thinning to 30cm/12in apart. Plant a few in a greenhouse for a late autumn crop. Where borage is required mainly for its leaves, cut off the flower stalks.

CHERVIL (Anthriscus cerefolium)

Chervil is a fast-growing, hardy annual or biennial about 25cm/10in tall. The feathery leaves have a refreshing aniseed flavor, and can be chopped like parsley into many salad dishes. Chervil remains green in winter, when it is invaluable. Except in mild areas it is normally best grown under cover.

It is not fussy about soil. For autumn to early-spring supplies, sow in situ in late summer either broadcast or in rows, thinning to about 10cm/4in apart, or sow in soil blocks for transplanting under cover in late autumn. For summer supplies, sow in spring in a slightly shaded situation. Keep the plants well watered. They can be cut back several times before they run to seed, but any which flower will usefully seed themselves.

DILL (Anethum graveolens)

This delicate annual is grown both for the seedheads, used in pickling cucumbers, and for the feathery, delicately flavored leaves, which can be chopped into various salad dishes.

For the foliage, grow it like coriander (see p.85), sowing in situ outdoors in a sunny sheltered spot in early summer. Keep the plants moist and start cutting when they are about 10cm/4in high. They normally resprout at least once. For the seedheads, sow in early summer broadcast, or in rows 23cm/9in apart, thinning to 7.5cm/3in apart.

HYSSOP (Hyssopus officinalis)

Hyssop is a very attractive, shiny-leaved, reasonably hardy little perennial shrub, growing about 45cm/18in high. The pungent minty leaves can be used, albeit sparingly, in salads. It grows best in light, well-drained soil. The blue, pink or white flower spikes attract bees and butterflies.

Sow indoors or out in spring and early summer, planting the seedlings about 60cm/24in apart when they are several inches high, or divide established plants in spring or autumn. Hyssop plants should be renewed every three or four years.

LOVAGE (Levisticum officinale)

This magnificent hardy perennial grows up to 2.5m/8ft tall, and is one of the first plants to emerge each spring. The glossy leaves have a deliciously strong, celerylike flavor. Rub them into a salad bowl, or chop them sparingly into salads. The leaf stalks can be blanched like celery.

Lovage thrives in rich, moist soil. Sow fresh seed, preferably in autumn, transplanting in early spring. Alternatively, divide old plants in spring, replanting pieces of root which have a shoot. Lovage often seeds itself, and seedlings can be transplanted when young.

MARJORAM (Origanum spp.)

There are many forms and varieties of this slightly tender Mediterranean herb, also known as oregano, growing from a few inches to about a foot in height. Their small leaves, used whole in salads, have a very pleasant characteristic flavor. Although naturally perennial, they are not very hardy so may have to be treated as annuals. For salads three types are recommended: sweet marjoram (Origanum majorana) has lovely soft leaves; pot marjoram (O. heracleoticum) remains green nearly all winter (it makes a lovely edging); while golden marjoram (O. aureum) is very pretty.

Marjorams grow best in well-drained soil in a warm situation. Sow sweet marjoram in spring indoors, planting out 13cm/5in apart after frost. For the other marjorams, buy plants initially, then propagate them by dividing established plants every two or three years. All can be potted up for use indoors in winter.

MINT (Mentha spp.)

The majority of the many hardy perennial mints can be used, chopped sparingly, in salads and salad dishes, to impart that special 'minty' flavor. Those listed below are my favorites: apple mint, spearmint and raripila mint for their flavor; pineapple and scotch mint for their decorative qualities.

All spread rapidly in moist, fertile soil and will grow in light shade. Plant small pieces of root 5cm/2in deep and 23cm/9in apart in spring or autumn. Move the plants every few years or they exhaust the soil. They die back in winter, but a few planted in a greenhouse in autumn, in the soil or in pots, start into growth very early in the following spring.

Among the many useful forms of mint are apple mint (Mentha suaveolens), spearmint (M. spicata), raripila or pea mint (M. raripila rubra), pineapple mint (M. suaveolens variegata), scotch or ginger mint (M. gentilis).

PARSLEY (Petroselinum crispum)

A biennial plant growing to 45cm/18in high, its mildly flavored serrated leaves are very widely used in cooking, and can be chopped into many salad dishes. There are curly and plain, or broad-leaved, types. The former are more decorative, but the latter, especially the 'Giant Italian' varieties, are hardier, more vigorous, more easily grown and, in my view, better flavored.

Parsley needs moist conditions and fertile soil: the many failures are due to neglect after sowing, starvation and thirst. For a continuous supply, sow twice, in spring for summer use, and in summer for autumn to spring supplies. Sow in situ or in soil blocks for transplanting when still young. Water drills well before sowing (see p.27), and keep them moist until germination. Thin or plant 23cm/9in apart. Plants die back in severe winter weather. Keep a few plants cloched or plant them in a greenhouse for later supplies. Always cut off flowering shoots to prolong the plant's useful life.

SAGE (Salvia officinalis)

The sages are perennial, mainly gray-leaved herbs, growing 30-60cm/12-24in high. They are reasonably hardy and keep their strongly flavored leaves in winter. Chop them sparingly into salads. Both the common narrow-leaved and broad-leaved sages are well flavored. There are also very colorful 'golden' and 'red' forms and a less hardy 'tricolor' (pink, purple and white) form. The red sage is frequently referred to in traditional salad lore. All have decorative value in salads.

Sages need well-drained light soil and a sunny sheltered position. Raise narrow-leaved sage from seed sown in spring, planting out 30cm/12in apart the following spring. Broad-leaved sage rarely sets seed, so buy plants or raise them from heel or tip cuttings taken in spring. Prune sage back lightly in late summer.

Raripila mint   Scotch mint   Apple mint   Pineapple mint   Spearmint

MINTS *Of the many colorful, distinctly flavored mints, these easily grown varieties are some of the best for use in salads.*

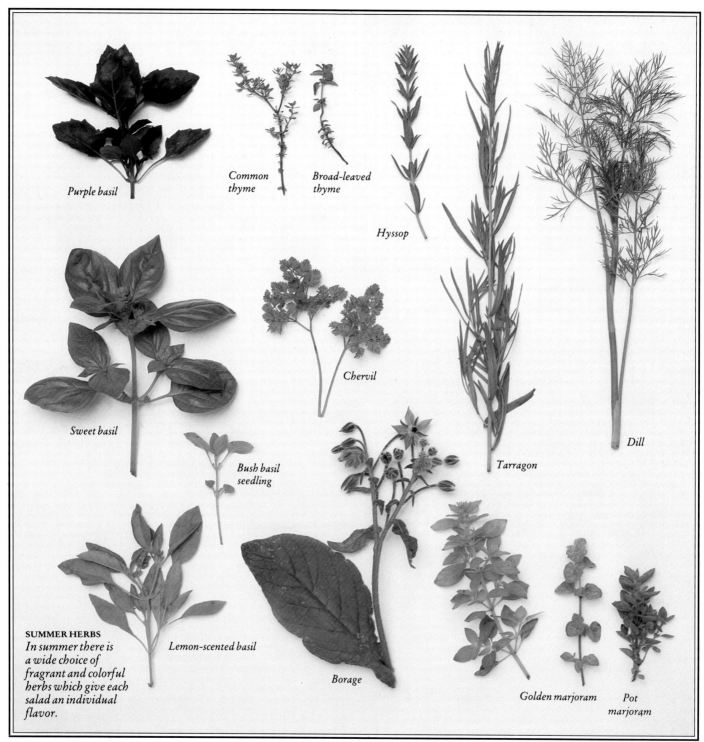

Purple basil

Common thyme

Broad-leaved thyme

Hyssop

Sweet basil

Chervil

Tarragon

Dill

Bush basil seedling

SUMMER HERBS
In summer there is a wide choice of fragrant and colorful herbs which give each salad an individual flavor.

Lemon-scented basil

Borage

Golden marjoram

Pot marjoram

SALAD BURNET (Sanguisorba officinalis)

A low-growing, very hardy perennial plant, salad burnet has pretty, lacy leaves which remain green all winter. They have a faint cucumber taste and are very decorative in salads. Use the youngest leaves whole in salads as the older leaves are rather tough-textured unless dipped in hot water for a few seconds before use.

Salad burnet grows wild on limestone, and will grow in full sun or semishade, even on dry soils. Sow *in situ* in spring, thinning to about 10cm/4in apart. Keep removing the flower stalks to concentrate the plant's energies.

SAVORY (Satureja spp.)

There are two main forms of savory: summer savory (*Satureja hortensis*) is an annual growing up to 30cm/12in high; winter savory (*S. montana*) is a more compact, hardy, evergreen perennial plant. Both have small, almost spicy leaves and are said to enhance other flavors in cooking. Use them sparingly in salads and salad dishes.

They require a sunny position and well-drained reasonably fertile soil. Sow in spring, preferably indoors, planting out about 15cm/6in apart. Winter savory can also be propagated by dividing old plants. Plant up in pots in summer, to bring indoors for use in winter. These plants are very pretty when they burst into fresh growth in spring.

SWEET CICELY (Myrrhis odorata)

An attractive feathery-leaved reasonably hardy perennial plant growing up to 1.5m/5ft high, sweet cicely has sweet, aniseed-flavored leaves. They are lovely chopped into salad or used whole for decoration – but pick them just before use as they wilt almost instantly. The substantial roots can also be boiled, cooked, and sliced into salads. Sweet cicely starts into growth early in the year and dies back late, so has a long season of usefulness.

It grows best in rich moist soil in a lightly shaded situation. Sow fresh seed outdoors in autumn, thinning to 8cm/3in apart, and plant in a permanent position the following autumn about 60cm/24in apart. Plants can also be propagated by dividing roots carefully in spring and autumn. Renew plants only if they are losing vigor.

TARRAGON (Artemisia dracunculus)

There are two forms of these narrow-leaved, perennial herbs with their unique, much-prized flavor. The smaller-leaved, more distinctly flavored French tarragon grows about 1m/3ft high, while the larger-leaved, hardier Russian tarragon is taller. Although always said to be inferior in flavor, the latter is quite adequate for use in salads and salad dishes, though French tarragon is probably better for flavoring vinegar and in cooking. French tarragon plants often deteriorate with age, whereas Russian tarragon may improve.

Grow tarragon in a well-drained, sheltered position, preferably on light soil. Russian tarragon can be raised from seed sown in spring and French tarragon, which rarely sets seed, by dividing old plants. Plant them about 60cm/24in apart. In cold areas, tarragon may need protection from frost by covering the roots with straw in winter.

THYME (Thymus spp.)

Many of these reasonably hardy, sun-loving, creeping and low-growing herbs have culinary uses: their tiny, characteristically flavored leaves can be added sparingly to salads, salad dressing and vinegar.

Grow them in a sunny situation in well-drained soil. Common thyme can be raised from seed sown in spring. Other forms, see below, can be raised by dividing old plants in spring or autumn, or taking cuttings in spring. Plant them 23-30cm/9-12in apart. Keep them well trimmed, and renew the plants every three years or so. They can be potted up for winter use indoors.

The following forms of thyme are well worth growing for salads: *Thymus vulgaris* and *T. pulegioides*, the common and large-leaved thymes, both with the traditional 'thyme' flavor; *T. citriodorus*, the lemon-scented thyme; *T. fragrantissimus*, which has an orange scent; and *T. herba-barona*, the caraway thyme.

FLOWERS

The use of wild and cultivated flowers in salads is one of the nicest traditions we have inherited from the past. While a few flowers have real flavor – most notably nasturtiums and pot marigold – their chief value lies in their colors. Small flowers and those with no hard parts can be used whole, but with any daisylike flowers the petals should be pulled off gently and sprinkled over the salad. It is best to do this after dressing the salad, just before it is served.

Gather flowers at their freshest, early in the day when the dew has just dried on them. They should always be handled very gently as they bruise easily; so cut them carefully, and keep them in a flat basket so that they won't be squashed. If necessary, wash them gently, lightly patting them dry with paper towelling. Keep them in a closed bag in a refrigerator until needed. Just before using they can be refreshed by dipping them in ice-cold water.

In the past many of the edible wild flowers were gathered from fields and hedgerows, but now they have become more scarce – in some countries it is illegal to dig up or gather wild plants. They need to be conserved, so why not cultivate them in your garden?

A few of the wild and cultivated flowers that can be used in salads are mentioned here, with brief information on how to grow and use them. For fuller information consult an appropriate gardening book (see p.167).

Althaea rosea (Hollyhock)

A tall garden plant that produces flowers of many colors, the hollyhock grows up to 2m/6ft high, though smaller forms have recently been introduced. The petals and cooked buds are used in salads.

Hollyhocks like rich, moist soil. Although perennial, they should be grown like biennials as they tend to become infected with rust. Sow in a seedbed in midsummer, thin to 15cm/6in apart and plant out in autumn 1m/3ft apart. In very cold areas, overwinter in frames and plant out in spring. Tall varieties may need staking.

Anchusa azurea (Anchusa)

A perennial garden plant growing 90-120cm/36-48in tall, its bright, gentian-blue flowers are at their best in early

EDIBLE FLOWERS *A few of the many flowers which can be used to decorate salads. They were photographed in late spring.*

Violets and pansies

Borage

Bellis perennis

Pot marigold

summer; in salads, they look particularly attractive mixed with rose petals.

Grow in ordinary soil in a sunny border. Although perennial, it is best grown as a biennial as it deteriorates with age. Sow in a seedbed in early summer, planting out in autumn or the following spring about 45cm/18in apart.

Bellis perennis (Daisy, wild and cultivated)

The ubiquitous little white lawn and field daisies can be used whole in salads. The flowers open in bright sunshine but quickly close: since they're far prettier in salads when open, pick just before use if possible or keep them in a sealed plastic bag at room temperature until they are wanted.

The much larger flowers of the cultivated forms are pink, red or white, and often double. Sprinkle the petals over a salad. Although perennial, they are best treated as biennials, to retain their vigor. They grow almost anywhere. Daisies are excellent for edging.

Sow in early spring to flower the same year, planting 13cm/5in apart. Sow in summer, planting in autumn, for flowers early the following year, and plant a few under cover for extra early flowers. Keep the flowers cut and remove the dead heads to prolong flowering. Lift and replant self-sown seedlings to avoid overcrowding.

Borago officinalis (Borage)

The brilliant blue flowers of this annual look marvelous and taste sweet. Sprinkle on salads and in salad dishes, but remove the hairy sepals behind the petals just before eating. (For cultivation, see p.122.)

For a succession from early spring until frost, supplement outdoor plants by planting a few under cover in late summer. They may well flower in autumn, winter and very early spring, depending on the severity of the winter. Established plants seed themselves everywhere becoming smaller with time, which is probably an asset where space is limited.

Calendula officinalis (Pot marigold)

Not to be confused with the African marigold (Tagetes erecta), or French marigolds (Tagetes spp.), these colorful annuals come in all shades of orange and yellow, with double or single flowers from early spring until the first frosts. They are of very ancient medicinal and culinary use in baking, in salads, for seasoning, for coloring, and as a saffron substitute. Sprinkle the petals on salads and in salad dishes for their bright color and pleasant, fairly strong flavor.

They are not fussy about soil or situation. For summer and autumn flowers, sow in early spring either indoors for planting out, or in situ: but thin early to 25cm/10in apart or they become floppy. Sow again in summer and plant under cover for very early flowers (a gamble which may pay off if mildew and frost don't take their toll). Sow also in autumn indoors or in situ to overwinter as seedlings for early outdoor flowers. Keep picking the flowers and dead leaves to prolong flowering. The flowers can be dried gently for winter use, or alternatively they can be pickled (see p.156).

Chrysanthemum spp. (Chrysanthemum)

Special varieties of chrysanthemum are eaten in Japan and China, but the many forms of tender 'florist's chrysanthemum' (Chrysanthemum morifolium, C. sinense) can be substituted. They grow on average 60-120cm/24-48in tall and come in all colors. Before using in salads, blanch the flowers by dipping them into boiling water for a second or two; then sprinkle the petals on the salad.

Grow chrysanthemums in ordinary garden soil. They are normally raised from cuttings taken in autumn or spring.

Cichorium intybus (Chicory)

Any cultivated or wild chicory plants left to run to seed in spring produce spires of blue, occasionally pink, flowers. Use the petals or whole flowers in salads: they have a slightly bitter 'chicory' taste. The flowers close and fade rapidly so, if possible, pick just before use. Flowers can be pickled (see p.156): the color is lost but a faint flavor remains. (For cultivation, see pp.64-70.)

Hemerocallis spp. (Day lily)

Hardy herbacious perennials, day lilies grow several feet tall with lily-like flowers. There are many forms with varying colors. Whole flowers and petals can be used in salads for their colors, their crisp texture and very delicate flavor. Don't use the buds: they have a bitter aftertaste.

Grow in ordinary soil, planting roots in spring or autumn about 1m/3ft apart, since they develop into large clumps.

Lavandula spp. (Lavender)

Lavender is a Mediterranean shrub growing 60-120cm/24-36in high, with beautiful purplish-blue flowering spikes – English lavender (Lavandula spica) is probably the hardiest form. The strongly flavored flowers and chopped leaves should be used sparingly in salads, though salads were traditionally served on beds of lettuce and lavender sprigs.

Grow lavender on very well-drained soil in a sheltered position. English lavender can be raised from seed sown in spring, or from cuttings taken in summer. Trim plants back in spring to prevent them from becoming straggly; replant every five years.

Monarda didyma (Oswego tea)

A favorite perennial garden plant, which is also known as sweet bergamot or bee balm, oswego tea grows up to 60cm/24in high, with scarlet or pink flowers in late summer. The flowers (traditionally dried to make delicately perfumed tea) look beautiful mixed with borage flowers in salads.

It grows best in slightly moist soil, from seed sown in spring, planted about 60cm/24in apart. Divide old clumps every three years or so, replanting the younger parts.

Pelargonium spp. (Geranium)

This is a tremendously varied group of tender plants, with fragrant pink, red, white or purple flowers; the leaves also exhibit an extraordinary range of scents and flavors, from orange and lemon to rose and mint. Both flowers and leaves can be used in salads: the flowers generously, the leaves more sparingly. Some *pelargonium* varieties can now be raised from seed, but the scented-leaved varieties need to be raised from cuttings taken from mature plants in autumn, and kept in frost-free conditions throughout the winter.

Hemerocallis

Nasturtium – red-, plain- and variegated-leaved forms

Hollyhock flower and bud

Cultivated rose

Pelargoniums

Wild rose

Anchusa

Lavender   *Clary sage*

MORE EDIBLE FLOWERS
These flowers (photographed here in midsummer) were all grown for culinary and salad use in the past.

Primula veris (Cowslip)
A beautiful perennial plant, it has yellow flowers in spring which can be used whole in salads. In the past, cowslip flowers were also pickled.

Grow in a sunny position. Sow fresh seed in autumn (germination is slow), planting out in spring about 23cm/9in apart.

Primula vulgaris (English primrose)
Similar to the cowslip (see above) in appearance, growth and use, English primroses are more ground-hugging, and prefer a slightly shaded position in humus-rich soil.

Sow in autumn in a shaded frame and plant out in spring or the following autumn 15cm/6in apart. Divide mature plants every three years or so.

Rosa spp. (Rose)
Any roses, wild or cultivated, can be used in salads. Select those with the most fragrance and sprinkle the petals over the salad, either alone or mixed with other flowers. They add color and fragrance and have a delicate taste.

Salvia sclarea (Clary sage)
A very hardy biennial growing up to 60cm/2ft tall, clary sage has spikes of deep purple and pink bracts. These look very striking sprinkled on salads and have an interesting pleasant taste of their own.

Not fussy about soil, clary sage can be sown either in autumn – being overwintered as seedlings and planted out up to 45cm/18in apart in spring – or in summer for later blooms. The flowers survive light frost.

Salvia officinalis (Sage)
The various forms of narrow-leaved sage have purplish-blue, pink and white flowers, which can be sprinkled on salads to add color and fragrance. (For cultivation, see p.123.)

Sambucus nigra (European elder)
This hedgerow shrub is covered in early summer with sweet-smelling creamy blossoms composed of myriads of tiny confettilike flowers. Shake the blossoms over a salad at the last moment, without even washing them, or the fragrance will be lost. Only a few are needed to impart a flavor: too many can impart an overpoweringly musty taste.

The North American Indians ate the leaves and flowers in salads, while in England the buds and flowers used to be pickled. The flowerheads are normally collected from the wild, but elder can quite easily be grown in a garden, if preferred.

Scorzonera hispanica (Black salsify)
Quite a substantial dish can be made of the flower buds, whether raw or cooked and cooled; the yellow petals can be strewn on a salad. Both have a distinct flavor of their own. The flowers tend to open only briefly in the morning, in sunshine, and then close firmly. Where petals are wanted either pick them just before required, or pick when the flowers are open and keep them in a closed bag in a refrigerator until needed: this may persuade them to remain open. (For cultivation, see p.115.)

Tragopogon porrifolius (Salsify)
The flowers are an exquisite soft mauve. (For cultivation, see p.113: for use of flowers, see *Scorzonera hispanica*, above.)

Tropaeolum majus (Nasturtium)
Brightly colored annuals, with trailing and dwarf forms, nasturtiums have a long and versatile history of use in salads. The flowers and flower buds have real piquancy, the seeds are pickled as capers, and the leaves have a peppery taste. Varieties with variegated leaves ('Alaska', for example) and small, neat red leaves ('Empress of India', for example) are especially pretty in salads. Nasturtiums are not frost-hardy but thrive in poor soil and dry conditions.

Sow *in situ* in late spring, or in soil blocks for transplanting. Thin or plant 25cm/9in apart. Sow again in summer, under cover, to extend the season a few weeks in autumn. Nasturtiums will often reseed themselves.

Viola odorata (Violet)
Small and dainty though they are, violet flowers were formerly eaten raw with lettuce and onions. They have a flavor of sorts and are very pretty in salads.

Grow them in a shady spot. Sow seed in autumn in a cold frame (germination is slow and erratic) and plant out in spring about 23cm/9in apart.

Viola wittrockiana (Garden pansy)
The velvety textures and marvelous range of colors and 'faces' in pansies transform any salad, the smaller, daintier forms such as heartsease (*Viola tricolor*) looking best of all. Pansies are short-lived perennials and can flower almost all year round.

Grow in good soil in light shade. Sow in spring for autumn planting, or in autumn for spring planting, spacing them 15cm/6in apart. Divide plants every few years, or propagate favorite plants with cuttings taken in autumn.

WILD PLANTS

Cultivated vegetables have all evolved from wild plants, so it is not surprising that the countryside is still a treasure trove of edible plants, most of which can be eaten raw. Over the course of the centuries some of these wild plants have become weeds, establishing themselves in the luxurious environments of gardens and cultivated fields. Here they thrive, growing soft, tender and succulent – a host of tasty leaves to add to salads. This is, in fact, the best way to use weeds and wild plants: to enrich a salad with their strong, sometimes strange flavors rather than to make a salad composed entirely of wild plants.

The golden rule is to pick the leaves when they are *small, young* and *tender*. The majority become tough as they mature. Aware of this, peasant communities all over the world scour fields and mountains for the very first leaves of spring: they are the most delicious of all. Peasants, of course, have always used wild plants for their medicinal and 'health giving' properties; today we know that many are also rich in the vitamins and minerals necessary for a balanced diet.

It is essential to identify edible plants accurately, as there are a few poisonous ones with which they can be confused. Identify them with a good botanical text or, if you have no botanical knowledge, be guided by an expert until you are sure of yourself. You will soon get to know the garden weeds and the wild plants common to your area. But never go just by a picture in a book. Two people I know who did so confused ground elder with

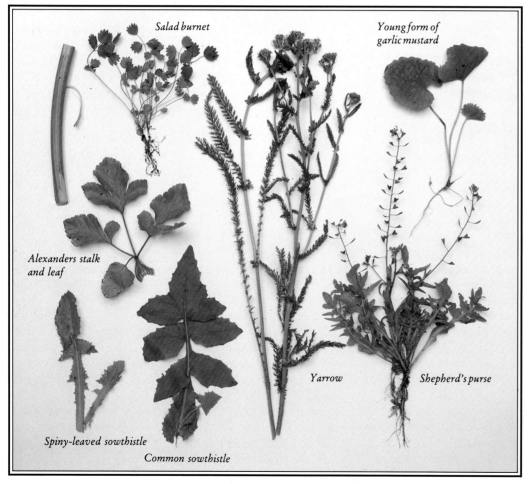

Salad burnet

Young form of
garlic mustard

Alexanders stalk
and leaf

Spiny-leaved sowthistle

Common sowthistle

Yarrow

Shepherd's purse

EDIBLE WILD PLANTS *Some of the many wild plants which were traditionally used in salads and can still be found in the countryside. They are often richly flavored, but, until you are very familiar with them, take great care to identify them correctly before picking them for use. They are quite easily cultivated in the garden.*

dog's mercury and found themselves in hospital as a result. To help with identification, edible plants are listed here under their Latin names, as common names (also given) can be very misleading.

Since some enterprising seedsmen are now selling seed of wild plants (see p.167), it is possible to cultivate them yourself.

Achillea millefolium (Yarrow, Milfoil)
Very common weed, green most of the year. Strongly flavored, so use sparingly.

Aegopodium podagraria (Ground elder)
Pernicious weed, but with delightful angelica flavor. (Don't confuse with *Mercurialis perennis* [dog's mercury]: similar, but poisonous.)

Alliaria petiolata (Garlic mustard, Jack-by-the-hedge)
Common hedgerow weed with faint garlic flavor.

Apium graveolens (Wild celery, Smallage)
Grows in damp places. Chop leaves and young stems into salads. Not to be confused with poison hemlock (*Conium maculatum*) or hemlock water dropwort (*Oenanthe crocata*).

Arctium lappa (Great burdock), A. minus (Common burdock)
Use cooked or raw. Pick the leafy stems of young shoots in spring, strip off peel, cut into 5cm/2in pieces for salads. Flavor described as 'intriguing and elusive'.

Capsella bursa-pastoris (Shepherd's purse)
Very common weed, green much of the year. Basal rosettes and stem leaves excellent raw; distinctive flavor due to sulfur. Cultivated in China for use raw and cooked. Said to be richer in vitamin C than oranges.

Cardamine hirsuta (Hairy bitter cress)
Very hardy, ubiquitous little weed appearing in moist sandy soils. Cut the tiny leaves for salads; they have a very 'cressy' taste. The seed pods virtually explode when touched: thin out seedlings to get plants of a reasonable size. If the plants are covered with a cloche, they will be large and tender!

Above *Buck's horn plantain, a curious, neglected wild salad plant which is useful both early and late in the year. Blanch the leaves in boiling water for a moment before use.*

EDIBLE WEEDS *These very common weeds, all picked from the author's garden, add interesting flavors to salads. All spread very easily, so it is inadvisable to cultivate them apart from a few horseradish plants, for making sauce, and some dandelions, for blanching.*

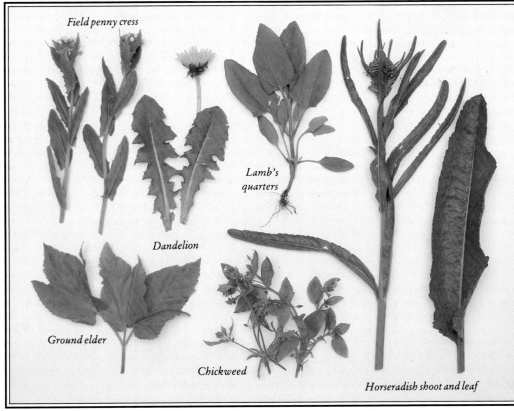

Field penny cress

Lamb's quarters

Dandelion

Ground elder

Chickweed

Horseradish shoot and leaf

Cardamine pratensis (Lady's smock, Cuckoo flower)
Plant of damp meadows; remains green late in winter. The leaves have watercress spiciness and are very good in salads.

Centranthus ruber (Red valerian)
Red- and white-flowered forms found on dry banks and walls. Often cultivated in gardens.

Chenopodium album (Lamb's quarters, Fat hen)
Very common arable weed, often found near manure heaps. Spinachlike flavor, and excellent cooked like spinach or raw. American Indians made the seeds into cakes and gruel.

Chrysanthemum leucanthemum (White weed, Ox-eye daisy, Marguerite)
Young leaves and flowers used in salads in Italy.

Chrysosplenium oppositifolium (Golden saxifrage)
The *cresson des roches* of the Vosges mountains. Found in wet places.

Cirsium palustre (Marsh thistle)
A plant of damp places. Use young shoots and the stalks after removing prickles and peeling them.

Crithmum maritimum (Samphire)
Fleshy-leaved plant found on cliffs and shingle. Leaves and stems cooked or pickled for salads.

Halimione portulacoides (Sea purslane)
Succulent gray-leaved plant of salt marshes. Gets muddy so needs careful washing before use.

Nasturtium officinale (Watercress)
(Confusingly sometimes also known as brooklime, the common name for *Veronica beccabunga*.) Grows in running water: never pick from stagnant or contaminated water in pastures because of risk of liver fluke infection. Preferable to cultivate (see p.86). Older leaves have more flavor than young.

Oenothera biennis (Evening primrose)
The leaves have quite a good flavor; the roots are edible before the plants run to flower.

Oxalis acetosella (Wood sorrel, Alleluia)
Delicate, folded, cloverlike leaves are among first to appear in woods in spring. They have a sharp sorrel flavor.

Papaver rhoeas (Corn poppy)
Common red-flowered poppy. Leaves eaten in Mediterranean region, and seeds used to decorate bread and buns. Not to be confused with *Glaucium corniculatum* (horned poppy).

Plantago coronopus (Buck's horn plantain)
A pretty plant, formerly much cultivated by the French. The tough but tasty leaves at their best in spring and autumn. Blanch in boiling water for a few seconds to make them more tender. Seeds itself once established in a garden.

Polygonum persicaria (Lady's thumb, Redleg)
Very common weed of arable land. Leaves used cooked or raw. Not to be confused with the very acrid *Polygonum hydropiper* (smartweed, water pepper).

Pyrola minor (Lesser pyrola)
Berried evergreen plant, found in woodlands, rocky ledges and sand dunes. Sometimes used in salads in North America.

Rumex sanguineus (Red-veined dock)
Dramatic-looking but coarse-textured leaves. Soften by blanching in boiling water for a few seconds. Easily cultivated.

Salicornia europaea (Glasswort, Marsh or Sea samphire)
Narrow succulent leaves: a primitive-looking plant found in salt marshes and on shingle beaches. Gather young leaves in summer. Excellent both raw and pickled.

Sedum reflexum (Reflexed stonecrop)
Succulent perennial found wild on walls and rocks, of ancient use in salads. Easily cultivated in dry places.

Silybum marianum (Milk or Holy thistle)
Striking plant, beautiful white-veined foliage. Use young leaves and peeled, chopped stems; roots are also edible raw and cooked. Easily cultivated.

Smyrnium olusatrum (Alexanders)
Tall, striking plant common in coastal areas. Buds, young leaves, stems, spicy seeds (a pepper substitute), all of ancient use in salads. Stems used to be blanched. Not to be confused with poisonous hemlock water dropwort (*Oenanthe crocata*), found in similar places.

Sonchus arvensis (Field sowthistle), *S. asper* (Spiny-leaved sowthistle), *S. oleraceus* (Common sowthistle)
Weeds found commonly on arable land; pleasant taste, but bristly parts should be trimmed off.

Stellaria media (Chickweed)
Perhaps the commonest of all garden weeds. Available almost all year round: best when grown in light shade. Use tiny seedlings or large plants if still succulent. Cut with scissors and leave to regrow.

Thlaspi arvense (Field penny cress)
Very common weed with delicious spicy leaves.

SALAD
MAKING

INTRODUCTION

Salad making is an art which can easily be mastered but, like any art, it demands good-quality materials and the expenditure of time, skill and that magic ingredient, creativity. So often salads are made for the wrong reasons: to avoid cooking, to save time or to use up unsuitable leftovers. And what horrible salads result: wilted lettuce, soggy coleslaw, dried mounds of grated carrots and gelatinous faded rings of egg white.

Such dishes are far removed from the salads that can be created with fresh homegrown salad plants. These have a richness of flavor, color and texture which are beyond the imagination of the salad maker restricted to shop-bought ingredients. Coupled with fresh herbs, delicately flavored dressings and carefully chosen garnishes, they are a marvellous basis for superb salads.

The historical background

The art of salad making has spanned centuries and continents. In Europe, it reached one of its most extraordinary heights in the 'crowned sallets' of Elizabethan times. These were elaborate constructions; sometimes a complete head of celery would be the centerpiece, mounted in a pot and surrounded by layer upon layer of sliced meats, eggs, shredded vegetables, nuts and fruits. Alternatively, the salad could take the form of a pastry castle with 'towers' and 'ramparts' of carrots, turnips and beets, and 'courtyards' planted with herbs and flowers.

One of the most articulate of all exponents of the art of salad making was the famous seventeenth-century diarist, John Evelyn. His book on the subject, *Acetaria. A Discourse of Sallets*, is full of wisdom and observation, most of it as pertinent today as it was nearly 300 years ago. Here's how he summarized the 'art' of salad making:

'Every plant should come in to bear its part and . . . fall into place like the notes in music, and there must be nothing harsh or grating. And though admitting some discords (to distinguish and illustrate the rest), striking in the more sprightly and sometimes gentler notes, reconcile all dissonances and melt them into an agreeable composition.'

Incidentally, John Evelyn's garden at Says Court was organized in such a way that a mixed green salad could be put on the table every day of the year.

Modern influences

Perhaps the finest twentieth-century examples of salad making are to be found in the Middle East, in the wonderful tradition of *mezze*, which stretches from Morocco to Afghanistan and from Greece to the Yemen.

Mezze can be anything from a simple snack to a banquet of 40 to 50 dishes. They look rather like *hors d'oeuvre* and consist of bowls of exquisitely prepared and displayed salads. Stuffed zucchini, peppers, or vine leaves might be cut in slices; crisp raw vegetables set against creamy fragrant dips; ripe, purple and green olives contrasted with chopped egg, eggplants served in yogurt, tomatoes in olive oil and dried lentil and bean salads decorated with cucumber and tomato wedges.

Whatever the source of inspiration, the culinary imagination can express itself in salad making, although the approach to any salad dish will be influenced by the way in which the salad will be used. For example, if it is to be an *hors d'oeuvre*, the salad will generally take the form of crudités, though indeed almost any light appetizing salad could be used. The exception is the simple green salad, which is best served between courses rather than at the start of a meal. Where a salad is an accompaniment to the main dish it should be chosen so that it contrasts or harmonizes with it – a colorful marinated pepper salad, for example, set off against the pale flesh of chicken. Finally, a salad dish can be substantial enough to make a meal in itself – the potato and dried bean salads come into their own here, as do composé salads where vegetables are mixed with pasta or rice.

Right *Spring 'saladini' in which the plants are (reading clockwise from the chopsticks): salad burnet, land cress, 'Pak Choi' flower, pansies, Bellis perennis, chickweed, curly-leaved endive, sprouted mung beans and lentils, broad-leaved endive, claytonia, 'Shanghai Pak Choi', corn salad, self-blanching celery, 'Ragged Jack' kale, 'Red Verona' chicory, Japanese mustard 'Miike Giant', 'Treviso' chicory, Japanese mustard 'Green in the Snow', Japanese 'Mizuna' mustard, hairy bitter cress, garden cress, angelica and Mediterranean rocket.*

TYPES OF SALAD

Salads can be divided into several fairly distinct groups according to the range of ingredients used and the way they are prepared. The salad recipes on pp.151-6 are arranged accordingly, although there is, naturally, some overlap between the groups. Most salad plants can be treated in a number of ways and part of the fun of growing your own, especially the more unusual plants, is in deciding how to use them to best advantage. Don't be afraid to follow your inclination and use your imagination, but bear in mind that the quality and flavor of homegrown salad vegetables will usually be so good that only the minimum of 'treatment' will be necessary – just enough to enhance, but never to disguise or conceal, the natural flavor.

RAW SALADS

Wherever possible, salad plants should be eaten raw since not only are the subtleties of flavor lost in cooking, but the vitamins are destroyed. Raw salads can take several forms, including crudités, simple salads in which the flavor of a particular plant predominates, and more complex mixed salads and 'saladini' (see below).

Crudités
In this, the most elementary, form of vegetable salad, beautifully fresh, prime-quality, chilled vegetables, daintily cut where necessary, are served with just a sprinkling of sea salt. Crudités are eaten with the fingers, as an *hors d'oeuvre* at the start of a meal, and can be served with a variety of dressings, sauces and purées into which they are dipped.

All kinds of salad vegetables can be used as crudités from root vegetables, grated and dressed with a vinaigrette, to cauliflower florets, either served whole or cut to look like miniature trees. Small lettuce heads, tiny new artichokes and young radishes can be served whole, as can scallions, crisped beforehand in iced water in the refrigerator. Celery and fennel can be cut into dainty matchsticks (see p.150).

Crudités should *look*, as well as taste, wonderful. Blend colors and textures to maximum effect, and serve them in attractive dishes with, for special occasions, finger-bowls of rosewater and scented geranium leaves.

Simple salads
The simple salad is made of one or at most only a few raw ingredients, which are dressed and garnished. The basic simple salad is the classic green salad – a few fresh, very crisp lettuce leaves or hearts, tossed in a vinaigrette dressing just before serving. The purpose of this superb but simple salad is to refresh the palate after the main course, in preparation for the cheese and dessert that follow.

Vary a simple salad by adding a few leaves of chicory, endive, purslane, dandelion and spinach, or any other appropriate salad plant. Or make a simple salad with any of these alone, or in simple combinations. Further variety can be created by using different vinegars and oils in the dressings, and by garnishing with herbs, flowers, nuts, sprouted seeds or seedlings.

Simple salads can also be made with nonleafy plants such as tomatoes (dressed just with basil and the lightest of vinaigrettes), or lightly dressed beansprouts on a bed of endive, or with purslane mixed with Mediterranean rocket. Almost any salad vegetable, in fact, can be treated 'simply'. These simple salads are unpretentious and quick to make, depending above all on the quality of their ingredients for their excellence.

Mixed salads and 'saladini'
Simple salads lead naturally into mixed salads. These are salads with a number of different ingredients and, perhaps, more complex dressings, but which are still subtly balanced and blended so they have character – not merely nondescript diversity for diversity's sake.

Into this category of mixed salads falls 'saladini', the modern incarnation of the sixteenth-, seventeenth- and eighteenth-century salads in which 20 or 30 ingredients were combined.

The term 'saladini' arose from our travels in Europe – the 'Grand Vegetable Tour', as we liked to call it. In Italy we had seen seedlings of lettuce, endive, chicory, Mediterranean rocket and corn salad, alongside baskets of small wild plants, being sold for salads in the markets. The idea was to buy a few handfuls of each and mix them into a salad at home. These small leaves were called *insalatine*, a dimunitive of *insalata*, the Italian word for salad – but my untuned ears misheard it as 'saladini'. We liked the word, it was associated in our minds with the unusual continental plants we began growing and using in mixed salads after our return from our European tour, and we adopted it as our own.

Virtually all the plants covered in this book can be used in 'saladini', and, like John Evelyn with his green salads, we find we can serve a freshly picked 'saladini' every day of the year. The midsummer 'saladini' are very different from those in midwinter but, however bizarre and diverse the individual plants, there will always be a delightful and exciting harmony of color, taste and texture in the finished result.

In mixing our 'saladini' we always try to balance flavors, contrast textures, and include a few ingredients for their form and color alone. When I started reading the seventeenth- and eighteenth-century gardening classics I discovered that they did the same. John Evelyn divided

salad plants primarily into 'blanched herbs', such as chicory, celery, fennel, various types of lettuce and endive, and 'green herbs', which included lettuce, corn salad, purslane, various cresses, sorrel, the seedling leaves of radish, turnip and mustard, and various wild plants. He suggested the proportions in which available salad plants could be mixed in each month of the year. For example, 'a pugil or handful of lamb's lettuce, three parts of radish, two parts of cresses . . .'. He also suggested that they should be enlivened with 'furnitures' – 'all hot and spicy herbs, mixed with the more cold and mild, discretely to temper and give them relish'.

The eighteenth-century gardening writer, Batty Langley, in his *New Principles of Gardening*, divided salads into 'raw sallets', 'boiled sallets' and 'pickled sallets', then further classified the plants according to the strength of their flavor. For example, among 'hot and dry' plants cress was a mere '2nd degree' on his scale of

Below left *Crudités, displayed in prettily shaped dishes and served with dips of puréed eggplant and yogurt. (For recipes, see p.151)*

Below *Zucchini salad dressed with a garlic vinaigrette and garnished with ripe olives and peppers. (For recipe, see p.151)*

Above left *Purslane and flower salad in which the succulent purslane leaves provide a perfect foil for colorful nasturtium, pot marigold and borage flowers, variegated nasturtium leaves and sprigs of red currant. (For recipe, see p.152)*

Above *Simple green salad, with 'Little Gem' and bronze 'Trotzkopf' lettuce, garnished with variegated lemon balm and borage flowers. (For recipe, see p.151)*

Left *Mixed cabbage salad, combining red and Chinese cabbage, kohlrabi, fennel and celery and flavored with a vinaigrette dressing. (For recipe, see p.153)*

Right *Pepper salad dressed with a light vinaigrette and garnished with olives, quartered tomatoes and coriander. (For recipe, see p.153)*

hotness, while garlic and mustard were 4th degree.

Elaborate classifications like these are, of course, unnecessary, but when making 'saladini', keep a balance in mind; make sure nothing is overpowering. Very strong or bitter plants such as chicories and mustards can be shredded (even blanched in boiling water for a second), and offset with mild, sweet or succulent leaves – such as the purslanes.

Use chopped herbs and flowers as a means of creating further variations. Start by rubbing the bowl with lovage or garlic, put in the salad plants and herbs, toss them with a simple vinaigrette dressing, and, just before serving, sprinkle flowers or flower petals over the bowl. No true salad lover will ever tire of this type of salad, and it tastes as good as it looks.

COOKED SALADS

Vegetables don't *have* to be used raw in salads. Many can be cooked first, then used in salads when cold – a few suggestions are given below. The main point to bear in mind is that they must never be overcooked, and must retain their crispness.

Of the root vegetables, potatoes are inedible raw, whereas parsnip, salsify and black salsify are generally more palatable cooked; while kohlrabi and Jerusalem artichoke have a markedly different and, many think, improved, flavor after cooking.

Many legumes, including fresh and dried green and runner beans, broad beans and various pulses must be cooked, as they are toxic in varying degrees when raw.

Left *Dried and fresh bean salad. Here the lightly cooked fresh broad beans and runner beans have been mixed with a range of cooked dried beans, and dressed with a vinaigrette made with olive and lemon juice, seasoned with garlic. Parsley, basil, marjoram and fennel have been used as a garnish. (For recipe, see p.155)*

Above right *Eggplant and yogurt salad. The cooked, sliced eggplant is arranged on a bed of red 'oak-leaved' lettuce and dressed with a yogurt dressing, flavored with fenugreek leaves and garlic. Powdered sumac has been used to decorate it. (For recipe, see p.155)*

Right *Beet and buckwheat salad. An unusual combination of cooked buckwheat, red and golden beets, blanched beet stalks and beet tops, stir-fried with scallions, garlic, chives and ginger. Dressed with a garlic flavored vinaigrette, the salad is garnished with fennel and tahini (pounded sesame seed). (For recipe, see p.155)*

Again, particularly with dried beans, the flavor seems best when cold.

A number of other vegetables *can* be used raw in salads, especially when very young, but on the whole they taste better cooked first and used cold. Asparagus, cauliflower, zucchini, calabrese and leeks come into this category.

Cooked leftover vegetables often make excellent salads, though they may need to be 'jazzed up' with a little extra seasoning, dressing or garnish. Any dressings can be used with cooked vegetables, the choice depending on personal taste and the dishes that are being served in the rest of the meal. For example, if the main course had a creamy sauce, you would not want to serve an *hors d'oeuvre* dressed with a rich mayonnaise or cream dressing.

Salads with hot dressings – and 'hot salads'

The classical hot dressing is the well-known French *aux lardons*: essentially this is hot bacon fat poured over salad leaves, which are eaten immediately. There are several variations on the theme, but it is always used for bitter and sharp-flavored leaves such as dandelion, endive, wild chicory and spinach.

The Italian *bagna calda* is made along similar lines, except that the hot sauce is made by heating garlic and anchovy in oil or butter, which is then poured over finely shredded endive.

In China and Japan the term 'hot salad' is used to refer to vegetables which are stir-fried for such a short time that they are still virtually raw, then served marinated or with a dressing, which may be hot. Sprouted seeds and any of the oriental mustards can be served this way.

COMPOSÉ SALADS

In a 'composé' salad the cooked vegetables are mixed with another main ingredient. This might be something starchy, say rice, pasta or grains, or, alternatively, fish, meat, chicken or even cheese or combinations of these, dressed and garnished as necessary. These mixtures can be deadly in the wrong hands. Meat, chicken and fish should be chopped by hand (don't use a food processor) into pieces of small but discernible size.

Where pasta is used, mix it with oil, not butter, as soon as it is cooked and before it has cooled, to prevent it

141

becoming lumpy. Use long-grain brown rice, American or Spanish rice, as the grains separate nicely and absorb dressings well – Patna and Basmati rice tend to congeal into a solid mass when cold.

Fine examples of composé salads are the various forms of 'salade Niçoise', in which tuna is combined with salad vegetables, or combinations of beans and peas with tagliatelle, or tomatoes provençale and *pain bagna.*

Below *Tomato and mozzarella cheese combine to make an excellent summer salad. The clove-like flavor of the green basil dressing is a perfect complement to the tomato. (For recipe, see p.156)*

Below right *Bean and pasta salad in which pink, green and white tagliatelle are mixed with cooked broad beans, and blanched sugar and garden peas, dressed with a garlic mayonnaise. (For recipe, see p.156)*

MARINATED SALADS

A marinade is a liquid (often flavored or spiced) in which raw food is soaked to tenderize and flavor it. A vinaigrette dressing is the most common marinade for vegetables, but light vinegar alone, or lemon juice, or olive oil can also be used.

Certain particular vegetables have the sort of texture which easily absorbs a marinade, acquiring a very special flavor as a result. Globe artichokes, peppers, eggplants, onions, leeks, and grated carrots come into this group, as do pulses such as dried beans and lentils, as well as grains such as Bulgar wheat. Slightly coarse roots (carrots just past their prime for example) can be tenderized with a vinaigrette marinade.

The vegetables can be sliced, chopped, grated, or blanched. Some will need to be marinated for no more than half an hour; some, such as the pulses, will need several hours, while others, like peppers and eggplants (see recipe suggestions, p.156), are best marinated over-night.

Pickling

A pickle is a long-term marinade, in which vinegar is used as a preservative. Before the advent of freezers and the virtually year-round availability of almost everything, pickling was one of the most important means of pre-serving food to brighten and enrich the dull diets of the winter months.

In the past an astonishing variety of plants were pickled for salads. These included globe artichokes, beet, green beans, cucumbers, leeks, mushrooms, onions, purslane, radish seedpods, herbs like summer savory and tarragon, the buds of broom, elder and nasturtium, flowers of chicory, cowslip, elder, goat's beard, salsify, clove-scented pinks, and nasturtiums, and even nasturtium seeds.

Although it is no longer essential to make pickles, a few salad plants still deserve to be pickled simply because their flavor is so good when marinated in this way – and here I'd include shallots, onions, pickling cucumbers, sweet peppers, globe artichokes, and nasturtium seed-pods. And it's fun to make a few old-fashioned pickles such as radish seedpods, glasswort, and black salsify, salsify and nasturtium flowers.

PREPARING SALADS

The way that salad vegetables are cut and prepared, the choice of garnish, and even the choice of a suitable bowl or dish to serve the salad in are all aspects of the 'art' of salad making.

PREPARATION

A few good kitchen tools help to make sure that preparation is easy and efficient.

For chopping and shredding, have a good selection of sharp *knives*, including a paring knife and a medium-sized chef's knife. A Japanese vegetable knife, which is rather like a lightweight cleaver, is an extremely versatile tool, excellent for shredding cabbage and chopping herbs. Always buy the best quality knives you can afford. *Boards* should be large, made of good hardwood and scrubbed clean with salt rather than washed in detergent. *Food processors* should be used with great discretion: their action on the vegetables is harsh and their crisp texture may be destroyed. But they are good for shredding and grating carrots and beets; for other root vegetables, use an ordinary *hand grater*.

Use a good-quality *pestle and mortar* (not made of wood) for pounding garlic, mustard seed, herbs and spices and for making dressings. A Japanese *sunibachi*, which has a grooved mortar, is excellent for grinding herbs. A *garlic press* is useful for crushing garlic.

For drying salads, a collapsible, hand-swung *salad basket* and the centrifugal-type of *salad spinner* are useful, particularly for small quantities of leafy salad, but there's nothing much wrong with swinging washed salad dry in a thin clean cheesecloth.

For cleaning salad plants, there's a stubby Japanese *vegetable brush*.

Left *Green salad with hot bacon dressing. Sharp-flavored leaves such as spinach, sorrel, endive and dandelion are well suited to this treatment. The blue and white dish sets off the salad to advantage. (For recipe, see p.155)*

Finally, when serving salads, remember that *wooden salad bowls* should be reserved for salads which are tossed in a vinaigrette dressing, and never used for mayonnaise, creamy dressings, or dressings made with animal fats, which give them a rancid smell. Season a new bowl, before it is ever used, by rubbing it hard with salt and oil. Wipe wooden bowls clean – never wash them.

Mixed leaf salads and colored vegetables like peppers, on the other hand, look marvellous in a *glass bowl*. But since glass goes streaky after tossing, you should toss the salad in another bowl, and then turn it into the glass bowl to serve.

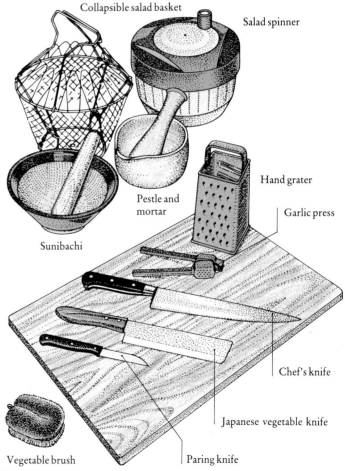

Collapsible salad basket

Salad spinner

Hand grater

Pestle and mortar

Garlic press

Sunibachi

Chef's knife

Japanese vegetable knife

Vegetable brush

Paring knife

Right *A selection of useful tools and equipment for preparing salad vegetables. Always buy the best quality equipment you can afford.*

Hints on preparation

Whenever possible, gather leafy salads just before you use them, though in hot weather it may be necessary to collect them early in the day before they wilt and keep them in a plastic bag in a refrigerator until required. Coarse and dirty outer leaves should, of course, be removed, but the less leafy salads are washed, the better. It is preferable to wipe them clean with a damp piece of paper towel. If washing is really necessary, pull the leaves apart and wash quickly in cold salted water: this encourages insects and slugs to fall off. Calabrese and cauliflower heads, which tend to harbor well-concealed caterpillars, should be left in cold salted water for about ten minutes.

Skin or peel salad vegetables only when it is essential to do so. Tomatoes, peppers, cucumbers, zucchini, young carrots, kohlrabi and new potatoes are all best unskinned, as their skin is nutritious, colorful and adds texture. Celery and fennel need careful scrubbing, however, and it may be necessary to peel off very stringy parts; the same is true with some varieties of string beans, and elderly sugar peas. Some roots which are used cooked are difficult to peel: for example, beet bleeds, salsify and black salsify discolor and are fiddly, and Chinese artichokes are *very* fiddly. Cook all these without peeling; the skins can then be removed easily. If beets are being used raw, they should be peeled thinly as the raw skin is unsightly and unpleasant to eat. Large potatoes will need peeling. Roots such as radishes dry out easily and can be kept in a bowl of cold water in a refrigerator. Globe artichokes are prepared by trimming off the stalks, the tough basal bracts and the pointed tips of the upper bracts.

CUTTING Cutting correctly has a bearing on both the taste and the appearance of the salad. It's important to cut to a uniform size. Vegetables look most attractive 'à la julienne', that is cut into matchstick-sized slivers, or diced, that is cut into cubes of about 1cm/½in diameter; or sliced. Don't slice too thinly: one needs to bite into something of substance. *Very* thin cucumber slices, for example, are sad things. Leaf vegetables should generally be torn rather than be cut with a knife; it gives them a better taste and texture, they last longer, and look more appetizing.

ACIDULATION Roots such as celeriac, salsify and black salsify become unpleasantly discolored on contact with air after being peeled. To prevent this, slice them into water acidulated with a few drops of vinegar or lemon juice, and leave them until required. Globe artichokes can be prevented from becoming discolored by rubbing the cut surfaces with lemon. Where roots have been blanched or cooked, there is no need for acidulation.

BLANCHING Vegetables can be dipped into boiling water for a few seconds to make slightly tough roots and leaves more tender and digestible, and also to prevent discoloration, but take care not to overdo it. Dip vegetables into boiling water – leaves for a few seconds, roots for a minute or two – then refresh them by immediately plunging them into cold water. This is also a good way of treating any vegetables which are cooked in advance, whether used cold or to be reheated. After cooking, turn them into a strainer, and run cold water through them until they are cold. This will preserve their flavor.

STIR-FRYING This is a very useful way of preparing oriental vegetables. Use a deep skillet or a wok, and cut vegetables into 2.5-5cm/1-2in lengths. Heat a small quantity of oil in the skillet. When it is moderately hot, add the vegetables, putting the thicker vegetables in first. Cover for the first minute or two to cut down on splash and smoke, but not for too long or the vegetables will lose color. Remove the lid; then add a little water if cooking firm vegetables. Cook for a further three to five minutes, stirring continuously.

TOSSING SALADS Leafy vegetables should be tossed in a very large bowl, as gently as possible to avoid any bruising. Chopsticks are ideal for tossing salads.

Garnishing

Garnishes can be purely decorative, or can add an essential culinary quality to a salad dish. Give rein to your imagination, creating original effects with, say, seeds, leaves and flowers from the salad garden, or spices from the store cupboard. A few suggestions are given below.

COLORED AND SPICY POWDERS Cayenne and chilli pepper, sumac (which is a purplish-red powder made from sumac seed), ground mustard seeds, cumin and sweet paprika. Sprinkle them on creamy dressings.

WHOLE SEEDS Sesame, caraway, squash, pumpkin, sunflower. Crisp them up by toasting them for a minute, either in the oven, or under a broiler in a tiny bit of oil.

NUTS All sorts of nuts (but not salted peanuts) can be used, whole or chopped, preferably lightly toasted.

HARD-BOILED EGG This is always best chopped rather than cut in rings. Nice patterns can be made by separating the white and yolk, sifting them, and sprinkling them in alternate bands of yellow and white on colorless salads such as celery. Chopped hard-boiled egg goes well with leeks, asparagus, lentil, beets and dry bean salads.

CROÛTONS Soak cubes of stale bread in garlic and olive oil and put them in the bottom of the salad, or fry them in garlic and olive oil and scatter them over the top.

FLOWERS The most colorful and appealing of all garnishes, sprinkled over the salad at the last moment. Use individual petals or the whole flower, whichever is appropriate. For gathering and use of flowers, see p.125.

HERBS Freshly cut green herbs make a wonderful final garnish to a salad, sometimes chopped, sometimes using the leaves whole, as well as being an integral part of some salad dishes. For ideas on choosing suitable herbs to accompany different salad plants, see the chart below.

PRESENTATION

The final touch of artistry lies in the choice of dish or bowl in which the salad is served. While bowls are undoubtedly best for tossed leafy salads, platters and shallow dishes are often more suitable for mixed and composé salads, and for salads with heavy dressings. The ingredients can be clearly seen rather than being lost in the depths of a bowl, so there is more scope for artistic decoration. It is worth collecting prettily shaped bowls and dishes for different types of salads. For example, soft-colored salads look best in soft-colored dishes; brightly colorful salads are set off perfectly in blue and white dishes; asparagus looks dramatic in tapered dishes, and so on. Attractive little dishes are particularly useful for serving crudités.

USES OF HERBS

BASIL Powerful, distinctive herb with a clove-like flavor. Unsurpassed as an accompaniment to tomatoes, peppers and eggplants and the key ingredient in the well-known Mediterranean sauce, 'pesto'. Use small leaves whole and tear, rather than cut, large leaves to preserve their flavor.

CHERVIL Faint aniseed flavor. The delicate leaves can be used generously in many salads. With tarragon, chives and parsley, it is one of the ingredients in the famous French *fines herbes* combination.

CHIVES Delicate onion flavor. Chopped chives make a refreshing garnish, suitable for most salads but especially good in potato dishes. The same is true of garlic chives, in which the garlic flavor is more pronounced.

CORIANDER A unique, musty, curry-like flavor. Use chopped as liberally as parsley on *mezze* and *hors d'oeuvre*, in yogurt dressings, and with cucumber and zucchini.

CRESSES All are peppery and so will enliven bland dishes. Watercress combines well with 'Witloof' chicory and oranges.

DILL An unmistakable, indescribable gentle flavor of its own. Fresh dill blends well in potato, cucumber, egg, bean and zucchini salads; dried dill in sour cream dressings for cucumber and beet salads.

FENNEL Aniseed flavor. Suitable for tomato, cucumber and salsify salads. It makes a delicate garnish on asparagus.

HORSERADISH Hot and pungent. The grated root is added to cream dressings for beet, apple and celery, and cooked root salads. Combines well with chives in mayonnaise,

provided the latter is not made with olive oil.

HYSSOP Strong, hot flavor. Use young leaves cautiously with cucumber, onions and pickles.

LEMON BALM Delicious, refreshing, slightly sweet lemon scent. Wonderful contrast to bitter-leaved plants like sorrel, chicory and endive.

LOVAGE Unique but dominating celery flavor, so use very cautiously in 'saladini' and composé dishes. Rub a wooden salad bowl with a lovage leaf to impregnate it with the flavor.

MARJORAM Sweet marjoram is fragrant, blends with most Mediterranean vegetables and enlivens a plain lettuce salad. Pot marjoram and winter marjoram are closer to the pungent 'oregano', the wild marjoram of the Mediterranean; marjoram is also used with peppers, tomatoes and eggplants.

MINTS The stronger mints go well with potato, cucumber, carrots, and Bulgar wheat salads. Chop sweeter, more perfumed mints onto green and fruit salads or mix with parsley in mayonnaise.

PARSLEY Mild but distinctive flavor, widely used in generous quantities in and on many salad dishes. It mitigates the smell of raw onion and garlic.

SAVORY Strongly flavored. Use like hyssop.

SWEET CICELY A sweet aniseed flavor. Use like fennel. Add to water when cooking old carrots as it rejuvenates them.

THYME Herbs of many fragrances and strengths. Strip the leaves from the stalks and scatter them on eggplant, tomato, carrot, zucchini, lentil and bean salads.

SALAD SUGGESTIONS

When you have an abundance of freshly picked home-grown salad vegetables, there is a great temptation simply to eat them as they come, with the simplest of dressings, or at most tossed into a 'saladini'.

But from time to time a vegetable cries out for different treatment. Perhaps the cry will come from a beautifully bulging fennel, perhaps from an extra special crop of tomatoes or from perfectly ripened peppers. The spirit of adventure is stirred, you decide to try a new or different recipe, and you are delighted with the result. I suspect that most of us at some time experience this tug of war between opting for the simple or experimenting with the more sophisticated.

The selection of recipes given here makes no claim to be comprehensive, but it does include a range of ideas for the plants covered in this book. While some suggestions are very simple, others are more sophisticated. Interpret them all freely – vary the herbs and garnishes, according to what is available. In salad making it is the spirit that counts, not the letter of the law.

The recipes that follow have been arranged in sections corresponding roughly with the main types of salad already described. Within the types, they have been arranged (again fairly loosely as there is a great deal of overlap) in the order in which the cultivation of the plants was covered in the text.

No specific 'saladini' recipe has been given in the recipe section, as the ingredients are largely a matter of what is available at the time. On the whole, the greater the range of plants and the more varied the mixture of mild- and sharp-flavored leaves, the better the resulting salad.

The opening section gives recipes for some useful basic dressings, together with a chart showing some simple variations on the basic dressings, and their possible uses. Much of the skill in salad making lies in knowing what dresing will bring out a salad's natural flavor. It's a skill that is acquired through experience, although there is plenty of scope for intuition and imagination, as there is with every aspect of salad making.

First and foremost, it is important to use good-quality ingredients in both dressings and salads. Boileau, in the reign of Louis XIV, described a dinner in which two salads were served – one of yellow purslane, the other of wilted greens. Both smelt of rancid oil and were swimming in strong vinegar. It can still happen!

DRESSINGS

The permutations on the basic types of salad dressing are infinite. Suggestions for some useful dressings are given overleaf, and the chart opposite indicates how some of the dressings, and their variations, can be used for different salads.

The principal ingredients in a dressing are oil and vinegar, with mustard a common accompaniment.

Oils

There are many different types of oil. The main ones are listed below:

OLIVE OIL This is the preferred oil for most salad dressings and, of the various kinds available, a dark, full-flavored, fruity, unrefined oil is best. Look for 'extra virgin' or 'first cold pressing' on the label. Excellent oils come from a number of countries, among them France, Italy, Greece and Spain.

Cheaper refined olive oil, labelled 'pure' or 'fine', can be used where 'lighter' dressings are required.

SUNFLOWER, GROUNDNUT OR SOYA OIL These are all neutral flavored oils, and can be blended with olive oil or used alone to produce a much lighter dressing.

SESAME OIL The very strong, distinctive flavor of this makes it ideal for use with Chinese vegetables.

WALNUT OIL Another distinctly flavored oil, it can be used as a substitute for, or an accompaniment to, olive oil in vinaigrettes. It is especially good with bitter salad plants.

Vinegars

As with oils, there are several types of vinegar, all with rather different flavors.

WINE VINEGAR The perfect accompaniment for olive oil, wine vinegar is normally used for a vinaigrette. It should also be used to make mayonnaise.

CIDER VINEGAR This delicately flavored vinegar makes a good light dressing.

SHERRY VINEGAR This is just right for a vinaigrette for Chinese vegetables, if a few drops of soya sauce are added.

FLAVORED VINEGARS Subtly flavored vinegars can be made by steeping shallots, herbs, fruit or flowers in good wine vinegar for anything up to a few weeks. These vinegars impart an unusual flavor to dressings, but must be mixed with a light oil or the flavor will be drowned. Raspberry flavored vinegar can be made by adding half a dozen raspberries to a small bottle of wine vinegar. Rose petals can be treated in the same way. Some people advocate straining these vinegars, but it is not really necessary.

Mustards

Mustards vary considerably in strength and flavor. Among the best known are:

DIJON MUSTARD Rather mild in flavor, it is generally suitable for salad dressings.

ENGLISH MUSTARD Much stronger in flavor, so especially good in rémoulades and in ravigotes.

MEAUX MUSTARD (*Moutarde de Meaux*) Aromatic, with partly ground mustard seeds in it, it is excellent in potato mayonnaise.

HERB MUSTARDS These can be used to add an extra quality to a vinaigrette – the flavor varies according to the herbs used.

SUITABLE DRESSINGS FOR DIFFERENT PLANTS

VINAIGRETTES	FOR USE WITH	MAYONNAISES	FOR USE WITH	MISCELLANEOUS DRESSINGS	FOR USE WITH
Basic vinaigrette (olive oil, vinegar or lemon juice, mustard, salt and pepper)	green salad, any leafy or crisp raw or cooked salads	**Basic mayonnaise** (eggs, oil, lemon juice, salt and pepper)	cooked vegetables, crudités	Buttermilk and mayonnaise dressing	spinach, sorrel, beetroot, cucumber
Basic vinaigrette with herbs, capers, gherkins, anchovies, for *sauce ravigote*	cooked root vegetables	Basic mayonnaise with herbs for *sauce verte*	ditto	Sour cream (or yogurt) with dill and mint	cucumber, beetroot, aubergine
Basic vinaigrette with hard-boiled eggs, for *sauce gribiche*	Chinese vegetables, cooked vegetables	Basic mayonnaise with mustard and anchovies for *rémoulade*	celery, celeriac, potato	Sour cream	chicory, sorrel, spinach, dandelion, endive
Basic vinaigrette with honey and hard-boiled egg, cream or yogurt for *honey vinaigrette*	bitter chicories, spinach, sorrel, mustard	Basic mayonnaise with garlic and chillies for *sauce rouille*	cooked salads, crudités	Skordalia	beetroot
		Basic mayonnaise with garlic for *aïoli*	ditto	Chinese hot dressing	Chinese vegetables
				Hot bacon dressing	dandelion, spinach, endive, sorrel, chicory
Basic vinaigrette with soy sauce, sesame seeds, ginger and garlic for *Chinese dressing*	sprouted seeds, cabbage, Chinese vegetables	Basic mayonnaise with garlic, herbs and egg white for *sauce mousseline*	green salads	Irish salad dressing	grated vegetables, tomato, cucumber
		Basic mayonnaise with curry powder for *curry mayonnaise*	cooked root vegetables, rice		
Basic vinaigrette with pounded basil and garlic for *green dressing*	tomato, potato, carrot, pasta	Basic mayonnaise with horseradish for *piquant mayonnaise*	tomato, beetroot, cooked root vegetables		

DRESSING RECIPES

The following are a selection of some of the basic dressings and dips that can be used with salads. Vary the ingredients according to taste. For suggestions on which dressings to use with different plants, see the chart on the previous page.

BASIC VINAIGRETTE (FRENCH DRESSING)

3 parts olive oil
1 part wine vinegar or lemon juice
mustard, crushed garlic and salt
* and pepper to taste*

Mix the vinegar or lemon juice and the mustard, garlic and seasoning in a jug or jar. Add the oil slowly, beating vigorously until the mixture emulsifies. The dressing will keep for a few days in an airtight container in a cool place. Stir well before using.

SAUCE RAVIGOTE

Make a vinaigrette, as above, but add a tablespoon of chopped herbs (chives, tarragon, parsley and chervil), and half a teaspoon of chopped onions and a few capers. Chopped anchovies and sweet dill pickles can also be added, if liked.

THICK VINAIGRETTE

Make a basic vinaigrette with Meaux mustard and add a tablespoon of yogurt or thin cream to the emulsion.

HONEY VINAIGRETTE

yolk of one hard-boiled egg
1 tbs raspberry (or other fruit)
* vinegar*
4 tbs olive oil
1 tsp coffee cream or yogurt
1 tsp honey

Pound the egg yolk. Add the vinegar. Then, stirring all the time, add the oil, drop by drop at first, then in a thin stream once

the mixture emulsifies. Add the cream or yogurt and honey.

BASIC MAYONNAISE

2 egg yolks
1 tsp lemon juice
salt and pepper
1 ¼ cups olive oil

In a good-sized bowl, mix the egg yolks, lemon juice and seasoning, stirring to a smooth paste. Add the oil drop by drop, until the mixture emulsifies, then add it in a thin trickle, stirring continuously. If the mixture becomes too thick, thin it with a few drops of lemon juice. (Should the mixture curdle, break another egg yolk into a clean bowl, and beat in the curdled mixture.) Mayonnaise is laborious to make by hand, but can easily be made in a blender or food processor. It will keep for several days in an airtight container in a refrigerator.

SAUCE VERTE (GREEN MAYONNAISE)

To a basic mayonnaise, add a few finely chopped fresh herbs; alternatively, a mixture comprising a few sprigs of chervil, tarragon, watercress and a couple of spinach leaves can be pounded in a mortar and added to the mayonnaise.

CURRY MAYONNAISE

To a basic mayonnaise, made with sunflower rather than olive oil, add a little curry powder to taste, pinch by pinch.

MOUSSELINE

To a basic mayonnaise, add a crushed clove of garlic and a handful of finely chopped chives and parsley. Then fold in one or two egg whites, previously whipped until thick.

AÏOLI (GARLIC MAYONNAISE)

To a basic mayonnaise, add several cloves of crushed garlic.

SKORDALIA

Make an aïoli, as above, but substitute a floury potato, well mashed, for the egg yolk of the mayonnaise. A lighter dressing results.

PIQUANT MAYONNAISE

To a basic mayonnaise, add a little grated horseradish and some paprika. Fold in an equal quantity of whipped cream to the flavored mayonnaise.

RÉMOULADE

2 ½ cups olive oil
1 egg yolk
1 large clove garlic
2 cooked shallots, chopped
2-3 anchovy fillets
1 tbs mustard paste
1 tbs capers
parsley and chervil, chopped and
* pounded to taste*
1-3 tbs tarragon vinegar
salt and pepper

Pound all the ingredients except the egg yolk and olive oil together. Stir in the egg yolk, then add the olive oil as for mayonnaise. If the sauce becomes too thick, thin with a little tarragon vinegar, drop by drop. (The pounded yolk of a hard-boiled egg may be used instead of a raw one, making the dressing very similar to a ravigote.)

YOGURT DRESSING

1 ¼ cups yogurt
½ tbs olive oil
juice of one lemon
2 garlic cloves, crushed
a small bunch of mint, finely
* chopped*
salt and pepper

Mix the yogurt, olive oil and lemon juice together, and add the garlic, mint and seasoning. (Dill or fennel can be substituted for the mint.)

SOUR CREAM DRESSING (1)

1 tbs wine vinegar or lemon juice
1 ¼ cups sour cream
½ tsp celery seed or finely
* chopped leaf celery*

Add the vinegar or lemon juice to the other ingredients, drop by drop.

SOUR CREAM DRESSING (2)

Mix together 1 ¼ cups sour cream with one teaspoon each of fresh fennel and chopped mint. (Yogurt can be substituted for the sour cream and dill leaves for the fennel.)

GREEN DRESSING

1 ¼ cups sour cream
lemon juice
4 tbs green onions, sliced
finely chopped parsley, basil
* or sorrel*
salt and pepper

Mix the sour cream with the lemon juice, and add the onions, herbs and seasoning.

IRISH SALAD DRESSING

yolk of one hard-boiled egg
1 ¼ cups olive oil or coffee cream
a little vinegar to taste
salt and pepper
pinch of mustard

Pound the egg yolk and mix in the olive oil or cream with the vinegar. Add seasoning and mustard.

GREEN BASIL DRESSING

a handful of chopped fresh basil
2 garlic cloves, crushed
3 tbs lemon juice
½ cup olive oil

Pound the basil in a mortar with the garlic and lemon juice; add the olive oil very slowly, drop by drop as for basic mayonnaise, until a good pouring consistency is reached.

CHINESE SWEET AND SOUR DRESSING

1 tbs sugar
juice of one lemon
salt
soy sauce
1 tbs sesame oil
1 tbs wine vinegar
a little sliced fresh ginger root
pinch of sugar

Make a syrup by warming a tablespoon of sugar in a little water. Add lemon juice and salt until sweet/sour balance obtained. Mix with soy sauce, sesame oil, wine vinegar, ginger and a pinch of sugar just before serving.

CHINESE DRESSING

3 tbs olive oil
1 tbs vinegar
1 tbs soy sauce
salt and pepper
3 tbs finely chopped shallots
3 tbs thinly sliced sweet peppers
1 tbs ground sesame seeds
1 garlic clove, finely chopped

Pour the oil and vinegar into a small basin. Gradually beat in soy sauce, seasoning, shallots, peppers, sesame seeds, and garlic. (Suitable for any type of bean sprouts.)

Dips

Any of the vinaigrettes, mayonnaises or creamy dressings above can be used as a dip for crudités. The following vegetable purées are also delicious with crudités.

PURÉED EGGPLANT

Wipe an eggplant and, leaving the skin on, steam it until it is very soft. While it is still warm, squeeze out the bitter juices and excess water, and purée the flesh in a blender with a little yogurt, olive oil, lemon juice, crushed garlic, salt and pepper to taste. Flavor with fresh or dried fenugreek leaves.

PURÉED TAHINI

Purée the tahini (pounded sesame seeds, usually available from Greek or Cypriot stores) with the juice of a large lemon, crushed garlic, salt, parsley, a little olive oil and some hot water, until it emulsifies.

HUMMUS

Make a purée from 1¼ cups cooked chick peas, three tablespoons of tahini, 1¼ cups of olive oil, paprika, lemon juice, lots of crushed garlic and the liquid in which the chick peas were cooked.

YOGURT DIP

Blend freshly chopped mint, a little chopped onion, crushed garlic, a little olive oil and lemon juice with yogurt. Flavor with cucumber, if liked.

SALAD RECIPES

These are some of my favorite salad recipes. Don't be afraid to vary the ingredients and experiment with whatever vegetables and plants are available. Specific quantities are not normally given unless they are essential to the balance of the recipe.

RAW SALADS

I have divided this category into three main groups: crudités, simple salads and more complex mixed salads.

Crudités

A large number of vegetables can be used for crudités. They must always be fresh, young and of prime quality. They can be used whole, cut or diced, sliced or grated. Some may need dressing with lemon juice to prevent discoloration.

Vegetables suitable for use when raw: asparagus, asparagus peas, beets, cabbage, carrots, cauliflower, celery, Chinese artichokes, cucumbers, fennel, pickling cucumbers, iceplant, kohlrabi, mitsuba, peppers, pickling onions, radishes, sprouted seeds, sugar peas, tomatoes, 'Witloof' chicory. Vegetables suitable for use when blanched: broad beans (preferably the red-seeded varieties), beets, celeriac and green beans.

Simple salads

RED LETTUCE WITH BORAGE FLOWERS

Tear the leaves off a large, very fresh red lettuce and a green lettuce heart, toss thoroughly in a walnut oil vinaigrette and garnish with variegated mint, lemon balm and borage flowers.
(Illustrated on p.138)

CABBAGE COLESLAW

Finely shred about 450g/1lb of white cabbage and dress with mayonnaise thinned with sour cream. Strips of finely sliced red pepper can be added as a colorful garnish.

CHINESE CABBAGE COLESLAW

This makes an excellent accompaniment to duck or pork. Finely shred a medium-sized Chinese cabbage, and add a small amount of thinly sliced fresh ginger root, a crushed garlic clove, and a tablespoon of soy or Tamari sauce. Toss with a vinaigrette made with sesame oil and wine vinegar. (Suitable also for any oriental brassicas, spinach or chard.)

ORIENTAL VEGETABLES

This is a very flexible recipe. Use any sharp-flavored leaves, such as oriental mustards, torn or shredded into small pieces, with leafy 'Pak Choi', shungiku and mitsuba stems. Incorporate a few mild-flavored leaves like purslane and claytonia for a contrast. Mix them together and toss in a large bowl with a thick vinaigrette, which will cling to the glossy leaves. Garnish with chopped fresh herbs or the flowers of Chinese chives.

'SUGAR LOAF' CHICORY SEEDLINGS

A refreshing early spring salad. Mix chicory seedlings with a small quantity of finely chopped or sifted hard-boiled egg. Eat plain or with a light vinaigrette dressing.

RED CHICORY AND 'SUGAR LOAF' CHICORY

Tear the larger leaves of a head of red and a head of 'Sugar Loaf' chicory into manageable pieces, but keep the smaller central leaves whole. Dress with a well-flavored vinaigrette, into which a tablespoon of yogurt or thin cream has been beaten. (Suitable also for lettuce hearts and endive.)

'WITLOOF' CHICORY AND ORANGE

This is a delicious salad incorporating an interesting contrast of flavors and textures. It hardly needs a dressing – just a sprinkling of light vinaigrette.

Arrange the spears of a couple of crisp 'Witloof' chicons like flower petals on a round plate. Slice a mild Spanish onion and two peeled, seedless oranges as thinly as possible and arrange in the center, with some whole ripe olives. Garnish with chopped coriander. (Suitable also for 'Sugar Loaf' chicory and curly-leaved endive.)

'WITLOOF' CHICORY WITH PIQUANT MAYONNAISE

Finely slice 'Witloof' chicons, and dress them with horseradish-flavored mayonnaise. Garnish with chopped parsley, chervil or winter savory.

ENDIVE, WATERCRESS AND ORANGE

Remove the leaves from a curly-leaved endive and a bunch of fresh watercress, and crisp them in the refrigerator for several hours. Make a vinaigrette with olive or walnut oil, mustard, garlic, lemon juice and the zest of a large seedless orange. Remove the orange pith and slice the flesh thinly, or divide the orange into segments and add to the watercress and endive. Toss the ingredients well in the dressing before serving.

PURSLANE AND FLOWERS

Arrange young purslane in a flattish bowl and add some chicory, nasturtium and bergamot flowers and a few rose petals. Sprinkle with chives, marjoram, and green and purple basil, and decorate with a few red currant sprigs. Splash with a light vinaigrette, made with walnut oil rather than olive oil, just before serving. Succulent yellow-green purslane leaves make a perfect foil for flowers. *(Illustrated on p.138)*

SALADE LORETTE

Mix several heads of corn salad with about the same amount each of thinly sliced celery and sliced or chopped boiled beet. Dress with vinaigrette. (Celeriac could be substituted for the celery, if wished.)

ICEPLANT WITH RASPBERRY VINEGAR DRESSING

Arrange iceplant in a dish and toss with a vinaigrette made with raspberry vinegar and walnut oil – it makes a lovely contrast in flavors.

RAW SPINACH

Use young and tender spinach leaves. As they tend to be gritty, wash them well, shaking dry before chilling. Make a vinaigrette well-flavored with garlic and mustard, and pour over the leaves. Garnish with quartered, hard-boiled eggs and sliced onion. (Suitable for all types of spinach, sorrel and amaranthus, or for lettuce and spinach mixed in equal quantities.)

DANDELION

Tear the green leaves of dandelions into small pieces and mix with equal quantities of blanched dandelion, endive or 'Witloof' chicory leaves. Rub the salad bowl with garlic before adding the mixed leaves and toss with a vinaigrette dressing. Garnish with olives. (Suitable also for sorrel, Mediterranean rocket, young spinach leaves, 'Sugar Loaf', red and wild chicory.)

SORREL, DANDELION AND RED LETTUCE

Toss torn leaves of more or less equal quantities of dandelion and lettuce in a garlic-flavored vinaigrette. Garnish with a few dried olives and some toasted sesame seeds.

LAND CRESS

To a bunch of land cress add some sliced radishes and a few chopped stalks of celery. Arrange the cress in a dish, with the radishes and celery mixed together in the center. Pour over a vinaigrette to which plenty of ground black pepper and a teaspoon of soy sauce has been added.

MEDITERRANEAN ROCKET, PURSLANE AND BROAD BEANS

Mix a few handfuls of rocket leaves with a handful of purslane leaves and a small quantity of very small blanched broad beans. Dress with a vinaigrette made with good olive oil. Garnish with a little sifted or chopped hard-boiled egg.

WATERCRESS WITH SOUR CREAM DRESSING

Watercress has such a sharp peppery taste that it normally requires little dressing. It is, however, good with a sour cream dressing, and when combined with claytonia. Crisp the watercress in the refrigerator beforehand.

FENNEL, AVOCADO AND PINK GRAPEFRUIT SALAD

Slice a large bulb of fennel thinly; cut a couple of ripe, but not too soft, avocados into strips (acidulate with lemon to prevent discoloration). Remove pith from two grapefruits and divide them into segments. Arrange the ingredients in circles on a shallow dish, and garnish with watercress and fennel fronds, if available. Sprinkle with a raspberry-flavored dressing made with walnut rather than olive oil. Chill before serving.

CELERY AND FENNEL

Although celery is generally best as a crudité or served with cheese, it is also good in salads. Finely slice a few celery stalks and a large bulb of fennel and mix together. Dress them with a vinaigrette incorporating a few tablespoons of blue-veined cheese.

CELERIAC RÉMOULADE

Peel one good celeriac, cut it into large pieces and blanch them (in boiling water with vinegar or lemon juice). Drain and shred the celeriac, dress with a rémoulade and garnish with chopped capers and sweet dill pickles. (Suitable also for salsify, black salsify, kohlrabi and cardoon.)

CUCUMBER SALAD

Choose a medium-sized cucumber. Peel it if you dislike the skin and slice it fairly thinly (but not too thinly). Arrange on a flat dish, sprinkle with fine salt and leave for an hour. Then drain and rinse with cold water, draining again and patting dry on a paper towel. Arrange on a shallow dish and pour over a yogurt dressing flavored with chopped mint and garlic, or a sour cream and dill dressing, and chill well before serving.

CUCUMBERS AND NASTURTIUM LEAVES

Mix peeled, sliced cucumber with plenty of small, variegated and red nasturtium leaves. Dress with a mustard-flavored vinaigrette and garnish with a few nasturtium flowers and buds.

TOMATOES WITH PESTO DRESSING

This is one of the simplest but very best ways of serving tomatoes. Cut well-flavored tomatoes into fairly thick slices. Cover with a pesto dressing made of olive oil, lemon juice, salt, a pinch of sugar, and a tablespoon of equal quantities of chopped basil and chopped chives and a large crushed garlic clove. (The tomatoes can also be dressed simply with olive oil flavored with salt, pepper and marjoram or coriander.)

HUNGARIAN TOMATO SALAD

Use small sweet tomatoes. Skin them (by dropping them into boiling water for a minute) and chill. Make a piquant mayonnaise. Place the tomatoes whole on lettuce leaves and cover with the mayonnaise. Garnish with a little paprika and chives.

PEPPER SALAD

Arrange rings of different-colored peppers on a bed of crisp lettuce leaves. Garnish with olives, coriander leaves and quarters of tomato. Pour over a vinaigrette made with good olive oil and plenty of garlic. *(Illustrated on p.139)*

WINTER RADISH

Although summer radishes are best eaten whole as crudités, winter radishes can be grated and mixed with a mayonnaise dressing. (Alternatively, lightly stir-fry the radishes and incorporate them into any recipes for Chinese vegetables.)

PLAIN CARROT

Finely grated carrots are excellent dressed with a vinaigrette flavored with chopped chervil, chives, parsley or fennel and salt.

ZUCCHINI AND RED LETTUCE

Thinly slice a few very young zucchini (those with different colored skins look particularly attractive) and arrange them on a bed of red lettuce. Dress with a light vinaigrette and garnish with chopped red sweet pepper, onion and broad-leaved parsley, and a few ripe olives. *(Illustrated on p.137)*

RAW CAULIFLOWER

Grate a very fresh small raw cauliflower. Finely chop a few carrots, a small bunch of parsley, a bunch of scallions and a bunch of chives; slice a few radishes into thin circles. Mix together with a bunch of watercress and toss well with vinaigrette. Scatter with fresh chervil before serving.

CAULIFLOWER AND HYSSOP

Mix a fresh cauliflower broken into florets with one tablespoon each of finely chopped hyssop and parsley and a chopped apple and chopped carrot. Toss well with a simple yogurt dressing.

GLASSWORT

Very freshly picked, clean young glasswort can be eaten raw. If it is muddy, wash it *very* thoroughly. Blanch it in boiling water for a minute, drain it, arrange on a plate and dress with vinaigrette made with olive oil and lemon juice. Garnish with sifted hard-boiled egg and bronze fennel. Serve with wedges of lemon.

FLOWER SALAD

Wash and dry a curly-leaved endive. Cut into very thin strips. Add a tablespoon each of finely chopped celery leaves and parsley, and some olives. Toss in a plain vinaigrette. Finally add plenty of violet and/or pansy petals and mix gently into the salad before serving.

Mixed salads

GREEK SALAD

1 crisp lettuce
a small bunch of broad-leaved
 parsley
a handful of corn salad
3 tomatoes, quartered
fresh basil
1 cup crumbled feta cheese
a few ripe olives
half a sweet pepper
2 small onions

Tear the lettuce and parsley, leave the corn salad leaves whole and thinly slice the sweet pepper and onions. Add the rest of the ingredients, and toss in a garlic-flavored vinaigrette made with

olive oil. Garnish with chopped fresh herbs. (Suitable also with cucumber and purslane included in the mixture.)

MIXED CABBAGE

Equal quantities of red cabbage, Chinese cabbage, kohlrabi, and fennel
Finely chopped scallions, red peppers, and toasted sesame seeds, to garnish

Shred the red and Chinese cabbage finely, cut the kohlrabi and fennel into julienne strips. Toss thoroughly in a full-flavored vinaigrette or a thin mayonnaise. Garnish with finely chopped scallions, red peppers, and toasted sesame seeds. *(Illustrated on p.138)*

RAW VEGETABLES WITH GREEN DRESSING

Equal quantities of baby carrots, baby turnips, baby beets and radishes
2 kohlrabi
a handful of crisp lettuce leaves

Shred the baby vegetables and the kohlrabi, doing the beets last to avoid staining the other vegetables. Toss each vegetable separately in vinaigrette. Line a shallow bowl with lettuce, and carefully place separate piles of vegetables on top.

PORTUGUESE TOMATO SALAD

450g/1lb tomatoes
1 large onion
a bunch of coriander, finely chopped
2 large garlic cloves, crushed

Slice tomatoes thickly and the onion finely and put in a salad bowl with the coriander and garlic. Pour vinaigrette over, and mix well.

ONION, CARROT, HAMBURG PARSLEY AND MINT

1 small onion, sliced or grated
1 cup fresh mint leaves
2 heaped tbs grated carrot
2 heaped tbs grated turnip-rooted parsley
a little lemon juice
salt and pepper

Pound the onion finely with the mint. Add grated carrot and turnip-rooted parsley. Mix well, and add lemon juice, salt and pepper.

MARIE STONE'S MIXED VEGETABLE SALAD

Equal quantities of carrots, turnips, celeriac, Jerusalem artichokes, kohlrabi, beets, hearts of red and white cabbage, radishes, and seakale.

This salad looks most pleasing if the vegetables are carefully cut small and then blanched. Dress with a generous quantity of vinaigrette, cream dressing or mayonnaise.

KOREAN BEANSPROUTS SALAD WITH CHINESE DRESSING

Put some mung beansprouts in a large salad bowl, pour in the Chinese dressing (see p.151) and gently toss the sprouts until they are evenly covered. Chill thoroughly before serving. (Suitable also for sprouted seeds.)

COOKED SALADS

CHARD WITH BUTTERMILK DRESSING

Wash about 900g/2lb chard well, drain and cut roughly into fairly thick slices, using the white part as well as the green. Steam for a few minutes until tender. Drain very well, put in a shallow dish and season well. Mix with a buttermilk dressing and garnish with a pinch of cayenne, chopped chives, and dill seed.
(Suitable also for any of the spinaches.)

TURKISH BEET SALAD WITH YOGURT

Boil or bake four beets until tender; cool and then rub off the skins carefully. Slice or dice the beets, season with salt and pepper and arrange in a dish. Beat 1¼ cups yogurt with crushed garlic, a little salt and a few caraway seeds and pour over the beets. Garnish with paprika.

POTATOES

All potato salads are best made with small, yellow or waxy potatoes. They should always be cooked with the skins on and peeled while still warm. Potatoes can be dressed according to taste, but vinaigrette dressings are best added while the potatoes are still hot. Cube or slice the potatoes evenly, and turn gently in the dressing. 'Extras' such as olives, chopped scallions, crushed garlic or herbs may be added later when the salad is at room temperature. Potato salads do not chill well, nor do they keep well in a refrigerator. If a mayonnaise or sour cream dressing is preferred, add a little vinaigrette when the potatoes are hot, then add the dressing later. Sliced salami, sausage, cooked ham, flaked tuna or chopped egg may be added to a potato salad along with the mayonnaise or sour cream dressing. A good ravigote sauce or anchovy-flavored mayonnaise is excellent with potato salad. Potato salads make a suitable accompaniment to a main dish, particularly when served with a green salad.

POTATO AND DANDELION

Thinly slice some cooked potatoes while still hot, and season. Add some chopped shallots and torn dandelion leaves. While still hot, pour on a generous amount of vinaigrette, well-flavored with Dijon mustard and garlic. Garnish with chopped chives and dill. Delicious hot or cold.

SALADE CRESSONIÈRE

The potatoes are prepared as above, and mixed with a bunch of watercress, and some chopped parsley, chervil and hard-boiled egg, dressed with vinaigrette.

HOT POTATO SALAD

6 good-sized cooked waxy yellow potatoes
2 bunches scallions, finely chopped
2 cups mayonnaise
3 tbs Dijon mustard
1 tbs grated horseradish
1 celery heart, chopped
seasoning of salt, pepper, and paprika to taste

Cube the potatoes while still hot. Mix them with the chopped scallions – green and white parts – and seasoning. In a pan stir together the mayonnaise, mustard and horseradish, and heat for two or three minutes; add the celery and pour the sauce over the potatoes. Finely chopped hot bacon may be added – it should be mixed in well with the other ingredients. Sprinkle with paprika before serving.

PARSNIP SALAD

Peel three or four parsnips and cook them until just tender. Remove the core and slice the parsnips into thinnish rings. Lay in rows on a flat plate and, while still warm, dress with a vinaigrette made with olive oil and lemon juice. Garnish with parsley, decorate with capers and peppercorns, and serve after an hour or so, when the flavors have had a chance to mingle.
(Suitable also for most cooked root vegetables such as celeriac, salsify, black salsify, turnip-rooted parsley and Jerusalem artichokes.)

CHINESE ARTICHOKES

Scrub the tubers (which are normally very small) and cook them in boiling salted water for a few minutes or fry them lightly, or steam them until just soft. Cool and serve with a well-flavored vinaigrette or light creamy dressing, and garnish with chopped green herbs.

SUMMER TOURANGELLE

225g/½lb green beans
350g/¾lb potatoes, cooked
60g/2oz carrots, blanched
60g/2oz kohlrabi, grated

Boil the beans, cut diagonally into 2.5cm/1in pieces, in salted water until tender. Drain and refresh with cold water. Cut the potatoes and carrots into julienne strips. Mix the ingredients together and moisten with some mayonnaise, thinned with a little boiling water. Arrange in a salad bowl and coat with the unthinned remainder of mayonnaise.

WINTER TOURANGELLE

Make as above, using celery, blanched celeriac, or blanched winter radish instead of beans.

JERUSALEM ARTICHOKES

Scrub a few artichokes very well. Then boil them in salted water until just tender. Drain and peel them while still very hot or, if preferred, leave them unpeeled. Slice them evenly and dress them while still warm with a ravigote sauce or a vinaigrette to which a little tomato purée has been added.

FRESH PEA AND GREEN BEAN SALAD

Cook equal quantities of whole sugar pea pods, shelled green peas, chopped green beans and diced carrots until just tender. Line a bowl with chilled red lettuce and arrange the vegetables on top. Make a sour cream or yogurt dressing flavored with mint and garlic. Mix well and pour over salad. Garnish with a few finely chopped dill or fennel leaves.

ITALIAN GREEN BEAN SALAD

Cook the green beans until barely tender, drain, season and mix with a vinaigrette and some chopped onion. Leave to cool before serving piled on lettuce leaves, and garnished with chopped hard-boiled egg, Parmesan cheese, and some chopped fresh coriander, parsley, basil and marjoram. For a more substantial dish, add quarters of hard-boiled egg and a few olives.

DRIED AND FRESH BEAN SALAD

Any attractive combination of dried beans, such as flageolet, pinto, Dutch and blackeye, can be used. Soak them overnight in separate containers, and cook separately until soft but not mushy. Drain them and mix with an equal quantity of lightly cooked fresh beans (broad, fava, runner and green). Dress while still warm with a vinaigrette made with olive oil and flavored with garlic.
(Illustrated on p.140)

ASPARAGUS SALAD

Tie about 450g/1lb of young, well-trimmed and scrubbed asparagus into bundles. Cook in boiling salted water until tender. Dress with a light tarragon-flavored mayonnaise or a vinaigrette flavored with fennel leaves.

WELSH ONIONS AND SCALLIONS

Wash and trim a bunch of scallions, tie them into a bundle, cook them in boiling salted water until just tender. Chop a bunch of Welsh onions and steam them, also until just tender. Dress both when nearly cool with a vinaigrette well flavored with herbs. Serve on a flat dish and garnish with chopped chervil and tarragon.

EGGPLANT AND YOGURT SALAD

Slice an eggplant thinly and sprinkle it with salt. Leave for about half an hour, to ensure that the bitter flavor is completely removed, then wash off the salt. Squeeze out any excess moisture. Drain and pat dry on paper towels and fry until crisp in olive oil. Place on a flattish dish and pour over a dressing made with yogurt, lemon juice, a little olive oil, a pinch of fenugreek leaves (dried or fresh) and a large clove of garlic. Sprinkle with sumac or paprika.
(Illustrated on p.141)

GLOBE ARTICHOKE SALAD

Prepare the artichokes, rubbing any cut surface with lemon to prevent discoloration. Cook in boiling water until soft, 15-20 minutes depending on size. Remove the outer leaves, then the pale central leaves, then the hairy

part from the 'choke'. Drain and cool. Dress with a garlic-flavored vinaigrette, and decorate with parsley, a little chopped hard-boiled egg and capers.

CARDOONS

The blanched stems can be cut into 8cm/3in lengths, tied in bundles like asparagus, and cooked in the same way until tender. Cool, and serve with a piquant rémoulade sauce, or a thick vinaigrette made with plenty of mustard.

Salads with hot dressings, and hot salads

GREEN SALAD WITH HOT DRESSING

Equal quantities of red lettuce, spinach and sorrel, endive, dandelion, and very young beet tops
a few slices of crispy bacon
a few pumpkin seeds
wine vinegar
croûtons

Choose leaves as small as possible, or tear them if large. Place in a glass bowl. To make the dressing, cube bacon slices and cook in a pan until the fat runs; take out the crispy bits, add to the salad. Add a little wine vinegar and pumpkin seeds to the fat in the pan, and cook for two minutes. Then pour over the salad. Decorate with croûtons. Serve immediately. (Suitable also for any bitter leaves such as chicory. The vegetables can be on their own or mixed.)
(Illustrated on p.144)

ENDIVES IN BAGNA CALDA

A Piedmontese method, literally a 'warm bath'. Warm together 300g/10½oz anchovy fillets, 6

crushed large garlic cloves, 1 cup each of olive oil and butter. Shred the endives very finely. Pour the *bagna calda* over them. Cover tightly. Eat when cold. (Suitable also for any other bitter leaves and for sweet peppers, with the skins removed. If charred under a hot broiler, the skins will peel off easily.)

COMPOSE SALADS

SALADE NIÇOISE

450g/½lb green beans, lightly cooked
450g/½lb cooked new potatoes, sliced
1 crisp lettuce heart
4 tomatoes, quartered
some ripe olives
a few quartered hard-boiled eggs
1 small can tuna fish, drained
a few anchovy fillets

Put the prepared vegetables in a bowl, and arrange the olives, egg, tuna fish and anchovies on top. Add a vinaigrette made with full flavored olive oil and plenty of garlic.

PROVENÇALE TOMATOES WITH PAIN BAGNA

This looks best made with a mixture of yellow and red tomatoes, and is excellent for picnics. Pound some garlic, parsley stalks and tops, basil, lemon thyme, and olive oil in a mortar to a smooth paste. Scoop out the insides of the tomatoes, add them to the paste, and stuff the mixture back into the tomatoes. Chill for several hours and serve with *pain bagna*. To make *pain bagna*: cut a thick French loaf in half, and soak it in olive oil for an hour or so until it is quite spongy. Strain off the oil, rub the bread with garlic. Spread the bottom with tomato sauce or ratatouille, then cover it with the top half. Place under a weighted plate and leave overnight.

TOMATO AND MOZZARELLA

Beefsteak tomatoes are well suited to this recipe. Slice a few large firm ones with an equal quantity of sliced Mozzarella cheese. Arrange in alternate layers and pour over a green basil dressing. Garnish with fresh basil leaves.
(Illustrated on p.142)

BEET AND BUCKWHEAT SALAD

Cook a small round red beet and a small yellow beet, each weighing about 225g/½lb, in salted water until tender. Cook 3½ cups roasted buckwheat in water for about 10 minutes. Drain. Steam fresh chopped beet stalks until tender. Then stir-fry torn beet tops with scallions, ginger, garlic, and chives, for two minutes; then add soy sauce. Arrange the stalks on top of the buckwheat. Cube the beets or cut into thin circles. Dress with a garlicky vinaigrette and arrange on the top of the salad. The dish may be decorated with chopped coriander or parsley.
(Illustrated on p.143)

BEAN AND PASTA SALAD

450g/1lb fresh green, white and pink tagliatelle – equal quantities each color
equal quantities of broad beans, sugar peas, and green peas
garlic mayonnaise
fresh basil, fennel, tarragon

Cook the pasta *al dente*. Blanch the broad beans, sugar peas and green peas. When the pasta is cooked, season and moisten with olive oil, then add the garlic

mayonnaise, mix well and arrange on a platter to display the different colors of pasta. Scatter the vegetables on top. Sprinkle with olive oil and garnish with chopped herbs.
(Illustrated on p.143)

MARINATED SALADS

SALADE MAROCAINE

Chop a large onion and thinly slice about 900g/2lb red and green peppers. Fry in the olive oil until just soft, then add a little tomato paste, about 900g/2lb skinned tomatoes, plenty of crushed garlic, and a little paprika (sweet and piquant, if available), cumin, salt and pepper. Cook for about 10 minutes. Cool, then add lemon juice. When ready to serve, cover with chopped fresh coriander, parsley, mixed olives, and lemon wedges (or a piece of Moroccan preserved lemon).

MARINATED PEPPERS

Peppers (a mixture of different colors)
olive oil
3 large garlic cloves, crushed
salt and pepper
fresh coriander, cumin, and paprika to taste

Put the peppers under the broiler at midheat. Keep turning until skin is black and blistered, and the insides are well cooked. Remove from broiler and wrap in paper towels for 10 minutes. The skins will then come off very easily. Cut in half, remove seeds and chop into thin strips. Add salt and pepper, a little coriander, cumin and paprika. Mix the olive oil with the garlic and pour it over the peppers. Leave them to marinate overnight, or for 24

hours. Serve garnished with chopped parsley and lemon wedges.
(Suitable also for eggplants.)

PICKLING ONION SALAD

60-80 small pickling onions
a little olive oil
1¼ cups white wine
1 tbs wine vinegar
bay leaf
bunch of thyme
6 whole cloves of garlic
1½ heaped tbs tomato paste
salt and black pepper
chopped fresh parsley and watercress sprigs, to garnish

Peel the onions, cook for a few minutes in a little oil, then add the wine, vinegar, herbs and garlic. Simmer until the onions are cooked but not falling apart. Add tomato paste and seasoning, then cook for another 15 minutes on a low heat. Turn the mixture into a glass dish and chill for several hours, then serve garnished with chopped parsley and sprigs of watercress.

MARINATED LEEK SALAD

1 bunch thin leeks, finely chopped
1¼ cups olive oil
1 garlic clove
juice of one lemon
salt and pepper
chopped parsley
green and ripe olives

Slice the leeks thinly, including the green part. Wash well to remove soil. Dry in a salad spinner. Steam until tender but not soggy. Mix olive oil, garlic, lemon juice, salt and pepper together and pour over leeks in a shallow dish, while still hot, and marinate for several hours before serving. Garnish with chopped parsley and olives.
(The same marinade is excellent with raw grated carrots.)

PICKLES

AMERICAN DILL PICKLES

In a large sterilized jar, put a clove of garlic, six peppercorns, a clove and a sprig of dill with seeds. Then scrub thoroughly and dry well a sufficient number of small or pickling cucumbers to fill the jar. Pack them closely together. To make the pickling vinegar, bring 2½ pints cider vinegar, mixed with 1¼ pints water and ⅓cup coarse salt, to the boil. Allow the vinegar to cool down before pouring it over the cucumbers, to fill the jar. Seal the jar and leave for at least five days before using.

PICKLED RADISH PODS

Make a brine by dissolving ⅓ cup salt in 1¼ pints water. Next bring the brine to the boil and turn off the heat. Then drop the radish pods into the hot brine and leave them to cool. Drain them well and pack them into sterilized jars. Cover with white vinegar (spiced if preferred) and seal the jars.

PICKLED FLOWERS

This is very successful with salsify, black salsify and chicory flowers. Lay the flowers down in layers in a sterilized container and cover each layer with sugar. Pack them down firmly and cover with cider vinegar that has previously been boiled up and allowed to cool. Seal the container and leave for about four days before using.

APPENDIX

SPECIAL SITUATIONS

Some plants are more tolerant than others of particular conditions. In the lists that follow, plants that thrive in semishaded, dry or moist conditions are given. A list of plants that can be grown in containers is also included.

Semi-shaded
These plants tolerate semishaded positions, provided they have adequate moisture:

Angelica
Balm
Chickweed
Chives
Endive
Good King Henry
Hamburg parsley
Japanese mustard 'Mizuna'
Jerusalem artichoke
Kohlrabi
Land cress
Mint
Mitsuba
Parsnip
Shungiku
Sorrel
Sweet cicely
IN SUMMER ONLY
Chard
Chervil
Coriander
Cress
Lettuce
Parsley
Peas
Radish
Spinach

Dry conditions
These plants can tolerate fairly dry conditions:

Alfalfa
Balm
Basil
Calendula officinalis
Claytonia
Iceplant
Kohlrabi
Lavender
Leaf amaranthus
Nasturtium
Pickling onions
Purslane
Sage
Salad burnet
Clary sage
Sweetcorn
Thymes

Moist conditions
The following tolerate moist conditions provided they are not waterlogged:

Balm
Celeriac
Celery
Chicory ('Grumolo', red and 'Spadona')
Chinese cabbage
Corn salad
Fennel
Jerusalem artichoke
Land cress
Leek
Mint
Mitsuba
Sweet bergamot
Watercress

Containers
These plants are suitable for containers, provided the containers are of an adequate size. Other plants can, of course, be grown in containers, but apart from herbs, which are useful over a long period, containers are best used for plants that give quick returns, either because they mature rapidly or have a relatively short season:

Basil
Carrots (short varieties)
Celery, leaf
Chervil
Chives, Chinese and garden
Endive, curly-leaved
Iceplant
Lettuce ('Little Gem', 'Salad Bowl' types and 'Tom Thumb' are the most suitable)
Marjoram
Onions, spring and everlasting
Peppers
Purslane
Radish, summer
Savory, summer and winter
Shungiku
Thymes
Tomatoes

THESE SEEDLING CROPS CAN BE GROWN IN CONTAINERS:
Abyssinian cabbage 'Karate'
Chicory, 'Sugar Loaf'
Claytonia
Coriander
Cress
Endive
Lettuce
Mediterranean rocket
Mustard
Radish
Salad rape
Spinach
Turnip

'SALADINI' CROPS

The salad lover wants fresh salad all year round. The ideal 'saladini' type of salad needs a bulky crop as the backbone, plus a few interesting or sharp-flavoured leaves, some bland leaves, something crisp and something colorful or decorative. The lists overleaf give some plants in each category and the season for which they can be grown. They are based on experience in the author's garden where winter temperatures generally fall to about −10°C/14°F and the mean midsummer temperature is around 15°C/59°F. In colder areas, winter cover would be essential for the winter crops suggested here; in warmer areas the summer crops could be grown in late spring and autumn, and the autumn and spring crops throughout the winter and so on.

In addition, seedling crops of garden cress, mustard, salad rape and coriander can be grown on windowsills all year round; sprouted seeds can also be grown indoors all year round.

The lists are a rough guide only. There is a tremendous variation from one season to the next. For other plants and full cultural information on those listed, see Salad plants, p.58-132. The plants are listed here in the order in which they appear in the main text.

It is suggested that beginners should start with just a couple of plants from each group and extend their range as they gain experience and confidence. A short list of easily grown crops is given below.

Easily grown salad crops
Lettuce: 'Salad Bowl' varieties
Brassicas: Abyssinian cabbage 'Karate', 'Mizuna'
Seedling crops: 'Sugar Loaf' chicory, curly-leaved endive, salad rape, turnip, garden cress, white mustard, rocket
Flowers: Bellis perennis, Calendula officinalis, nasturtium
For seed sprouting: alfalfa, lentils, mung beans, radish

PLANTS FOR 'SALADINI'

BULKY	SHARP AND/OR DISTINCTLY FLAVOURED	MILD AND/OR CRISP-TEXTURED	COLOURFUL AND/OR ORNAMENTAL	BULKY	SHARP AND/OR DISTINCTLY FLAVOURED	MILD AND/OR CRISP-TEXTURED	COLOURFUL AND/OR ORNAMENTAL
For spring Lettuce, 'Little Gem', overwintered varieties Chicory, 'Sugar Loaf', red, 'Witloof' Endive, broad-leaved curly-leaved Cabbage, spring, 'Dutch winter white', Chinese* Claytonia	Chicory, all mature types, 'Sugar Loaf' seedlings Curly kale Hardy leafy oriental mustards Other hardy oriental brassicas Spinach/chard Sorrel Shungiku Coriander Cress, garden, land Dandelion Rocket White mustard Celeriac Hardy green onions Radish, summer, winter	Lettuce seedlings Chinese cabbage* Abyssinian cabbage 'Karate' Corn salad Claytonia Rape Seakale Leaf celery Radish, seedlings, pods Hardy roots Sugar peas Chickweed	Lettuce, 'Salad Bowl' varieties, red overwintered varieties Red chicory Cabbage, red, ornamental Kale, 'Ragged Jack', ornamental Flowering oriental mustards Salad burnet Bronze fennel Flowers, *Bellis perennis, Calendula officinalis, Viola spp.*	**For autumn** Lettuce, 'Little Gem', autumn varieties Chicory, 'Sugar Loaf', red Endive, broad-leaved, curly-leaved Cabbage, red, 'Dutch winter white', ornamental, Chinese Oriental brassicas Oriental leafy mustards	Green chicories Curly kale 'Mizuna' Spinach/chard Sorrel Shungiku Coriander Cress, garden, land Dandelion Rocket White mustard Fennel Celeriac Radish, summer, winter, pods Chinese chives	Abyssinian cabbage 'Karate' Corn salad Iceplant Purslane Claytonia Salad rape Fennel Kohlrabi Celery, leaf, self-blanching, trench Cucumber Carrots Hardy root crops Chickweed	Lettuce, 'Salad Bowl' varieties, other red varieties Red chicory Cabbage, red, ornamental Kale, ornamental 'Ragged Jack' Flowering oriental mustards Yellow and ornamental tomatoes Peppers Salad burnet Flowers, *Bellis perennis,* borage, *Calendula officinalis,* nasturtium
For summer Lettuce, 'Little Gem', summer varieties Endive, broad-leaved, curly-leaved Cabbage, summer varieties, red, Chinese Claytonia	Seedlings of 'Sugar Loaf' chicory, curly endive, rocket, garden cress, white mustard, coriander, turnip 'Mizuna' Shungiku Land cress Fennel Spinach/chard Sorrel Radish, summer, pods Scallions Chinese chives Field penny cress	Lettuce seedlings Chinese cabbage Abyssinian cabbage 'Karate' Alfalfa Corn salad Iceplant Purslane Salad rape Celery, leaf, self blanching Kohlrabi Cucumber Carrots Chickweed Fat hen	Lettuce, 'Salad Bowl' varieties, other red lettuces Red cabbage Peppers Yellow and ornamental tomatoes Bronze fennel Flowers, *Bellis perennis,* borage, *Calendula officinalis,* nasturtium, rose, *Viola spp.* Variegated and red nasturtium leaves	**For winter** Winter lettuce Chicory, all green types, red, 'Witloof' Endive, broad-leaved, curly-leaved Cabbage, red, savoy, 'Dutch winter white', ornamental Chinese*	All chicories Curly kale Hardy oriental mustards Spinach/chard Coriander* Cress, garden,* land, hairy bitter Dandelion Rocket* White mustard* Leaf celery* Celeriac Winter radish	Cabbage, Chinese* Abyssinian cabbage 'Karate' Corn salad Claytonia* Salad rape* Celery, trench Hardy root crops Salad burnet Chickweed	Coloured winter lettuce Red chicory Cabbage, red, ornamental Flowering mustard flowers* Flowers, *Bellis perennis Viola spp.*

Plants for saladini (left)
Note: Plants requiring cover for satisfactory overwintering are marked with an asterisk.
Colored varieties of lettuce, marked with a double asterisk, include: 'Brune d'Hiver', 'Continuity', 'Marvel of Four Seasons', 'Red Lollo', 'Red Oak-leaved', 'Red Salad Bowl', 'Rossa Friulana' and 'Trotzkopf'.

Crop facts (right)
Note: *Normally grown from tubers
Fertility index denotes crop requirements: **1** moderate fertility; **2** fertile; **3** highly fertile. Germination temperature denotes the range within which seeds will germinate.

CROP FACTS

CROP	VITAMIN CONTENT	SEED LIFE (YRS.)	GERMINATION TEMPERATURE °C/°F	FERTILITY INDEX
Lettuce	A, B_1, B_6, C, E	5-7	5-17/41-63	3
Chicory, leaf	A, B_1, C	6-8	5-19/41-66	1-2
Chicory, forced	A, B_1	6-8	5-17/41-63	2-3
Endive	A, B_1, B_2, C	7-8	5-20/41-68	3
Cabbage	A, B_1, B_2, B_6, C	5	5-20/41-68	2-3
Oriental mustard	A, B_1, B_2, B_6, C	5-6	5-18/41-64	2-3
Spinach, true	A, B_1, B_2, C	4-5	5-20/41-68	3
Sorrel	A, B_1, C	6-7	5-16/41-61	2
Alfalfa (sprouted)	A, B_1, B_{12}, C, D, E, K, U	2-3	7-19/45-66	–
Corn salad	B_1, C	4	6-20/43-68	2
Cress, land	B_1, C	2	7-18/45-64	2-3
garden	B_1, C	2-3	7-21/45-70	1-2
Watercress	B_1, C	3	7-16/45-61	1-2
Dandelion	A, B_1	2	7-16/45-61	2-3
Florence fennel	B_1, C	4	5-21/41-70	2-3
Kohlrabi	A, B_1, C	6	5-21/41-70	2
Seakale, forced shoots	B_1	3-4	5-16/41-61	2
Mitsuba	B_1, C	2-3	5-15/41-59	2
Celery	A, B_1, B_2, C	2-3	10-23/50-73	2-3
Celeriac	A, B_1, B_2	5	10-21/50-70	3
Tomato	A, B_1, B_2, B_6, C	6	10-21/50-70	3
Cucumber	B_1, C	4-5	13-23/55-73	3
Peppers, sweet	A, C	3-4	15-25/59-77	2-3
Onion	B_1, B_2, B_6, C	3-4	10-18/50-64	3
Radish	A, B_1, B_2, B_6, C	5	4-15/39-59	1-2
Beetroot	B_1, B_2, C	2-3	7-18/45-64	2
Parsnip	A, B_1, C	2	5-15/41-59	2
Turnip-rooted parsley	A, B_1, C	2	5-16/41-61	2
Salsify	B_1, C	5	5-16/41-61	2
Carrot	A, B, B_2, B_6, C, E	3	5-18/41-64	2
Peas, garden	A, B_1, B_2, C	3	4-18/39-64	2
Beans, broad	A, B_1, B_2, C	3-4	4-18/39-64	2
dwarf	A, B_1, B_2, C	3	10-20/50-68	2
runner	A, B_1, B_2, C	3	13-22/55-71	2-3
Potato	A, B_1, B_2, C, D	– See note *	–	2-3
Aubergine	B_1, B_2, C	5	13-23/55-73	2
Calabrese	A, B_1, B_2, B_6, C	5-7	5-18/41-64	3
Cauliflowers	A, B_1, B_2, B_6, C		7-18/45-64	3
Zucchini	B_1, B_6, C	4	13-20/55-68	3
Leek	B_1, C	2-3	7-18/45-64	2
Sweetcorn	A, B_1, B_2, C	3-4	13-20/55-68	2
Parsley	A, C	2	5-18/41-64	2

GLOSSARY

Acid (soil) Deficient in lime. Soil-testing kits can be used to measure the degree of acidity on the pH scale, which ranges from pH1 (very extreme acidity) to pH14 (very extreme alkalinity). The neutral point is pH7. Overacidity is harmful to plant growth and is remedied by the addition of some form of lime. It occurs mostly on peat soils, on some sandy soils, and in areas of high rainfall.

Alkaline (soil) Soils with a high lime or calcium content. High alkalinity, which is much less common than high acidity (see above), can, where necessary, be corrected slowly by measures such as the addition of sulfur.

Annual Plant that grows from seed and completes its lifecycle in less than 12 months.

Axil Angle between a leaf stalk and its parent stem, at which point buds and new stems arise.

Base dressing Fertilizer worked into the soil prior to sowing or planting.

Biennial Plant whose lifecycle spans two years. The seed germinates and grows into a leafy tuft or rosette the first year, then the plant flowers, seeds and dies in the following year.

Blanch (gardening) To exclude light from plants to render them white and tender; (culinary) to immerse vegetables briefly in boiling water to make them tender.

Bolt To flower prematurely, usually owing to unsuitable growing conditions or the effect of day length.

Bract Small modified leaves at the base of the flower stalk or beneath the flower head. They sometimes look very like petals.

Brassica Large genus (q.v.) of plants popularly known as the 'cabbage' family, which includes turnip, mustards and cauliflower, for example.

Bulb/bulblet Usually an underground part of the plant, composed of thick, fleshy leaves or leaf bases packed tightly together. It stores food reserves. A bulblet is a small bulb formed at the base of, or on the stem above, a mature bulb.

Bulbil Small bulb-like organ which sometimes forms in place of flowers.

Check Growth halted through adverse conditions such as drought, cold, starvation or delayed planting.

Clamp Method of storing root crops, to protect them from frost, in which the roots are piled on a base of straw, then covered with straw and earth, either outdoors or on a shed floor.

Cordon Plant growing up a single stem.

Cover Term used to describe any form of protection for plants, such as a greenhouse, frame, cloche, or a windowsill indoors.

Crown Term used to describe the top of the root system of a perennial plant, or sometimes the whole root system.

Cultivar A variety raised in cultivation. So-called vegetable 'varieties' should, strictly speaking, be called cultivars, but this is not yet common practice.

Cutting Piece of leaf, stem or root used for propagation (q.v.). Softwood cuttings are taken from young growths early in spring; hardwood cuttings from mature growths towards the end of the growing season. Heel cuttings are sideshoots pulled away from the main stem with a tiny piece of main stem attached.

Dormant period Natural resting stage in the annual cycle of a plant's growth.

Earthing up Drawing up soil around the base and stem of a plant.

F_1 hybrids Plants grown from seeds resulting from the controlled crossing of carefully selected parent plants. F_1 hybrid plants have greater vigor and uniformity than ordinary seed raised cultivars. Seeds saved from F_1 hybrids have to be recreated each time by crossing the same parents or parent stocks.

Forcing Bringing a plant into earlier growth, generally by raising the temperature under which it is grown.

Genus (plural **genera**) Category of plant classification in which are placed all species (q.v.) with characteristics in common.

Green manure The practice of growing crops which are later dug into the soil either as a source of humus or a source of minerals, depending on the crop used.

Growing days The number of days in a year between the point when average daytime temperatures reach about 6°C/43°F in spring, and fall back to that point in winter. Most plants cease to grow below that temperature.

Growing point The tip of the plant's stem.

Harden off The process of gradually acclimatizing a plant that has been raised indoors to lower temperatures, so that it is not severely checked (q.v.) when it is planted outside.

Hardy/half-hardy Term used of plants in the temperate zone that live outside from year to year without any kind of protection. Half-hardy plants can survive only limited cold and need a sheltered or protected site, or removal to a more or less frost-free place for winter.

Heat treatment Special treatment of onion sets, carried out by seedsmen, to prevent them from bolting. If the treated sets are planted out into cold soil, the beneficial effect can be reversed, so planting must be delayed until the ground is warm, but moist.

Indoors see **Cover.**

In situ Used for seed sown where the plant is to grow, to avoid transplanting.

Leaching Used of soluble fertilizers and such substances as lime that are washed deep into the soil out of reach of plant roots, or out of the bottom of containers by rain or continual watering.

Legumes Term used to describe plants in the *Leguminosae* family whose fruits take the form of pods.

Loam Ideal soil type in which particles of clay, silt, sand and organic matter are well balanced and blended.

Long day/short day plants Plants in which flowering is governed by day length. Long day plants flower naturally after the longest day is passed in midsummer; short day plants in the period before the longest day.

Microclimate The climate of a very localized area, such as a garden or part of a garden, or even the immediate surroundings of a plant.

Monocropping Cultivation of only one crop.

Mulch A protective layer of material, anything from polyethylene film to manure, laid over the soil to prevent weed germination, to conserve moisture, or to improve the condition of the soil.

Offset Plant produced at the base of a parent plant.

Open pollinated Seed produced from natural, random pollination, as opposed to the production of F₁ hybrids (q.v.).

Perennial A plant that lives for several years.

Pinching out (or **Stopping**) Removing the tip of a stem, or a whole sideshoot, by nipping it off with the fingers.

Potting Placing a plant in a flower pot or similar container with suitable soil or potting mix. **Potting on** is the term for moving an established pot-grown plant into a larger container. **Repotting** involves taking a well-rooted or pot-bound plant out of its container, removing some of the soil and maybe outer roots, and returning it to the cleaned pot, or another pot of the same size, with fresh potting mix.

Potting mix, soil or compost Growing medium, containing minerals essential for growth, formulated for growing plants in various types of container. Loam-based mixes were widely used in the past, but nowadays moss peat, with or without sand or grit, is a more common base.

Propagation Increasing the stock of a plant, either by sowing seeds, by taking cuttings, or by dividing up the plant.

Ring culture A system of growing plants in greenhouses where the soil has become 'sick', using bottomless pots, filled with compost mix, standing on an inert base of shingle or weathered cinders.

Seed leaf The first tiny leaf or leaves (developed from the seed coat), produced by the seedling after germination. **True leaf** is the larger leaf (or leaves) that emerge next.

Self-fertile Plants that will set seed without cross pollination.

Short day See **Long day.**

Species Grouping of plants which differ only slightly and will freely cross with each other. Fairly closely related species are grouped together as a genus. See also **Genus.**

Stopping see **Pinching out.**

Strip cropping An efficient method of using cloches where sowing and planting is planned so that cloches can be moved between two adjacent strips of land, to allow cloches and land to be continually utilized.

Temperate Climatic zone roughly halfway between the arctic or antarctic and tropical latitudes.

Tender Plants that can be injured by cold weather or frost.

Topdressing Generally the application of fertilizer to growing plants; also used to describe the replenishment of the top layer of soil in a pot or container.

True leaf See **Seed leaf.**

Truss Vernacular name for a flower cluster, the botanical name for which is an inflorescence.

Tuber Enlarged root or stem which functions as a storage organ and is usually, but not invariably, underground.

Variegated Used mainly of leaves that are variously patterned, spotted or blotched with another color.

Variety Distinct form of a species that occurs as a true breeding entity in the wild.

GENERAL INDEX

PLANT INDEX

Bold type denotes illustrations

SEED SUPPLIERS

The following seedsmen have good general lists, which include some of the more unusual salad vegetables.

W. Atlee Burpee Co., Warminster, PA 18991, or Clinton, IA 52732, or Riverside, CA 92502 (mail to your nearest address)
Demonchaux Co., 827 North Kansas, Topeka, Kansas 66608
Epicure Seeds Ltd., PO Box 95, New Lebanon Center, NY 12126
Gurneys Seed and Nursery Co., Yankton, SD 57079
J. L. Hudson, PO Box 1058, Redwood City, CA 94064
Johnny's Selected Seeds, Albion, Maine 04901
Le Jardin du Gourmet, West Danville, Vermont 05873
Le Marche, Seeds International, PO Box 566, Dixon, CA 95620
Nichols Garden Nursery, 1190 North Pacific Highway, Albany, Oregon 97321
Redwood City Seed Company, PO Box 361, Redwood City, CA 94064
Seeds Blüm, Idaho City Stage, Boise, ID 83707
Stokes Seeds Inc., 737 Main St., PO Box 548, Buffalo, NY 14240
Thompson & Morgan, PO Box 100, Farmingdale, New Jersey 07727

The following seedsmen in the UK are specialists in unusual seed, and will send orders by post. A free catalogue can be obtained by sending an international postal coupon.

John Chambers, 15 Westleigh Road, Barton Seagrave, Kettering, Northants NN15 5AJ (Edible wild plants and herbs)
Suffolk Herbs, Sawyers Farm, Little Cornard, Sudbury, Suffolk, CO10 0PF (Unusual European salad and general vegetables; herbs)

BIBLIOGRAPHY

General gardening
Creasy, Rosalind, *The Complete Book of Edible Landscaping* (1982), Sierra Club Books, 530 Bush Street, San Francisco, CA 94108
Fell, Derek, *Vegetables, How to Select, Grow and Enjoy* (1982), HP Books, PO Box 5367, Tucson, AZ 85703

Regional
Solomon, Steve, *The Complete Guide to Organic Gardening West of the Cascades* (1981), Pacific Search Press, 222 Dexter Avenue North, Seattle, WA 98109

Herbs
Foster, Gertrude and Rosemary F. Louden, *Park's Success with Herbs* (1980), George W. Park Seed Company, PO Box 31, Greenwood, SC 29646
Garland, Sarah, *The Complete Book of Herbs and Spices* (1979), The Viking Press, New York, NY 10010
Gibbons, Euell, *Stalking the Healthful Herbs* (1962), David McKay Co., New York, NY 10016
Lathrop, Norma Jean, *Herbs, How to Select, Grow and Enjoy* (1981), HP Books, PO Box 5367, Tucson, AZ 85703

Flowers
Smith, Leona Woodring, *The Forgotten Art of Flower Cookery* (1973), Harper and Row Publishers, New York, NY

Pests
Carr, Anna, *Rodale's Color Handbook of Garden Insects* (1979), Rodale Press, Emmaus, PA 18049
Insects and Diseases of Vegetables in the Home Garden, USDA publication obtainable from the local county extension offices. (Good for identification; controls are mostly cultural and chemical).

Greenhouse culture
Smith, Shane, *The Bountiful Solar Greenhouse* (1982), John Muir Publications, PO Box 613, Santa Fe, NM 87501
Wolfe, Dolores, *Growing Food in Solar Greenhouses*, Doubleday and Co. Inc., New York, NY 10167

Wild edible plants
Gibbons, Euell, *Stalking the Wild Asparagus* (1962), David McKay Co., New York, NY 10016
Peterson, Lee, *Field Guide to Eastern Edible Wild Plants*, Houghton Mifflin Co., Boston, MA 02108

Mail-order gardening books
Capability's Books, Highway 46, Box 114, Deer Park, WI 54007

ACKNOWLEDGMENTS

Author's acknowledgments

It is extraordinary how many people, wittingly or unwittingly, become involved in the creation of a book, and I would like to take this opportunity to thank those who helped with *The Salad Garden*.

First, I would like to thank Roger Phillips and his assistant Jacqui Hurst for the tremendous enthusiasm and care that went into taking the photographs, which I hope will encourage people to try out the plants which are new to them.

I would like to extend a very warm thank you to Ethel Minogue and Paul Laurenson, for their invaluable assistance on the recipes, for dealing so patiently with our endless queries, and for their painstaking efforts in preparing the salad dishes for photography.

Several people kindly read through different parts of the manuscript. My particular thanks to David Carr, who read the bulk of the text. His very constructive criticisms and his work on the tables in the appendix have, I am sure, resulted in a far more accurate book. Thanks also to Kit Anderson for her very valuable comments on the manuscript, and to Rob Johnston of Johnny's Selected Seeds for information on available varieties.

On the production side of the book, I would first like to thank June Pattinson who, with unstinted willingness, burnt the midnight oil to complete the typing, and retyping: none of the deadlines would ever have been met without her. It is, of course, almost mandatory to thank everyone concerned in the publishing company but I would like to make a very 'unmandatory' thank you to Frances Lincoln and her staff, particularly the editor, Susan Berry, for the tremendous personal effort that has been put into this book and the interest everyone has shown in the outcome. It is not often one has the pleasure of working with such an enthusiastic team. So thank you also to Debbie MacKinnon, Mark Richards, Caroline Hillier and Louise Tucker on the design side, and to Penny David, Miren Lopategui, Joanna Jellinek and Joanna Chisholm, for their editorial work, as well as Anne Hardy for providing the index. Thank you, too, to the illustrators for their painstaking work on the drawings.

Last, but by no means least, a thank you to my family – my husband Don and my children Brendan and Kirsten – for their tolerance during the long period of neglect during which the book was written. There is nothing now between me and the mending pile!

Publisher's acknowledgments

The publishers would like to thank the following individuals and organizations for their help in putting this book together: Penny David for her editorial work in helping to shape the synopsis; Caroline Hillier for initial work on the design; Gillian Bussell, Caroline Smee and Elizabeth and George Galfalvi for typing the manuscript; David Carr for providing technical advice; the typesetters for meeting impossible deadlines; Liz Strauli for work on picture research; and Anne Hardy for compiling the index.

General editor: **Susan Berry**
Art editor: **Mark Richards**

Editors: **Joanna Jellinek, Miren Lopategui**
Designer: **Louise Tucker**

Art director: **Debbie MacKinnon**

Illustrations

All illustrations by Jane Cradock-Watson except for the following:
Nick May: 28, 34, 35, 42, 43, 44, 45
Jim Robins: 38, 39, 46, 47

Photographs

All photographs by Roger Phillips except for the following:
Pat Hunt: 14
Joy Larkcom: 18 (right)
Gary Rogers: 6 (left, bottom right), 7, 22 (bottom)
Michael Warren: 51, 52
George Wright: cover, 21 (right)

Filmset by SX Composing Ltd, Rayleigh, Essex
Originated by Amilcare Pizzi, Milan